T0138633

The ROI
from
Software Quality

The ROI
from
Software Quality

Khaled El Emam

Auerbach Publications
Taylor & Francis Group
Boca Raton London New York Singapore

Published in 2005 by
Auerbach Publications
Taylor & Francis Group
6000 Broken Sound Parkway NW, Suite 300
Boca Raton, FL 33487-2742

Library of Congress Cataloging-in-Publication Data

El Emam, Khaled
    The ROI from software quality / Khaled El Emam.
        p. cm.
    Includes bibliographical references and index.
    ISBN 0-8493-3298-2 (alk. paper)
    1. Computer software--Development. I. Title.

QA76.76.D47E424 2005
005.1--dc22
                                                  2004061902

Taylor & Francis Group
is the Academic Division of T&F Informa plc.

Visit the Taylor & Francis Web site at
http://www.taylorandfrancis.com

and the Auerbach Publications Web site at
http://www.auerbach-publications.com

Contents

APPENDICES

Additional tools for performing ROI calculations and for illustrating the examples in this book may be found at the Ottawa Software Quality Association Web site: <http://www.osqa.org/roi>

Preface

Over the past ten years, I have been doing research on how software metrics can be used to predict software quality, and how important decisions can be informed by such prediction models. While the companies that I was working with found all of this quite interesting, my sponsors were having a more difficult time justifying further expenditures on this kind of work. So I focused on building economic models to make the business case that software metrics can really reduce costs and have an impact on the bottom line. I did this by being precise about how metrics can help inform very specific decisions, and then evaluated the economic benefit of making the optimal decision.

This was successful. In fact, its success was such that the economic benefits became the main criterion that I used to evaluate the utility of new software metrics and prediction models. At the end of the day, that is what really mattered to the sponsors. This is not to say that other accepted ways of evaluating metrics, such as validity and reliability, were not useful. Of course they are! However, nothing beats making a good business case that the metrics will save real dollars.

As I presented these results to the academic and developer communities, I kept getting questions about how other practices (not just metrics-based decision making) would fare. The answers to these questions were only a small extension to the existing work. It was relatively straightforward to build an economic model focusing on software quality practices in general. There is a clear and hard-to-dispute economic benefit to improved software quality. This is a benefit to the developer of the software, as well as to the purchaser of the software. If developers will not provide quality, the purchasers should demand it. It will save the purchaser money to acquire a better-quality product.

Furthermore, the years 2001 to 2003 saw a substantial and painful upheaval in the world in general, and in the software engineering community specifically. On the one hand, many software companies were reducing their expenditures on quality assurance and quality control — they had to reduce costs to survive and quality was one of the first victims. But also, security vulnerabilities became a major issue of concern to governments and enterprises. Security vulnerabilities are a manifestation of low quality. There was a need for more QA and QC ... rather than less.

Paying attention to the quality of software is good business for the vendors. It is good business for the buyer. And this book shows you how.

Additional tools for performing ROI calculations and for illustrating the examples in this book may be found at the Ottawa Software Quality Association Web site: <http://www.osqa.org/roi>

The approach in this book is decidedly evidence based. Some of the early readers of the manuscript described it as "too academic." This was not meant to be complimentary. Some were pleasantly surprised by the volume of data, the studies that have been performed, and how straightforward it is to perform return-on-investment calculations. I hope you will fall into the latter group.

I think that providing evidence and substantiating arguments by numbers from methodologically defensible studies is important. Software engineering has traditionally not been an evidence-based discipline. This has resulted in over-blown expectations and marginally useful practices being adopted by large segments of the community. It has resulted in bad practices that have been rejected in the past making comebacks. It has also resulted in very beneficial practices taking a very long time to migrate into the mainstream. This pattern of behavior is a sign of immaturity, and we should strive to move away from it and to being able to substantiate the claims that we make. If we do not rely more on evidence to make decisions voluntarily, it will be imposed through regulation, legislation, and lawsuits. It is not too late to make the right choice.

Acknowledgments

This book was born when I first did some work for Klocwork Inc. in Ottawa, Ontario, Canada. Klocwork develops static analysis tools, with a strong product in the software metrics area. Klocwork's interest was to evaluate the ROI of static analysis. They asked me to write a report on that. After this report was written, it was used by Klocwork staff in the field to make the business case for their tools. The interactions with Klocwork over a period of a year and a half resulted in me putting together this book, which builds on that initial report and those exchanges. You can find out more about Klocwork at www.klocwork.com. Special thanks to the Klocwork team, including: Chris Fedorko, Donn Parker, Anthony Mar, Djenana Campara, and Norm Rajala.

Some of the material in this book was conceptualized while I was writing some reports for the Cutter Consortium. Cutter provides an excellent source of information on contemporary IT issues relevant to executives and senior management decision-making. You can get to Cutter through www.cutter.com.

Parts of this book were reviewed at various points by Dr. David Zubrow (of the Software Engineering Institute at Carnegie Mellon University) and Victoria Hailey (of the Victoria Hailey Group). Lynn LaRouche from London Life, Dr. Ho-Won Jung from Korea University, and Pierre Labreche from CMC Electronics in Montreal all kindly provided detailed comments and suggestions on an earlier version of this book, for which I am very grateful. I also wish to thank Peter Hill from the ISBSG in Australia for inviting me to be involved in the 2003 release of the ISBSG benchmark, as well as for his support of benchmarking efforts and the dissemination of their results: this is truly valuable for the software engineering community.

I have presented the material in this book at various conferences and other technical events throughout 2002, 2003, and 2004. I wish to thank all of the attendees at these talks for their tough questions and illustrative examples of ROI. These have helped to evolve the book during that time period. I would especially like to thank Compuware Corporation in Canada for organizing seminars to present this work.

I also wish to thank Virginia Sanchez for her valuable help in preparing the final copy of the manuscript for publishing and a special thanks to John Wyzalek of Auerbach Publications for his strong support in bringing this manuscript to publication.

About the Author

Khaled El Emam, Ph.D., is Chief Scientist at TrialStat Corporation, as well as a Senior Consultant with Cutter Consortium's Agile Software Development and Project Management Practice and Risk Management Intelligence Network. He is a Senior Scientist at the Children's Hospital of Eastern Ontario Research Institute, where he is leading the eHealth research program; an Associate Professor at the University of Ottawa, Faculty of Medicine, president of the Ottawa Software Quality Association; a visiting professor at the Center for Global eHealth Innovation at the University of Toronto (University Health Network); and visiting professor at the School of Business at Korea University. In 2003 and again in 2004, he was ranked as the top systems and software engineering scholar worldwide by the *Journal of Systems and Software* based on his publications. He holds a Ph.D. from the Department of Electrical and Electronics Engineering, King's College, at the University of London (U.K.).

Previously he was a senior research officer at the National Research Council of Canada, a group leader for quantitative methods at the Fraunhofer Institute for Experimental Software Engineering in Germany, and a Research Officer at the Computer Research Institute of Montreal.

Chapter 1

Introduction

When MyClinical Inc. bought a back-end encryption server to secure communications between client hospitals and their data center, they focused their pre-purchase efforts on negotiating very attractive licensing arrangements.* Little did they realize the true costs of this purchase: the product they just bought had frequent failures. The continuous reliability problems and connection failures from the diverse client platforms disrupted their customers' businesses. This did result in a decimation of goodwill from their customers, unawarded contracts down the line, and a tremendous amount of executive energy spent on damage control with key clients. When MyClinical could not take it any more, they replaced the faulty software. The subsequent infrastructure reconfiguration and the replacement costs of the back-end server dwarfed any expenditure thus far. While the company survived, MyClinical paid a heavy price for purchasing low-quality software.

This is not really that surprising. Most companies, just like MyClinical did, do not carefully consider many aspects of quality when making software purchase decisions. The vendor of the encryption server knew that. However, that vendor did not even release a new version of the product with bug fixes for another 18 months after MyClinical dumped the product. And, the vendor posted dramatic sales growth during that same period.

---

* While the name of the company has been changed, the story is a true one.

The consequences of low quality are clear for the customers. More than 60% of manufacturing companies reported major defects in software they had bought, and just fewer than 80 percent reported minor defects.[1] These organizations experienced an average of 40 major defects and 70 minor ones in purchased software.*

Customers today are generally not that satisfied with the quality of the software that they buy.[2,3] In fact, dissatisfaction is so widespread that it has spurred recent legislation activity in the United States governing software quality and the responsibilities of suppliers.[4]

It is clear then that low-quality software can be very costly for purchasers, and low quality is making those customers unhappy. As for vendors themselves, a cursory examination suggests that they can get away with it.

1.1 Profiting from Defects

Much of the software industry has been slow in its response to this customer dissatisfaction. It is quite common for software companies to compete on features and price. Rarely do they attempt to differentiate themselves by delivering high-reliability software.

To some extent, this casual approach to quality is justified because not all customers place an emphasis on software reliability. One large-scale study of the relationship between product attributes and customer satisfaction** found that, for example, network, mainframe users, and systems programmers valued reliability and performance most. However, end users and users of shrink-wrap software valued capability (features) and usability more than they did reliability.[5]

Therefore, focusing on delivering highly reliable software may not even be necessary for certain market segments. As long as the software works (more or less), then features, ease of use, and ease of learning trump quality. In fact, one can go further and assert that shipping software with defects can be quite profitable. Here is how this works.

Software contractors receive payments regardless of the delivered software's reliability and are frequently given additional resources to correct problems of their own making: it is often lucrative to deliver poor-quality products sooner rather than high-quality products later.[6] Bug fixes are typically packaged as new releases and sold to generate more revenue.

---

* This was for CAD/CAM/CAE/PDM software only. However, the U.S. Department of Commerce-sponsored study made the case for generalizing that result to all software in the manufacturing sector.

** There is evidence that satisfaction is a determinant of adoption and use of software.[27, 28]

Some organizations walk the extra mile. They make a deliberate decision to insert or retain defects in their software for which they already have fixes. When customers contact customer support, they are provided with exceptionally good service and an instant patch. This good service, as marketing intelligence has determined, breeds customer loyalty and ensures that the customer will be calling back the next time they have to make a new purchase. Over time, because of this loyalty, bugs can be a very profitable strategy for a firm.[7]

Another reason why defects are more profitable is that if a product has a reputation of never failing in the field, then customers may decline to purchase the support contracts. If, however, there is a possibility of needing support, then customers are more likely to buy and renew these customer support contracts.[2] Support can contribute 30 to 40 percent of a vendor's revenues.[8] If done properly, support can be a very high profit margin operation within a company. Therefore, maintaining support licenses is important for the bottom line of the vendor, and defects in shipped software justify to the customer the need to pay for support.

1.2 Losing from Defects

Does that mean software developers should ignore quality? Absolutely not. There are serious consequences to the vendor from low-quality software as well.

The threat of costly litigation due to failed software projects is increasing. Demarco and Lister[9] state: "As impressive as growth of the software industry has been, it is outpaced by the growth of software-related litigation. It is not unusual for a large software development organization today to have upwards of 50 active cases on its hands ... We are experiencing an epidemic of litigation on software projects." They continue to note that litigation costs constitute a larger component of the IT budget than coding itself. Jones[10] estimates that approximately 1 percent of outsourcing contracts result in litigation after 24 months and 4 percent are at a high risk of going to litigation. Lawrence[11] emphasizes the inability to meet quality requirements as an important cause of software litigation.

The carefully crafted warranty disclaimers that are frequently used in today's software contracts and license agreements are intended to protect vendors from litigation. Despite that, there are already examples of lawsuits related specifically to low software quality.[12] Furthermore, when safety is at issue, disclaimers have been invalidated by the courts.[13] Therefore, this suggests that there is at least a class of software products for which liability arguments can be made successfully in the United States.

There is also increasing concern about software bugs leading to security vulnerabilities.* This is generating momentum for making software vendors liable for quality problems. For example, recent articles published by the National Academy of Sciences suggest that the government should consider a policy of making vendors liable as a way to ameliorate security problems in software.[15,16] The argument is that such an increase in liability and consequent damages would change the cost-benefits calculations that vendors do before releasing software,[17] and tilt the scale toward greater investments in quality.

Some companies are demanding liability clauses in contracts with their vendors, holding them responsible for any security breach connected to their software.[13] There are suggestions that vendors should cover the costs consumers incur due to undisclosed bugs in their software.[17] If implemented, this could be very costly indeed for software vendors. Some of my clients are starting to see contracts with extended warranties and clauses on liability for damages due to software defects.

Even if there are no lawsuits, the cost of low quality can still be large. Estimates of rework (defined as the effort to fix defects in the software) can be as high as 80 percent of total development costs.[18] Overall, Canadian software companies spend 35 percent of their maintenance resources on fixing bugs, and 28 percent of maintenance resources in the United States.[14] A breakdown by business domain is shown in Table 1.1. A survey of development organizations found that 40 percent of respondents have maintenance teams that visit customers to correct software problems, and 18 percent of respondents said that they would recall their software products if severe defects were discovered in the field: both are costly to development organizations.[19] Field defects in software can be very expensive to fix and disruptive to a product's standing in the market.

When such a large proportion of a company's resources are devoted to bug fixing, the company's ability to innovate is very limited. In fact, it is not uncommon to find organizations in constant firefighting mode, unable to add features that their customers are demanding. They become completely consumed by reacting to emergencies and making quick fixes to their software. The staff starts to burn out and their ability to provide good service diminishes. This ultimately results in the loss of business.

There is a positive relationship between the reliability of software and the vendor's reputation and its credibility.[20] Therefore, delivering low quality can damage a company's reputation. There is evidence that a good

---

* Lindqvist et al. highlighted contemporary security vulnerabilities in a study they performed.[29] Students attacked some COTS products. Almost all attackers performed successful intrusions using mainly exploit scripts available on the Internet. In some cases, they managed to get administrator privileges.

TABLE 1.1 Percentage of Resources Devoted to Bug Fixes during Maintenance (post-release) in Various Industries in the United States and Canada

Business Domain	United States (%)	Canada (%)
Aerospace	33	30
Financial	22	40
Software	55	41
Distribution	18	N/A
Telecom. equip.	86	50
Telecom. service	46	31

Source: From Rubin, H. Yourdon, E. *Industry Canada World-wide Benchmark Project*: Industry Canada, April 1995.

reputation can increase sales.[21] Therefore, it is worth having a good reputation. Furthermore, with few exceptions, people will not (continue to) buy a product with many defects.[2]

At a broader level, the U.S. Department of Commerce estimates that the cost to the U.S. economy of inadequate software quality management practices — namely, testing — amounts to more than U.S.$59 billion per year.[1] This is an astounding number at a national level and represents a nontrivial fraction of the GDP of the United States. Any, even modest, improvements to the quality of software can have significant financial impacts on the cost structure of individual organizations and on the overall economy.

1.3 Investing in Quality

The reality is that defects play a starring role in most software projects (see Chapter 5 on "A Software Quality Benchmark" for further details). This translates to considerable development inefficiencies and lost revenue. On the other hand, the optimal level of software quality does not mean zero defect software.

It is important to make clear that zero (field) defect software is rarely, if ever, realized. There are at least two reasons for this. First, it is practically impossible to verify with certainty that a commercial software product is free of defects. Second, even high-reliability systems that have been tested extensively still have defects in them.[22,23]

Rather than aim for zero defects, one can evaluate the costs and benefits of specific investments in software quality. Then, based on economic arguments, a decision is made on where and how to improve quality. The required level of quality for a particular organization is a business decision.[26] However, to make that decision, management needs the right tools to determine how much to invest in quality, what the benefits would be, and when the benefits will be realized. Also, management needs to be able to compare alternative investment options to determine which one to focus on first.

Investment in quality should not be taken for granted. A business case must be made for doing so. In many companies there are always competing interests and demands, and limited resources. Should management hire more developers to add this new feature or invest in more testing? For example, if they can increase sales from the new feature, then testing may not be financially more attractive than a sale. There are also executives who strongly believe that any quality problems can be ameliorated through good support, and that is where the money should go.

Improving quality may be a no-brainer for QA (Quality Assurance) folks and software engineers. But many of the people who control budgets did not rise through the QA ranks, and may not have had a formal software engineering background. That is why the remainder of this book is important for putting quality in a business perspective.

1.4 The Benefits of Software Quality Practices

There are many practices and tools that a software vendor can employ to improve software quality (henceforth referred to as *quality practices*). A handful of these are discussed in the following chapters.

There does exist a general framework for understanding how such quality practices influence the outcomes of software projects. The smart implementation of quality practices can result in the following measurable benefits:

- A reduction in software development costs (i.e., an increase in productivity pre-release)
- Reducing time-to-market (i.e., shorter delivery schedules)
- A reduction in software maintenance costs (i.e., an increase in productivity post-release)
- The delivery of higher-quality software and consequently reducing the customer's cost of ownership

The specific relationship between quality practices and outcomes is shown in Figure 1.1. The diagram shows outcomes in circles. The minus

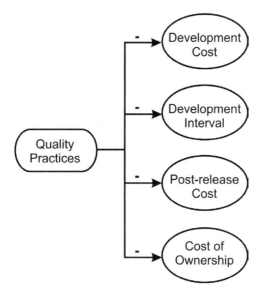

FIGURE 1.1 **The macro-level effect of implementing quality practices in terms of the four main outcomes. The diagram shows that the implementation of quality practices decreases cost and schedule as defined by the four outcomes in circles.**

signs above the arrows indicate that the implementation of quality practices reduce the value of the outcome measures.

This book is based on research demonstrating that for specific quality practices, the above four benefits can be quantified. This research has resulted in a comprehensive model mapping the relationships among quality practices and various outcomes (i.e., the details behind Figure 1.1).

It is easiest to look at the benefits of quality practices separately in terms of pre-release benefits (i.e., to development) and post-release benefits (i.e., to maintenance).

A causal model showing how practices influence outcomes during development is shown in Figure 1.2. The plus signs on the diagram indicate that this is a positive relationship. For example, the more quality practices you implement, the higher the pre-release quality. The minus signs indicate a negative relationship. For example, the higher the pre-release rework, the lower the development productivity.

Now let us go through this diagram to understand its implications. Pre-release quality is measured by the number of defects the development team discovers during inspections and testing. The defects may be in requirements documents, high level or detailed design, code, test cases, and project management documents.

When quality practices are implemented, the pre-release quality is better. This means that fewer defects will be inserted to start off with (for

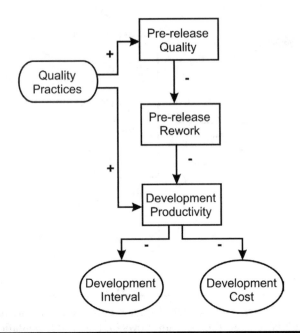

FIGURE 1.2   Illustration of the sequence of mechanisms that will lead to reductions in development cost and schedule from deploying quality practices.

example, there will be fewer defects in code because design reviews are performed), and defects will be discovered close to where they were inserted. This is called defect containment. It is much cheaper to find and fix a defect close to where it is inserted.

Higher pre-release quality means that pre-release rework is also reduced. Rework means fixing defects. It is not atypical for 50 percent or more of a project's pre-release cost to be reworked. If the quality of the software is higher, then less effort will be spent on rework because fewer defects need to be fixed. The less rework, the higher the productivity. Higher productivity means that the delivery schedule would be reduced and the project costs would go down. We will look at some examples of this in later chapters. Quality practices can also improve productivity directly.

Let us take a specific example: reuse. There is evidence that reuse of existing artifacts can improve quality.[25] Revised object-oriented classes tend to have a lower defect density than classes that were new or reused with modification.[20] In general, it was found that reuse reduced the amount of rework. This quality practice, through improving pre-release quality, reduces rework and hence increases overall productivity. In addition, productivity also increases because reuse is cheaper than developing from scratch.

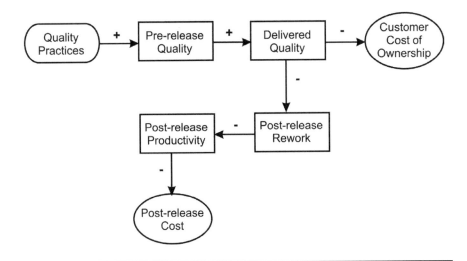

FIGURE 1.3   Causal mechanisms showing the relationship between quality practices and post-release outcomes.

The post-release causal model is shown in Figure 1.3. Here we see that when quality practices are implemented, the post-release quality (measured as the reciprocal of defects that the customer discovers) goes up. Therefore, the customer will discover fewer defects. Lower defects means a lower cost of ownership by the customer. This is indicated by the negative relationship between delivered quality and the customer cost of ownership. There is also a negative relationship with post-release rework. This indicates that as delivered quality improves, rework decreases. When rework decreases, maintenance productivity goes up and therefore total maintenance costs go down.

Much of the remainder of the book focuses on developing a quantitative understanding of these relationships. Most importantly, my objective is to illustrate how quality practices can lead to all of the outcomes that are shown in Figures 1.2 and 1.3.

1.5 Using Return-On-Investment (ROI) Analysis

When an ROI analysis is performed, it is possible to provide concrete numbers about the four types of benefits alluded to above. These can be in terms of percentage savings, person-months saved, or dollars saved. And we provide examples of all of these in later chapters.

ROI analysis can be performed before or after the introduction of a quality practice. The principles and techniques of evaluating the ROI from deploying quality practices are the same irrespective of whether it is being done before or after the fact. The only difference is whether the data used in the analysis is estimated (in the *before* analysis) or measured (in the *after* analysis).

When performed before deploying a quality practice, an ROI analysis can:

- Inform management of the potential savings from implementing a new quality practice.
- Help choose among a number of competing quality practices.

Being able to verify that ROI has materialized *after* implementing a new quality practice has a number of advantages, as follows:

- The analysis can help decide whether to expand the deployment of the quality practice from a pilot project to the wider community, such as the whole enterprise.
- It is very likely that during or after the implementation of a quality practice on a project someone will question whether it was useful. There may be schedule pressure to drop everything but the 'basics' (i.e., back to the code-and-fix mode of operation). There may be budget pressures and different development groups may be maneuvering for funds. Having an ROI after the fact is very useful for maintaining funding for the quality practices and protecting quality improvement budgets and resources.
- Comparing the before and after ROI analyses can be very instructional. For example, it may be discovered that assumptions were not realistic. This type of feedback is useful for improving future ROI studies.
- The before-after comparison could highlight incomplete implementations of the practices that would otherwise not be visible. In some cases, the actual ROI may be much lower than the projected ROI. For example, if a new tool is purchased and the staff is not trained appropriately, then the ROI may not match expectations. There may also be cases of resistance to change by staff that may hamper realizing all projected benefits. The actual ROI may also be much higher than projected if the team discovered optimizations and implemented them.

Therefore, it is important to be able to evaluate ROI both before and after implementing quality practices.

Reading this book should equip you to collect the appropriate data and to perform this kind of analysis rather easily. I will give examples of calculating ROI before introducing a quality practice and after introducing it. Performing an ROI analysis before introducing a practice is essentially predicting the future. Accounting for the uncertainty that is inherent when predicting the future is important. We can achieve this through a sensitivity analysis. Examples of performing a sensitivity analysis are also presented.

References

1. NIST. *The Economic Impacts of Inadequate Infrastructure for Software Testing*: National Institute of Standards and Technology, U.S. Department of Commerce, 2002.
2. Kaner, C. and Pels, D. Article 2B and Software Customer Dissatisfaction. Available at http://www.badsoftware.com/stats.htm, 1997.
3. Bennatan, E. A fresh look at software quality. II. Agile Project Management Advisory Service — Executive Update. *Cutter Consortium.* 4(5), 2003.
4. Kaner, C. Software engineering and UCITA. *Journal of Computer and Information Law,* 18(2):Winter 1999/2000.
5. Kekre, S., Krishnan, M., and Srinivasan, K. Drivers of customer satisfaction for software products: implications for design and service support. *Management Science,* 41(9):1456–1470, 1995.
6. Offutt, J. Quality attributes of Web software applications. *IEEE Software,* pp. 25–32, March/April 2002.
7. El Emam, K. *Software Defect Management Best Practices.* Cutter Consortium, Agile Project Management Advisory Service, Executive Report, 3(4): April 2002.
8. ASP. *Trends in Fee-Based Support*: The Association of Support Professionals, 2000.
9. Demarco, T. and Lister, T. Both sides always lose: the litigation of software intensive contracts. *Cutter IT Journal,* 11(4):5–9, 1998.
10. Jones, C. Conflict and litigation between software clients and developers. *Cutter IT Journal,* 11(4):10–20, April 1998.
11. Lawrence, B. Learnings of an expert witness. *IT Litigation Strategies*: Cutter Consortium; 2001.
12. Kaner, C., Falk, J., and Quoc Nguyen, H. *Testing Computer Software,* 2nd ed. John Wiley & Sons, 1999.
13. Mead, N. *International Liability Issues in Software Quality*: Software Engineering Institute, 2003. CMU/SEI-2003-SR-001.
14. Rubin, H. and Yourdon, E. *Industry Canada Worldwide Benchmark Project.* Industry Canada, April 1995.
15. Berkowitz, B. and Hahn, R. Cybersecurity: who's watching the store? *Issues in Science and Technology,* National Academies Press, 2003.
16. Personick, S. and Patterson, C. *Critical Information Infrastructure Protection and the Law: An Overview of Key Issues.* The National Academies Press, 2003.
17. McLaughlin, L. Buggy software: can new liability rules help quality?. *IEEE Software,* pp. 104–108, September/October 2003.

18. Shull, F., Basili, V., Boehm, B., et al. What we have learned about fighting defects. *Proceedings of the Eighth IEEE Symposium on Software Metrics,* 2002.

19. Beck, K., Bennatan, E., Evans, D., El Emam, K., Guttman, M., and Marzolf, T. *Software Quality Management Best Practices.* Cutter Consortium, 2003.

20. Garsombke, F. and Garsombke, H. The impact of vaporware, reliable software, vendor dependence and fulfilled promises on customers' perceptions/experiences and vendor reputation. *Software Quality Journal,* 7:149–173, 1988.

21. Fitzgerald, T. Understanding the differences and similarities between services and products to exploit your competitive advantage. *Journal of Services Marketing,* 2(1):25–30, 1988.

22. Myers, W. Can software for the SDI ever be error-free? *IEEE Computer,* 19(10):61–67, 1986.

23. Myers, W. Shuttle code achieves very low error rate. *IEEE Software,* pp. 93–95, September 1988.

24. Bach, J. Good enough quality: Beyond the buzzword. *IEEE Computer* pp. 96–98, August 1997.

25. Thomas, W., Delis, A., and Basili, V. An evaluation of Ada source code reuse. *Proceedings of the Ada-Europe International Conference,* 1992.

26. Basili, V., Briand, L., and Melo, W. How reuse influences productivity in object-oriented systems. *Communications of the ACM,* 39(10):104–116, 1996.

27. Alavi, M. and Henderson, J. An evolutionary strategy for implementing a decision support system. *Management Science,* 27:1309–1323, 1981.

28. Swanson, E. *Information Systems Implementation: Bridging the Gap Between Design and Utilization.* Irwin, 1988.

29. Lindqvist, U. and Jonsson E. A map of security risks associated with using COTS. *IEEE Computer,* 31(6):60–66, June 1998.

Chapter 2

Measuring
Software Quality

Thus far I have been rather loose with the definition of quality — although you probably gathered that I view quality as the (lack of) defects. Before moving into the quantitative aspects of the return on investment (ROI) from software quality, it is necessary to be more precise about what quality is and how to measure it. As you will see, counting defects is not a simple affair.

2.1 Definition of Quality

A commonly mentioned measure of software quality is customer satisfaction. However, there are a few problems in using customer satisfaction as a measure of quality:

- Not many software organizations actually measure customer satisfaction — therefore, it is not a good measure if few organizations actually collect the data. In an analysis of the 2003 ISBSG international benchmark data set performed by the author (see http://www.isbsg.org for more information about ISBSG), only 26 out of 2027 software projects in the database (approximately 1.3 percent of projects) admitted to collecting any customer satisfaction metrics. The ISBSG data set is collected through national software metrics associations in various countries across the world. Further information about the ISBSG data set is included in Appendix B of this book.

■ A survey of representatives from more than 150 IT departments[1] found that only 15 percent of respondents define software quality solely in terms of customer satisfaction.

■ Customer satisfaction embodies much more than the software product itself. For example, the quality of service, prestige, and reputation of the vendor play a role in satisfaction. The focus here is on the software product itself.

2.1.1 Pre- and Post-Release Quality

I use detected defects as the measure of software quality. The more defects, the lower the quality. Defects can be detected before or after release.

If a defect is detected before release, then it is a measure of pre-release quality. A pre-release defect can be found in any of the development artifacts, such as the design, the requirements, test plans, test cases, and project management documents.

If a defect is detected after release, then it is a measure of post-release quality. Post-release quality is really what matters to the customer. These defects are detected mainly in the code.

A defect is an incorrect step, process, or data in the software. If a product does not adhere to its requirements and a fix to the code or documentation was required, then that is considered a defect. If it does not meet customer expectations for performance, reliability, and security, then that is a defect. We can all agree that software with many such defects causes low customer satisfaction.[2]

2.1.2 Counting Minor and Major Defects

Defects are typically classified as major or minor. A good distinction between the two is by the extent to which the defect inconveniences the customer or damages the customers' business. Major defects are those that will have a substantial influence on the behavior or characteristics of the software that is noticeable by the customer. Minor defects are internal to the program and would affect its complexity, ease of understanding and modification, and efficiency. Also, problems with the user manual, help system, installation instructions, and error messages are considered minor defects. Minor defects neither make the software unusable nor cause major damage.

An important consideration is whether minor defects should be counted when measuring quality. From a customer perspective, minor defects also have a substantial cost and are therefore important to count.[3] The same is true from a developer's perspective; for example, in one organization it was found that fixes of minor defects pre-release would have prevented more than half of the technical support costs for a software product.[4]

Furthermore, there is evidence that detecting and fixing minor defects is important for improving the maintainability of a software application.[5] Therefore, maintenance cost is kept under control through inspection of changes and fixing all minor defects. Otherwise, the risk of the structure of the system deteriorating over time and becoming too expensive to maintain increases. We therefore include minor defects in the total defect count.

2.2 Types of Defects

The following are definitions of terms and explanations of software defect concepts that are used throughout this book.

A **failure** is an incorrect result produced by the software. It may be incorrect according to a requirements specification, a design, or because it does not meet customer expectations. A failure may be functional (i.e., the software does not implement a feature properly) or nonfunctional, such as a failure in performance (e.g., the software is too slow). Failures can only occur in executable software. For some types of systems, a simulation environment may exist to simulate various parts of the design. In such a case one may have a failure in the design.

A failure is caused by one or more **faults** or **defects**. We use these two terms interchangeably throughout.

Of course, a failure can be caused by multiple faults, not just one. However, a fault does not guarantee that a failure will occur. For example, some faults are never discovered. Some faults are minor and never result in a visible failure (e.g., efficiency or problems with the tenth most significant digit). Some faults never manifest themselves because that part of the code is never executed (e.g., code that deals with a very rare condition).

Some failures occur but are not observed. For example, on some aircraft there are multiple computers running in parallel with each one having software developed by independent teams. A failure can occur in one of the computers, but this does not result in an overall system failure because the other computers produce the correct result and out-vote the malfunctioning computer.

A fault is an incorrect step, process, or data in the software. When a programmer fixes a piece of software, he or she is fixing defects. We cannot really count the *true* number of defects in the software because some defects may never be discovered. We can only count defects that are discovered and fixed. From now on when we talk about defects, we mean those that are discovered and fixed. Therefore, to count defects, we usually count the number of fixes. The number of defects can be counted only after the fixes have been implemented.

Counting the number of fixes also means that if a failure is not dealt with (i.e., no fixes are implemented to resolve a failure), then we cannot count the defects associated with it. Perversely, this means that if no failures were ever fixed, then a product would be defect-free because no fixes have been applied.

An **error** is a human action that causes a defect to be inserted in the software. A single error can lead to many defects being inserted in the software. Understanding errors is important because if the frequency of a certain type of error can be reduced, then the number of defects prevented can be large.

Once software is released, either to customers internal or external to the organization, then **problem reports** (PRs) can be opened in response to a failure. A PR is a description of a failure. Different organizations will use alternative terminology, but almost all software organizations will have a problem reporting process. A PR reflects a single instance of a perceived failure. This means that a problem report may not necessarily be a true failure. If there are many customers, then there may be many problem reports describing the same failure.

A **rediscovery** occurs when someone identifies, a failure or defect that has already been discovered previously. For example, assume that a customer complaint results in creating a problem report. If another customer experiences the same failure, then this is a rediscovery. Similarly, if a tester detects a failure that has already been detected by another tester, then this is a rediscovery. Rediscoveries are expensive because effort is spent in making the rediscovery and in deciding that the incident is a rediscovery. For problem reports, a nontrivial amount of the support organization's effort is spent matching problem reports to determine if a new PR is similar to a previous one.

When a defect is fixed, the fix itself can introduce one or more new defects. This is called a **bad fix**. Depending on the schedule pressure, the code structure, and the quality of the existing test suite, bad fixes may actually be a major problem by themselves.

2.3 The Defect Life Cycle

Each defect goes through a number of states during its life. We cannot really say much about defects that are not detected at all. Hence, the

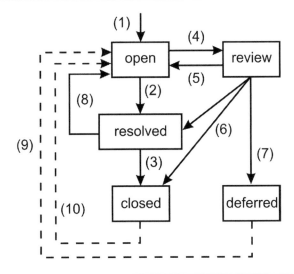

FIGURE 2.1 **A state-transition diagram showing the possible states of a PR's life cycle. This life cycle is described in the text in terms of PRs reported during testing and from the field, but the same life cycle applies to defects detected during inspections. This model is based on one in Patton.[6]**

focus is on defects that are detected. Figure 2.1 shows the states of a detected defect's life. In explaining this, I will use the example of a PR rather than a defect because that is the more complex case. However, the diagram still applies whether we are talking about defects or PRs.

A problem with the software is experienced either by a customer or by testers. A PR is opened. This is path (1). When a PR is opened, it is matched against existing PRs to determine if it is a rediscovery. If it is, then the new PR adopts the state of the original PR. It is important to count such duplicates because this is how the organization will be able to gauge the cost of rediscoveries. The cost of rediscoveries can be reduced by sending out preventative patches to existing customers.[7]

The PR is assigned to a developer who will work on it. This involves recreating the problem as described, and tracing from the symptoms to the defects in the code. Then the defects are fixed, the regression test suite is executed, and new unit test cases are written to detect those particular defects. The new test cases are added to the regression test suite. Once the programmer is happy with the fix, then the defect is resolved. This is illustrated in path (2) in Figure 2.1.

Note that multiple defects might have to be fixed for a PR to be resolved. Also, it is important to emphasize that PRs must be documented clearly and accurately; otherwise, matching with previous PRs may take more time than it should, and programmers may have a difficult time recreating the problem.

Typically, once a PR is resolved, it is sent on to the tester who confirms that the PR is resolved by running the system and integration test suite. If the tests pass, then the PR is closed. This is shown in path (3) in Figure 2.1. If the PR was not dealt with appropriately, then the tester may open the PR again and send it back to the programmer. This is shown in path (8).

The project manager should review all the PRs [this is path (4) in Figure 2.1] to determine which ones will be dealt with right away, which ones are not really a PR that will be dealt with at all, and which ones will be deferred to the next release. In some organizations, a Change Control Board plays that role. This board might consist of technical staff, customer representatives, and project management. Depending on the decision they make, paths (5), (6), or (7) can be taken.

Deferred PRs should be opened in, say, a subsequent release as shown in path (9). Sometimes, when there is a bad fix, a closed PR is opened again, as shown in path (10).

The roles that exist in this life cycle and the decisions they make are as follows:

- The programmer who resolves a PR
- The Change Control Board (which may consist of only the project manager or technical lead) that prioritizes PRs
- The project manager who should assign PRs to programmers and may make the close or defer decisions
- The tester who decides whether a PR is closed.

The above is a generic description of the states. In particular projects, some of these states may not exist. For example, a Change Control Board may not exist and the project manager may not review PRs, and the programmers make the decision on what to work on and what to defer. In that case, the "review" state may not exist.

Most defect or PR tracking software tools on the market today follow a life cycle similar to that presented in Figure 2.1. Thus, it is useful to understand this life cycle in order to use these tools more effectively.

2.4 Defect Undercounting

Although rarely discussed, most defect counts in practice are undercounts. It is important to understand the reasons for defect undercounting, especially if defect count data is going to be used to make important decisions. This is more of a problem for testing and post-release defect counts than it is for inspection defect counts.

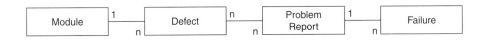

FIGURE 2.2 **Basic entity-relationship model showing the relationship between failures, PRs, defects, and modules.**

Typically, one talks about the number of defects in a piece of software. So essentially, the number of defects is counted and reported. The counting is done by looking at the changes in the version control system that is in place. Each delta (change to the code that is then checked in) is examined and if the delta was to make a fix, then this indicates that there was a defect in the module. By counting the number of deltas to implement fixes, one can get at the number of defects in a module. Recently, some work was done on automatically detecting whether or not a delta is a fix with good accuracy;[8] therefore, the defect count can be automated. This is achieved using some basic natural language processing logic on the comments provided with each delta. The total amount of defects in the system is the sum of defects counted per module.

In many organizations whenever a failure is observed (through testing or from a customer), a problem report (PR) is opened. A PR typically describes symptoms and how to recreate them. It is useful to distinguish between a failure and a failure instance. Consider the relationships in Figure 2.2. This shows that each failure instance can be associated with only a single PR, but that a PR can be associated with multiple failure instances. Multiple failure instances may be the same failure, but detected by multiple users, and hence they would all be matched to a single PR. For example, the program cannot open files with long filenames. This is a problem that multiple users might experience and so there will be multiple failure instances. A single problem report would be opened for all these failure instances explaining that the program cannot save files with long names.

A defect occurs in a single module, and each module can have multiple defects. A PR can be associated with multiple defects, possibly in the same module or across multiple modules. Also, the same defect might cause multiple unique PRs to be opened if the defect has multiple symptoms.

Counting inaccuracies can occur when a PR is associated with multiple defects in the same module. These inaccuracies are due to developers taking shortcuts. For example, because of schedule pressures, the developers fix all defects due to the same PR at the same time in one delta. A single delta means that they have to run all the regression tests once and document the fix once. Therefore, when defect count data is extracted from a version control system, it appears as if there was only one defect, when in fact many were fixed. Furthermore, it is not uncommon for developers to fix multiple defects due to multiple PRs in the same delta. In such a case, it is not known how many defects were actually fixed because each PR may have been associated with multiple defects itself.

The above scenarios illustrate that, unless the data collection system is fine-grained and followed systematically, one can only reliably say that there was at least one defect, but not the exact number of defects that were found per module. Therefore, typically the number of defects in the software is undercounted.

Another difficulty is whether the definition of a defect includes all instances of a defect or just defect types. For example, say a module has a memory leak because the developer did not know how to write good memory management code. The same error is made in three different places in the same module. Is this one or three defects?

In practice, this should be counted as a single defect. The reason is pragmatic. A tester or programmer is not going to check in the module three times into the version control system so that three deltas can be counted. At least if all programmers know this counting rule, the defect counts will be consistent across all programmers in the organization.

When defect measurements are used to give rewards or make punitive decisions, then there is motivation by staff and management to undercount. In one example, a corporate metrics program was set up,[9] and all the projects had to report "customer found defects" to corporate staff. Because of uncertainty about how this data was going to be used, some projects interpreted this to their advantage. Typically, while testing, both internal users and external customers will find post-release defects. Interpreting the definition literally means not counting defects found by internal customers and testing performed after the release date, and only reporting defects found by customers. This inevitably reduces the total defect count. Also, projects were required to report only high severity defects (those that fell into the top two severity categories on the company's defect severity scale). Consequently, the definition of severity was "adjusted" in practice so that fewer defects would be classified into the top two categories. The result was again an undercount.

Another ambiguity in the definition of defect counts that sometimes causes confusion is whether all defects should be counted or only closed ones. If only closed defects are counted, then the total number of defects

FIGURE 2.3   Entity-relationship model showing the relationship adopted frequently in practice when counting testing and customer defects.

will be much smaller than the actual. The total defect count, open and closed, gives a more accurate picture.

The point to be aware of is that when there is uncertainty about how critical performance data, such as the number of defects found, will be used or if it is known that the data will be used for reward and punishment, then there is always the risk of "creative undercounting." If the data is important for decision making, then some form of regular audits should be put in place to act as a deterrent to systematic undercounting.

For bugs found during testing and by customers, many organizations do not make a distinction between defects and failures. The entity-relationship model used to account for bugs is shown in Figure 2.3. One reason is pragmatic: counting defects accurately is difficult and can only be done after the fixes have been implemented. As shown later, many organizations have not reached a level of maturity where they can count actual defects. Therefore, they will count the number of unique failures as a surrogate for defects. This is usually operationalized by counting the number of PRs. This means that, in practice, many organizations count PRs as a surrogate measure for defects.

For bugs that are found during inspections, fixes can be counted rather easily. Therefore, inspection defect counts tend to be more accurate than testing and post-release defect counts.

Thus, we end up with a sum of inspection defects and (testing and post-release) PRs as the total number of "defects" in a software product throughout its life.

For all of the above reasons, defect data is, at best, approximate. Despite its limitations, however, defect data can serve (and has served for many years) as a reasonable basis for making management decisions and for evaluating trends in quality.

For simplification, I will continue to use the term "defects" irrespective of how they are actually counted.

2.5 Interpreting Defect Counts

Now that defect data has been collected, we need to be able to interpret the numbers. Some basic principles are presented below.

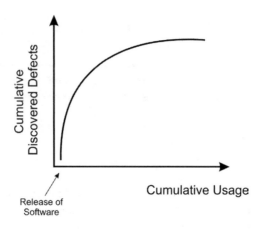

FIGURE 2.4   The relationship between usage and defect discovery.

2.5.1 Defects and Usage

Defects found post-release by customers are a function of usage. Usage is a function of:

- *The number of end users using the product.* The more end users that a product has, the more defects will be found. Therefore, everything else being equal, more defects will be found for products with thousands or millions of users compared with products that are custom made for a single client with, say, a few hundred end users.
- *The number of actual machines executing the product.* Usage increases the more physical machines using a product. In many instances, this will be correlated with the number of users.
- *The time since release.* The more time that passes since release, the greater the cumulative usage.

Figure 2.4 shows the relationship typically seen between usage and defect discovery. Usage starts right after the release of a product. Most defects are found soon after release. If the product interfaces with other vendors' products (e.g., a database or communications package), then every time that vendor releases a new version of its product, defects can be exposed at the interface. This is illustrated in Figure 2.5.

Early defects are the most "virulent" in that most users discover them. It is important to fix these virulent defects because they will affect most customers. Assuming a technical support process that is functioning well, the frequency of defects discovered over time tends to plateau. The rate

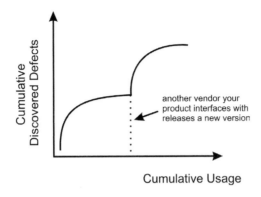

FIGURE 2.5   A step function defect discovery process.

of increase will not necessarily reach zero because there are people who will use the software in a slightly different way and uncover latent defects. These people can be current or new users. Current users may start using the software differently as they evolve from "novice" to "expert" users.

Defects discovered much later after release may be those that are rare and will only be found by a few customers. Alternatively, they may be defects that reflect the evolving feature usage of the product. For example, if novice users take the time to become "experts," then defects in the "expert" features may be discovered later.

2.5.2 Raw Defect Counts

One must be careful in interpreting defect counts. Let us say, for example, that we have two modules, A and B. Module A has a low pre-release defect count and B has a high pre-release defect count. This could mean:

- Both modules have the same number of latent defects, and module B has been tested more thoroughly and therefore has more defects discovered.
- Module B is larger than module A, and both modules received the same amount of testing. Therefore, testing detected more defects in module B because it had more defects in it.
- Both modules are the same size and were tested with the same effort, but module A has fewer latent defects (i.e., it is higher quality).

If we are talking about post-release defects, then it is also plausible that module B has been used more (e.g., its functionality is executed more often or it is used in more products).

It would be reasonable to conclude then that raw defect counts are difficult to interpret and therefore should not be used directly.

A better measure is defect density, which is defined as:

$$\text{Defect Density} = \frac{\text{Number of Defects Found}}{\text{Size}}$$

Defect density can be localized to a specific phase (e.g., defect density for the testing phase). The more common way of defining defect density is in terms of delivered defects to the customer (i.e., post-release defects).

The size of the system can be measured in many different ways. The most common are thousands of lines of code (KLOC) or function points (FPs).

2.5.3 Defects and Size

There are very few things that we know with high confidence in software engineering. One that can be easily supported with ample data is that size matters. This can be system or module size.

Larger modules tend to have more defects in them than smaller modules. This relationship is quite strong. Reasons for this include that larger modules present more opportunities for defect insertion, it is more difficult to find defects in larger modules through inspections and testing; and larger modules are more difficult to understand (more complex) so it is easier to make mistakes in their usage or their interfaces.

What is less clear is the nature of the relationship between size and defects. Figure 2.6 shows examples of linear and nonlinear relationships. A linear relationship implies that the number of defects increases steadily as the module size increases. This means that defect density is fixed. In

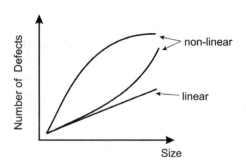

FIGURE 2.6   Possible linear and nonlinear relationships between size and defects.

practice, this is not true because modules tend to have a big variation in their defect densities. One nonlinear relationship states that defect density increases as a module's size increases. This means that larger modules tend to have relatively more defects than smaller modules. Another possibility is that larger modules tend to have relatively fewer defects than larger modules.

The relationship between size and defects, and the fact that this relationship is expected to be nonlinear, will have important influences on the way defect data should be interpreted and used.

2.5.4 Adjusted Defect Density

Because the relationship between defects and size is likely not linear, defect density is not really the ideal measure of quality. However it is better by far than raw defect counts.

Defect density is commonly used and is well understood. Therefore, it would be premature to suggest that it be abandoned for something else. However, below I explain why adjusting defect density is a good idea in some cases. If nothing else, the following exposition should help you interpret defect density better by alerting you to one of its weaknesses.

Assume that we have two companies and we wish to compare their performances. Both companies have ten products. Because the sizes of these products across the companies do differ, we will normalize the number of post-release defects by the size in LOC for each product. Now we can compare the two companies by their post-release defect density.

It would seem that because the defect counts have been normalized by size, that the size issue has been taken care of. However, this is only true if the relationship between size and defects is linear. If the relationship between size and defects is nonlinear, which is what I have argued above, then defect density is not that good for comparative purposes because it does not really eliminate the size effect.

Consider the two projects in Figure 2.7. These projects can have exactly the same process, methodologies, tools, and even people. But because project B is much larger than A, project B is going to have a larger defect density simply because it is larger. So, normalizing by size does not actually eliminate or control the fact that project B is larger than project A. The simple size differential between A and B can explain the defect density difference between the two projects. The same would be true for any nonlinear relationship between size and defects.

Consider the two companies shown in Table 2.1. Each has ten projects, but the project sizes differ. By computing the defect density (which is the total number of defects divided by the total size) we can see that company

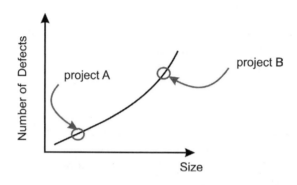

FIGURE 2.7 **With a nonlinear relationship between defects and size, two projects of different sizes will not have comparable defect densities. In this example, project B will have a higher defect density.**

TABLE 2.1 **Comparison of Defect Density for Two Companies, Each with Ten Projects**

Company X		Company Y	
Defects Found	*Size (KLOC)*	*Defects Found*	*Size (KLOC)*
22	10	2475	100
22	10	2475	100
22	10	2475	100
22	10	2475	100
22	10	2475	100
22	10	2475	100
22	10	2475	100
22	10	2475	100
2475	100	22	10
2475	100	22	10
Defect Density	18.3 defects/KLOC	Defect Density	24.2 defects/KLOC

Note: This example is based on the one from my Cutter report on the topic.[10]

Y has a larger defect density. One can then conclude that company Y is doing worse than company X in terms of delivered quality.

Note that company Y tends to have larger projects and the defect densities do not take this into account properly. As shown above, because

TABLE 2.2   Calculating Defect Density for Small and Large Projects Separately

	Company X	Company Y
SMALL (10 KLOC)	2.2 defects/KLOC	2.2 defects/KLOC
LARGE (100 KLOC)	24.75 defects/KLOC	24.75 defects/KLOC

Note: This example is based on the one from my Cutter report on the topic.[10]

TABLE 2.3   Calculating the Adjusted Defect Density for Each Company

	Total Size (KLOC)	Total Standard Defects for Company X	Total Standard Defects for Company Y
SMALL (10 KLOC)	100	220	220
LARGE (100 KLOC)	1000	24750	24750
Adjusted defect density		22.7 defects/KLOC	22.7 defects/KLOC

Note: As one can see, the adjusted defect density is exactly the same for both companies. This example is based on the one from my Cutter report on the topic.[10]

of size alone, the projects in company Y will have a higher overall defect density, just as we calculated. This does not mean that company Y has worse practices, only that it performs larger projects.

An alternative measure, *adjusted defect density*, is required. This adjusted measure is similar to what is used frequently in epidemiology to adjust for, say, age when comparing populations (mortality tends to be higher with older populations and older populations tend to have a higher incidence of disease).

The first principle of adjustment is to consider projects of different sizes separately. In our example we have two groups of projects: the 10 KLOC (SMALL) projects and the 100 KLOC (LARGE) projects. Table 2.2 shows the defect densities within company X and company Y for SMALL and LARGE projects.

The second principle of an adjusted defect density is to compare the two companies to a "standard company." The standard company can be the combination of companies X and Y. The standard company therefore has 20 projects. Ten of these projects are SMALL and ten projects are LARGE. The standard company has 100 KLOC of SMALL projects and 1000 KLOC of LARGE projects. This is illustrated in Table 2.3. If the standard company used the methods, tools, and people of company X, then the total number of defects for SMALL projects would be 220. This is calculated by multiplying company X's SMALL project defect density by the total size of the standard company's SMALL projects (2.2 × 100). Similarly, the LARGE project number of defects is computed for company X. The final set of calculations is shown in Table 2.3.

The final adjusted defect density shown in Table 2.3 makes it clear that, after eliminating the effect of project size, both companies actually have the same delivered quality. This is a markedly different conclusion that one would draw by comparing the unadjusted defect densities.

The above calculations can be easily generalized. For example, the definition of SMALL and LARGE projects can be a range rather than exact values. Note also that adjusted defect density will work irrespective of whether the relationship between size and defects is linear or nonlinear, so it is the safest approach.

The example above is one way of making adjustments. There are other ways that require making some assumptions about the functional form of the size versus defect relationship. The approach presented herein makes minimal assumptions.

It is not always possible to calculate the adjusted defect density after the fact (i.e., from defect density data) because one needs access to the raw defect and size data to do so. Therefore, for the purposes of this book, I will stick to the commonly used measure of defect density to allow comparison of data from different sources, and also to use a measure that a lot of people are familiar with and can understand.

2.6 Defects and Corporate Evolution

Software companies go through stages in implementing software measurement. The stages are shown in Figure 2.8 with examples. The stages represent the measurement evolution ladder, whereby software companies implement the lower stages before they implement the higher stages. Note that this staged model is descriptive rather than prescriptive; that is, it describes what actually happens rather than stating that this is the only way.

These stages were defined based on an analysis of very large multi-year data set collected by the European Commission on software companies.[10] Basically, software companies tend to go through stages of measurement implementation.

The first stage is product support measurement (i.e., problem reports). Almost all software companies collect that kind of data because they need it to remain in business. The next stage is basic project planning and tracking measurements, such as resources (effort) and time. They need

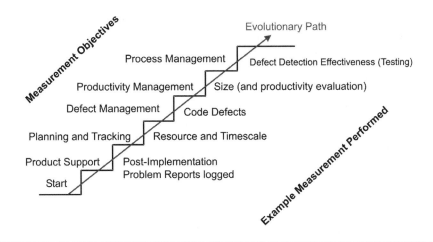

FIGURE 2.8   A staged model showing the stages of measurement that software organizations typically go through.

this data to bill their customers and have some form of budgeting. The next set of data collected is coding defects. Few companies actually collect defect data (i.e., relatively few reach that stage in the measurement ladder). Productivity measurement comes later, when proper size data is collected. Size measurement comes at a late stage of a company's measurement evolution, and surprisingly few organizations and projects collect decent size data.

The interpretation of this ladder is that organizations collect data that serves their needs, and the ladder reflects the needs of software companies as they evolve. Their needs move from ensuring delivery of a product, to better project management disciplines (generating revenue and making a profit), to controlling quality (customers complaining), managing productivity, and then sustained improvement. Few companies make it to the higher stages.

From a defect counting perspective, a software company is much more likely to have post-release PR data than to have data on actual defects and PRs during development. Also, a company is not likely to have good size data. This means that defect density data from organizations that are in the early stages or "maturity" in measurement should be suspect.

2.7 Defect Classification

Throughout a project, defects are classified in different ways to help make decisions. This section presents three classification schemes that are common and that relate to project decision making: (1) priority, (2) severity, and (3) fix type. The former two schemes must be assigned before a defect is fixed, while the latter can only be assigned reliably after the defect has been fixed.

2.7.1 Defect Priorities

When a defect is discovered, it is typically prioritized. A prioritization is a reflection of how urgent a fix for that defect is needed. The urgency of a fix is not necessarily a reflection of the severity of the defect. Severity is another kind of classification that is discussed below.

In practice, it is not always possible to fix all the defects that are found (either pre-release or post-release). Therefore, some prioritization scheme is needed so that the development team knows which defects to fix first.

Common reasons why defects are knowingly not fixed (once they are discovered) include:

- There is insufficient time or insufficient resources to fix all discovered defects.
- Reported defects may not be a problem in the software, but rather, the software is being used out of context or in away for which it was not intended.
- It is too risky to fix the defect because the code is badly structured, or the person who knew the code well has the left the company or retired and no one else has the courage to make changes.
- It is not worth expending the effort to fix the defect, as a small number and mostly small clients use the features affected by the defect, or the defect manifests itself so rarely that few customers will actually experience it.
- There is an easy workaround for the defect that does not inconvenience customers too much, and therefore the actual fix can wait.
- The defect is not documented or reported properly. If the staff involved in finding and reporting failures or PRs do not document them clearly and accurately, then it may not be possible to reproduce the problem.
- The equipment or infrastructure needed to recreate the problem is not available at the company. For example, if a customer has some very expensive hardware that causes a defect to occur when it interacts with the software, the development team may be unable to get access to this hardware to recreate and diagnose the problem, and fix the defect.

A defect prioritization scheme allows the development team to focus on the most urgent defects first. It is very possible that the lowest-ranked

TABLE 2.4   Two Defect Prioritization Schemes

Defect Prioritization Scheme I:
1. Immediate fix, blocks further testing, very visible
2. Must fix that defect before release
3. Should fix if time permits
4. Would like to fix but can release as is
Defect Prioritization Scheme II:
1. Fix immediately
2. Fix before alpha release
3. Fix before beta release
4. Fix before general availability
5. Fix before next release

Note: A defect with a priority of (1) requires more immediate attention than a defect with a priority of say (2). The second scheme is based solely on when the defect should be fixed. These schemes are described in El Emam.[10]

defects do not get fixed at all or their fixes may be delayed to the next patch or next release.

A defect's priority may change over the course of a project. For example, resources may become available and a defect that was once a low priority may be elevated to a higher priority.

The mechanism to decide on the priority of a defect will take into account the business context. For example, in one instance in a start-up, a customer had the same venture capital (VC) firm financing them as the start-up, and hence all defects from that customer were always high priority. This ensured that the VC firm heard about the great service provided by the start-up.

Lower-maturity organizations have an informal process for prioritizing defects. A more formal process assigns a specific priority value to each defect and then they are all ranked. The highest priority defects get treated first. Examples of prioritization schemes are shown in Table 2.4.

2.7.2 Defect Severities

Defect severity is another classification scheme. It is more concerned with how the defect affects the usability and utility of the product. A high-severity defect may mean that the product is unusable (e.g., the program crashes every time you open it).

The severity of a defect does not change over time, unlike priority. Therefore, if a defect is very severe, it will always be very severe.

TABLE 2.5   A Defect Severity Classification Scheme

A Defect Severity Scheme
1. Corruption or loss of data:
Inability to meet response or capacity constraints
Unintentional halt or failure
Failure that does not return to service within meantime to repair
2. System Inadequate:
Noncompliance of main function with specifications
Any critical fault that occurs during system testing
3. Unsatisfactory:
Noncompliance of auxiliary function to specifications
Noncompliance with standards for deliverable items
Layout or format defects in presentation that do not affect the
operational integrity of the system
Inconsistency or omission in documentation
4. Suggestion:
Suggestion for improving the software or documentation

Note: This scheme is described in El Emam.[11]

A high-severity defect may legitimately have low priority. For example, the program may crash only when there is less than 32 MB of memory in the computer and a vast majority of the clients have high-end machines. Hence, because the problem might affect too few low-end clients and the vendor can argue that the end-user machines are below minimal requirements, the defects associated with the system crash may not get fixed.

An example of a defect severity classification scheme is shown in Table 2.5. This scheme has been used in a number of software projects around the world.

The management for a project must take into account the severity of the defect when assigning it a priority.

2.7.3 Classification by Problem Type

One way to classify defects is to look at the type of problem that is fixed by the defect. Typically, developers would assign each defect to one of the problem categories after the fix has been made. One classification scheme that has been demonstrated to be reliable (i.e., different developers would assign the same defect to the same category) is shown in Table 2.6.[11] This type of defect classification is most useful for process monitoring and improvement. For example, the defects that are found during the various phases of a project can be plotted (see Figure 2.9). This would represent the "defect signature" for this kind of project. If the defect

TABLE 2.6 A Subset of a Defect Classification Scheme That Is Based on the Fix That Is Made

Type	Description
Documentation	Comments, messages:
	Is the function described adequately at the top of the file?
	Are variables described when declared?
	Does the function documentation describe its behavior properly?
Interface	Procedure calls and references, I/O, user formats, declarations:
	Does the library interface correctly divide the functions into their different types?
	Do the functions follow the proper object access rules?
	Are the declared and expected interface signatures the same?
Function	Logic, pointers, loops, recursion, computation:
	Are all branches handled correctly?
	Are pointers declared and used as pointers?
	Are arithmetic expressions evaluated as specified?
Build/Package/ Merge	Change management, library, version control:
	Is there a version number defined for the file ?
	Are the correct versions of functions included in the build?
Assignment	Declaration, duplicate names, scope, limits:
	Are variables initialized properly?
	Are all library variables that capture a characteristic or state of the object defined?
	Are all return values that are special cases (e.g., an error return) really invalid values (i.e., would never occur unless there was an error)?
Memory	Memory allocation, leaks:
	Are objects instantiated before being used?
	Do all objects register their memory usage?

Note: This particular scheme has the advantage that there is evidence to its reliability.[11] Each category is characterized by questions that if answered negatively would indicate a defect of that type.

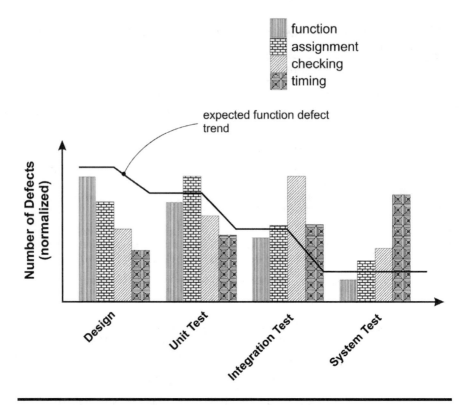

FIGURE 2.9 **An example of how a defect classification based on fix type can be used to characterize the process signature. Here we see the types of function defects that are typically detected throughout the various defect detection phases as the black line. The histogram shows the actual distribution of defect types for an ongoing project.**

discovery in subsequent projects is different from the signature, then it indicates that the process has changed or that there are quality problems with some of the project artifacts.

References

1. Beck, K., Bennatan, E., Evans, D., El Emam, K., Guttman, M., and Marzolf,T. *Software Quality Management Best Practices*, Cutter Consortium, 2003.
2. Kekre, S., Krishnan, M., and Srinivasan, K. Drivers of customer satisfaction for software products: implications for design and service support. *Management Science*, 41(9):1456–1470, 1995.
3. NIST. *The Economic Impacts of Inadequate Infrastructure for Software Testing*: National Institute of Standards and Technology, U.S. Department of Commerce, 2002.

4. Kaner, C., Bach, J., and Pettichord, B. *Lessons Learned in Software Testing*: John Wiley & Sons; 2002.

5. Siy, H. and Votta, L. *Does the Modern Code Inspection Have Value?* Bell Labs — Lucent Technologies, 1999.

6. Patton, R. *Software Testing*, SAMS Publishing, 2001.

7. Adams, E. Optimizing preventive service of software products. *IBM Journal of Research and Development*, 28(1):2–14, 1984.

8. Mockus, A. and Votta, L. Identifying reasons for software changes using historic databases. *International Conference on Software Maintenance*, 2000.

9. Herbsleb, J. and Grinter, B. Conceptual simplicity meets organizational complexity: case study of a corporate metrics program. *International Conference on Software Engineering*, 1998.

10. El Emam, K. *Software Defect Management Best Practices*: Cutter Consortium, Agile Project Management Advisory Service, Executive Report, 3(4), April 2002.

11. El Emam, K. and Wieczorek, I. The repeatability of code defect classifications. *Ninth International Symposium on Software Reliability Engineering*, 1998.

Chapter 3

Software
Quality Practices

There are many software practices that can improve quality. Before proceeding further in describing how these practices can provide benefits to software projects, it is useful to examine some quality practices to develop a better understanding of what they are and how they work.

This chapter briefly presents the low hanging fruit — the practices that:

- Are relatively easy to implement
- Have a substantial ROI
- Can be easily automated
- Have a strong track record or evidence base that their benefits are difficult to question.

Later in this book we will quantify the benefits from these quality practices.

3.1 Software Inspections

Software inspections constitute one of the most powerful methods for detecting defects in software artifacts. In practice, the most inspected software artifact is the source code, but there are other types of documents that can be inspected. For example, one can inspect design documents, project plans, and test cases. If your software process eliminates or

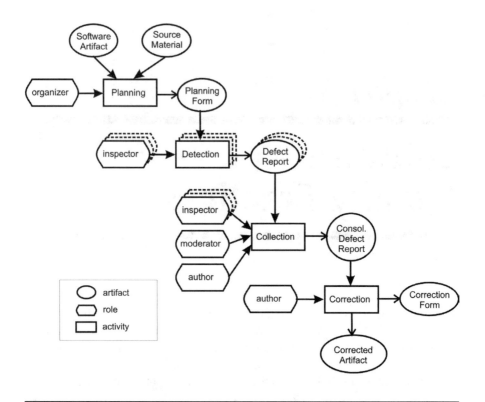

FIGURE 3.1   An overview of the inspection process.

minimizes documentation, then the source code will be the main document that is inspected (e.g., if an agile process is being followed). For the following exposition it is assumed throughout that the document being inspected is source code.

Defects are found through a manual process whereby a group of engineers read the source code, looking for defects. A classic inspection process looks like Figure 3.1. This shows the activities, and the inputs and outputs. The process has four main steps; a quick overview of them appears below.

The first activity in an inspection is **planning**. To start planning, the author of the code submits it to an inspection. This is usually done after the author has successfully unit tested the code. She can nominate a peer to organize the inspection or organize it herself.

The organizer first checks the code to make sure that it is of sufficient quality to be inspected. If the code was obviously of such low quality then it would be a waste of other people's time to find defects that the author should have easily found herself. In such a case, the organizer can refuse to initiate the inspection.

Second, the organizer identifies peers who are qualified to perform an inspection. Peers should have the technical expertise to identify defects in the code. It is also advisable to include peers who are knowledgeable about the components interfacing with the code being inspected.

Assuming that the identified peers accept to inspect the code, then the inspection goes ahead, and the organizer arranges the logistics of the inspection (such as book any required meeting rooms). The organizer also identifies the other material that needs to be made available to all of the inspectors and distributes it.

The inspectors perform defect **detection** individually during the detection activity. Each inspector will independently read the code and identify perceived defects in it. These defects and their locations are marked on the code. This activity is also sometimes referred to as **preparation**.

The main objective of the inspectors during preparation is to identify major defects. These are the defects that will be observable by the customer if they remain. Minor defects are things such as bad programming style and modifications to comments and documentation. While these are useful from a software maintainability perspective, they are optional.

The **collection** activity involves the inspectors and the author meeting to consolidate the defects that each of the inspectors has found. A trained moderator runs the inspection meeting. Usually, the moderator is also the organizer.

The purpose of the meeting is only to log the unique defects found by each inspector and not to discuss why a defect exists or what are the possible solutions. Some of the items identified by the inspectors during their individual search for defects may be false positives. The false positives should become apparent during the meeting.

The unique set of defects is then given to the author of the code, who fixes all of the defects. This is the **correction** activity. The inspection is over when all of the defects have been fixed.

3.1.1 Why Inspections Work

While there are many ways to find defects in code, inspections are much cheaper. Two other means for finding defects are testing and customers finding the defects.

When a defect is found during an inspection, the cause of the defect is already known. Thus, the effort to identify the cause of a symptom is minimal or nonexistent. Compared to testing and customer detected defects, this can be a dramatic cost saving.

During testing, one observes symptoms and then has to trace back from the symptoms to the cause and fix the cause. Furthermore, for many large systems, setting up the test environment can be time consuming because specific hardware and network configurations need to be prepared beforehand. For example, it is not uncommon for test labs with specialized equipment to be in use 24 hours a day by different groups trying to test their software.

When a customer finds a defect, then you must have a support organization that will log customer problem reports. The more problems that are reported, the larger this support organization must be. The more customers you have, the more likely that they will repeatedly report the same problems (rediscoveries). Although they are repeats, you will need an even larger support organization to respond and log these problem reports. Then, these reports must be consolidated and the causes of the problems identified. The code is fixed and then re-tested. An intermediate release or patch is prepared and shipped to all the customers. This whole process, and its concomitant costs, is unnecessary if there are no problems reported by the customers. In addition, there is the dissipation of reputation and goodwill as more problems are found by your customers.

3.1.2 The Benefits of Inspections

Inspections have qualitative or "soft" benefits in addition to the their ability to detect defects. The main benefits of inspections include:

- Inspection participants learn about the types of defects that are typically introduced and try to avoid them in the future. Therefore, inspections provide a feedback loop where developers can learn from their and their peers' mistakes.
- Inspection participants learn good practices from carefully scrutinizing the work of their peers. Again, this is part of the feedback mechanism where good practices can be learned.
- They convince participants to develop more understandable products. Because each person's work will be scrutinized by peers, there is a motivation to deliver work that is of good quality. So inspections encourage engineers to be more careful.
- Inspections are an excellent source of data for quality management. Even minimal data collected during inspections can allow management to make estimates of how many defects are in the software.
- Reduce the possibility of a "single point of failure" where all domain or technical knowledge is vested in a single individual — inspections are a vehicle for sharing knowledge across the project.

Some claimed benefits of inspections that are more qualified include:

- Inspections help create a "team spirit" (during inspection meetings). For large projects where the project team is distributed in multiple floors, buildings, or sites, then this is an important benefit. However, for smaller projects where the whole team is co-located, this is a weak advantage.
- It has been argued that inspection can be used as part of the training for new staff. In general, this is not an effective way to train staff. If new engineers need to be trained, they should attend a proper training program. Participation in inspections is a useful complement to reinforce the training program.

3.2 Risk Assessment Using Metrics

In many projects there are insufficient resources to test all of the code very thoroughly and there are insufficient resources to inspect all of the code. In such a case, it is necessary to make choices. For example, the project team must decide which part of the code will receive the most thorough testing or which subset of the code will be inspected.

The idea behind risk assessment is to find the modules or components of the system that have the highest risk of failing. The project team can then focus its efforts on these parts rather than indiscriminately across the whole system. This allows a much more efficient use of resources.

Static metrics collected during a software project can be used to identify high-risk modules or components. This section describes a methodology that employs metrics to identify such high-risk modules.

An illustration of this methodology is given in Figure 3.2. The first step is to collect the static metrics from an earlier release. These metrics are then used as the basis for risk assessment in current and future releases.

To perform risk assessment using metrics, it is necessary to build a risk model. Figure 3.2 illustrates where the risk model fits into the risk assessment process. A risk model is a statistical model that can be used to predict the probability that a module will have a post-release defect. As shown in the figure, one typically uses historical data to build such a model. The historical data may come from a previous release of the same product or even from another similar product within the same organization.

A risk model is typically a statistical model relating the metrics to the probability of a defect. Although many different statistical modeling techniques can be used, I have always obtained good results with a technique called logistic regression, which is well suited to this kind of modeling problem.

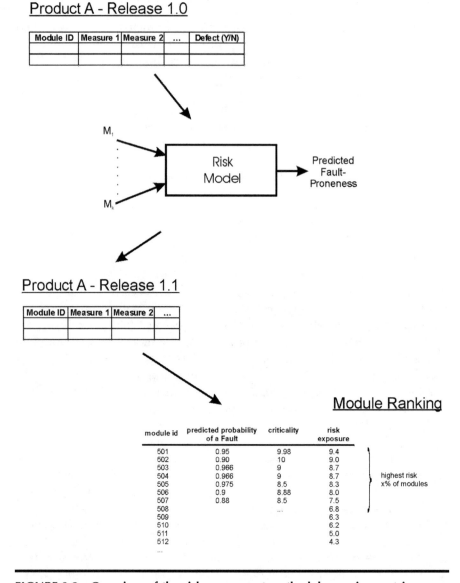

Product A - Release 1.0

Module ID	Measure 1	Measure 2	...	Defect (Y/N)

M₁ ⋮ M_k → **Risk Model** → Predicted Fault-Proneness

Product A - Release 1.1

Module ID	Measure 1	Measure 2	...

Module Ranking

module id	predicted probability of a Fault	criticality	risk exposure	
501	0.95	9.98	9.4	
502	0.90	10	9.0	
503	0.966	9	8.7	
504	0.966	9	8.7	highest risk
505	0.975	8.5	8.3	x% of modules
506	0.9	8.88	8.0	
507	0.88	8.5	7.5	
508		...	6.8	
509			6.3	
510			6.2	
511			5.0	
512			4.3	
...				

FIGURE 3.2   Overview of the risk assessment methodology using metrics.

The risk model can then be used to predict the probability of a post-release defect for the current and subsequent releases. In the example in Figure 3.2, we assume that the risk model is built from release n and we want to identify the high-risk modules for release n+1. Once the risk model is built from the release n data, the same metrics are collected from release n+1. The release n+1 data excludes post-release defects because we do not know that (if we did, we would not need a risk model). The new data is entered into the risk model that then produces the predicted probability.

The probability is a number between 0 and 1. The modules are then ranked by their predicted probability of a post-release defect, as shown in Figure 3.2. The top x percent are considered the highest risk modules.

The risk assessment approach so far does not take into account the business importance of the modules. Some modules perform critical functions for the software. If these modules have a defect, then the entire system will not function as expected. Even if the probability of a defect for these critical modules is relatively small, it is still important to pay attention to them. Similarly, some modules may have a high probability of a post-release defect but they perform very auxiliary functions. So if we have to make a choice, the low criticality modules would not be given much attention. It is therefore important to take into account how important a module is (in terms of the functionality it provides) when deciding where to focus the inspections and testing resources.

Criticality is a business decision. In my practice, we usually use a 1 to 10 scale to assign criticality to the modules. For large systems this is not plausible. So, use cases or requirements scenarios are assigned criticality values. Use cases are frequently used to describe "features" or a coherent set of functionality that the software is expected to perform. Some of these use cases have a very high business value. The project team would assign criticality values to the use cases on a 1 to 10 scale. Modules that implement highly critical scenarios are then considered very critical. So we essentially trace from the business requirements to the modules, see which modules implement the use case, and assign the module the same criticality as the use case. Because a single module can implement many use cases, some summary measure such as the average criticality can be used for each module. This process is much easier if a design tool is used to document use cases.

Multiplying the probability of a post-release defect with the criticality for each module gives the **risk exposure**. This is a summary measure that can be used to rank modules. The big advantage of risk exposure is that it captures the quality of the module as well as its business value. Ranking by risk exposure is illustrated in Figure 3.2.

The top x percent of the modules are then the high-risk modules. Depending on the scenario you are in, these modules are then inspected, or tested first.

One example of where this was applied is a project that was being developed in Java and used UML design models.[1] The project manager wanted to start design inspections but he did not have the resources to inspect everything. So a risk model was developed from a previous release

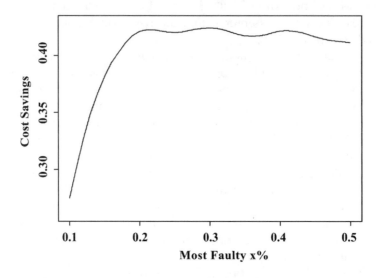

FIGURE 3.3 **Example of post-release cost savings as the number of classes inspected rises (i.e., as x percent rises). The x-axis shows the percentage of Java classes that would be inspected expressed as a fraction. For example, if the x-value is 0.1, this means that the top 10 percent of the classes in terms of risk would be inspected. The y-axis shows the effort savings expressed as a fraction. For example, a y-value of 0.2 means that in total 20 percent of the post-release effort would be saved.**

and was used to identify the high-risk Java classes for the current release. The post-release cost savings using this strategy were calculated as illustrated in Figure 3.3. Here we see that if the highest-risk 20 percent of the classes were inspected, the post-release cost savings would be around 42 percent. This means that the post-release costs would be 42 percent less compared to no inspections being performed.

The above methodology works whether one is using object-oriented techniques or structured techniques. It also works well irrespective of the size of the project.

3.3 Test-Driven Development

Test first programming (also known as Test-Driven Development or TDD) is a recently popularized approach to programming that stipulates writing unit test cases before writing the code.[2,3] To succeed, it relies strongly on test automation. It is one of the main practices in Extreme Programming. It became popular as Extreme Programming became more widespread.

TDD is different from the common practice of writing code first and then testing it. In common practice, the amount of unit testing done is driven by how much time is available — which is usually not enough. This results in many unit test suites being weak and covering only the most obvious cases. In fact, there are many organizations that either do not perform unit testing at all or where the performance of unit testing is rather poor and is not automated.

TDD effectively forces a certain level of discipline in unit testing. This by itself is a major advantage. To write tests before programming, the developers also need some definition of the API before they start. This ensures that there is a design. Again, forcing the developers to start with a design is a substantial advantage compared to what is typical today.

With TDD, the developer incrementally writes a test for the next smallest piece of functionality that should be implemented. Then that functionality is written and the test executed against the new code. Any bugs are fixed immediately. Given that the tests are automated, all tests can be executed at every iteration, ensuring that all functionality is still working.

Evidence is accumulating that TDD results in improved quality. There are two mechanisms that explain why under the TDD paradigm software quality improves:

1. The number of test cases that are written is higher compared to the more traditional testing approach of testing programs after they have been developed. This is because testing is not left to the end; it is the first thing programmers do.

2. The quality of the tests written is better when using TDD. The tests developers write with TDD tend to be more generic and cover the boundary conditions much better. This means that TDD tests are more comprehensive and deal with erroneous inputs more thoroughly. It makes sense because it is well known that programmers who test their own code typically write tests to deal with the situations that they have already thought of. If they have already thought of a situation or condition, then their code deals with it correctly. Therefore, the post-code tests are not going to be very effective at finding defects. With TDD, the tests are written from an understanding of the requirements rather than of the code that has already been written.

A recent study at IBM reported a 50 percent improvement in quality with TDD compared to the incumbent unit testing approach. Additional experimental studies that have just been completed at the time of writing demonstrate similar benefits in quality using TDD.

3.4 Automatic Defect Detection

Automatic defect detection implies using a tool. The tool would analyze the source code and look for defects. This can be considered an automation of the more manual software inspection. However, tools can only find a small fraction of the defects that a manual code inspection can find. Nevertheless, because the effort required to detect these defects is quite small, the effort savings from these tools can be considerable. Furthermore, these tools are constantly improving and therefore their "hit rate" is increasing.

The types of defects that an automatic inspection tool can identify are (I am assuming a language such as C or C++): NULL pointer dereferencing, out of bounds array access, memory management (checking the value of new calls and checking for memory leaks), bad deallocation of memory, uninitialized variables, identification of dead code, things to watch out for when moving from C to C++ (e.g., using new and delete instead of malloc and free), constructors and destructors (e.g., defining a copy constructor and assignment operator for classes with dynamically allocated memory), inheritance (e.g., defining inherited non-virtual functions, and the use of casts down an inheritance hierarchy), and ambiguous or bad constructs (e.g., assignments within conditions, the use of goto statements).

One way such a tool would be used in practice is that before manual inspections it would be executed to analyze the code. As a consequence, a list of potential defects is flagged. Developers then go through the flagged defects and remove the false positives. The remaining defects are true defects that need to be fixed.

3.5 Other Practices

There are additional quality practices that will not be covered in detail here but they are important to note. These include:

- *Code base reduction.* One thing we know in software engineering with considerable confidence is that larger units (be they functions or classes, for example) tend to have more defects. Reducing the size of these units and of systems in general (e.g., through refactoring and removing cloned code) can reduce total defects in the system.
- *Efficient changes.* When a failure is discovered in a system, a considerable amount of effort is spent looking for the defects to fix. This is called defect isolation effort. A software failure can occur during testing or operation. Code search and visualization

tools can help programmers see which modules are connected to each other, and this can assist in navigating the software to where the defect is. In addition to reducing isolation effort, a visualization tool can help a programmer avoid bad fixes. These are code fixes that introduce new defects. Bad fixes are typically due to the programmer not realizing the module that has been changed is being used by another module. When one module is changed, the other module breaks because now their behaviors are not compatible.

■ Reduction of code clones. A nontrivial percentage of the code in software applications today is cloned. This means that programmers copied the code from somewhere else and modified it to fit the new context. While a form of reuse, cloning is also ad hoc (i.e., opportunistic) and increases the risk of defects being propagated throughout a system (if the cloned code has a bug). Clone detection tools can help detect all copies of a code fragment that have a bug that should be fixed.

Subsequent chapters look at the costs and benefits of some of these practices as we develop ROI case studies.

References

1. El Emam, K., Melo, W., and Machado, J. The prediction of faulty classes using object-oriented design metrics. *Journal of Systems and Software,* 56(1):63–75, 2001.
2. Beck, K. *Test-Driven Development By Example*, Addison-Wesley, 2003.
3. Astels, D. *Test-Driven Development: A Practical Guide*, Prentice Hall, 2003.
4. Maximilien, E. and Williams. L. Assessing test-driven development at IBM. *International Conference on Software Engineering,* 2003.

Chapter 4

The State of the Practice

Chapter 3 contained an overview of some ROI quality practices. It is informative to find out how many software organizations and projects actually implement such quality practices. As you will see, for many industries and countries, these practices are not widespread. Furthermore, it is useful to see what other quality and general software practices are widely deployed.

This chapter summarizes much of the publicly available data on the adoption of good software engineering practices — practices that result in improved quality. To the extent possible, I have tried to categorize the findings by country, project size, and industry.

In the next chapter we look at an international software quality benchmark. The summaries presented here on the extent of implementation of quality practices provide the context for interpreting the benchmark data.

Because there are many studies to be referenced and many data summaries, the data are grouped. For example, I will look at all of the studies that evaluate how often software inspections are used under one heading. Because many of the studies look at more than one practice, the same studies may be referenced repeatedly.

4.1 Quality Assurance (QA) Function

The first issue we address is how often an actual quality assurance function does exist on the project or within the organization.

TABLE 4.1 Percentage of Organizations Having QA and Metrics Efforts in Place Based on a Worldwide Survey

Business Domain	Existence of a QA Function (%)	Existence of a Metrics Program (%)
Aerospace	52	39
Computer manufacturing	70	42
Distribution	16	—
Finance	57	25
Government	30	5
Health	51	8
Manufacturing	52	25
Oil and gas	40	20
Software	60	36
Telecommunications	54	44
Transportation	33	33
Utility	40	10

Source: From Rubin, H. and Yourdon, E. Industry Canada Worldwide Benchmark Project, Industry Canada, 1995.

A survey of representatives from 150 IT departments[1] found that 31 percent of the respondents do not have software quality professionals in their organizations (69 percent claimed that they do), and 38 percent believed that their SQA capabilities were unsatisfactory.

The results in Table 4.1 indicate that in certain application domains, the QA function is not common in software projects;[2] for example, Distribution (16 percent), Government (30 percent), and Transportation (33 percent). Other domains, such as the software/IT industry and computer manufacturing, are more likely to have a QA function (60 percent and 70 percent, respectively). This is not very surprising, as one would expect that companies that cater to software developers would have a better awareness of quality practices. What is surprising is that in the Health industry, only 51 percent of the organizations stated that they have a QA function. Health care is largely a regulated industry with serious safety implications if there are software defects (whether we are talking about medical devices or general information systems). A similar argument applies to the Aerospace domain, where only half the respondents claim to have a QA function.

TABLE 4.2   Likelihood of Implementing Various Software Engineering Practices based on the Project Size in Function Points (thousands)

Development and Maintenance Activity	1	10	100	1K	10K	100K
Requirements	✔	✔	✔	✔	✔	✔
Prototyping				✔	✔	✔
Architecture					✔	✔
Project plans				✔	✔	✔
Initial design		✔	✔	✔	✔	✔
Detailed design			✔	✔	✔	✔
Design reviews					✔	✔
Coding	✔	✔	✔	✔	✔	✔
Code inspections				✔	✔	✔
Change control				✔	✔	✔
Format integration				✔	✔	✔
User documentation			✔	✔	✔	✔
Unit testing	✔	✔	✔	✔	✔	✔
Function testing			✔	✔	✔	✔
Integration testing				✔	✔	✔
System testing				✔	✔	✔
Beta testing					✔	✔
Acceptance testing				✔	✔	✔
Quality assurance						✔
Installation and training				✔	✔	✔
Project management			✔	✔	✔	✔

Note: This data is based on the presentation in Jones, C. Variations in software development practices. *IEEE Software*, November/December, 22–27, 2003.

The data in Table 4.2 show that only the very large projects are likely to have a QA function (around 100,000 function points). Medium-sized projects and small projects are not likely to have a distinct QA group.

Table 4.3 looks at this issue from an application domain perspective. Here we can see that MIS-type projects are not likely to have a QA

TABLE 4.3   Likelihood of Implementing Various Software Engineering Practices Based on Project Type

Development and Maintenance Activity	MIS	Commercial	Systems	Military
Requirements	✔	✔	✔	✔
Prototyping	✔	✔	✔	✔
Architecture		✔	✔	✔
Project plans	✔	✔	✔	✔
Initial design	✔	✔	✔	✔
Detailed design	✔	✔	✔	✔
Design reviews		✔	✔	✔
Coding	✔	✔	✔	✔
Code inspections				✔
Change control	✔	✔	✔	✔
Formal integration	✔	✔	✔	✔
User documentation	✔	✔	✔	✔
Unit testing	✔	✔	✔	✔
Function testing	✔	✔	✔	✔
Integration testing	✔	✔	✔	✔
System testing	✔	✔	✔	✔
Beta testing		✔	✔	✔
Acceptance testing	✔	✔	✔	✔
Quality assurance		✔	✔	✔
Installation and training	✔	✔	✔	✔
Project management	✔	✔	✔	✔

Note: This data is based on the presentation in Jones, C. Variations in software development practices. *IEEE Software*, November/December, 22–27, 2003. For a definition of these application domains, refer to Appendix A.

function. However, systems software, commercial, and military projects are likely to have a QA function.

These tables indicate that we can be almost certain that small MIS projects will not have QA and large military projects will. This is somewhat consistent with the data in Table 4.1 where, for example, applications in

TABLE 4.4   Percentage of Respondents in a European Survey that Implemented the Following Organizational Structure and Management Practices

Organizational Structure and Management Practices	Adoption Percentage
Nominating software project managers for each project	92
Having the software project manager report to a business project manager responsible for the project's overall benefits to the business	81
Software quality assurance function with independent reporting line from software development project management	48
Establishing a change control function for each project	55
Required training program for new project managers to familiarize them	40
Maintaining awareness of CASE or other new software engineering technologies	41
Ensuring user/customer/marketing input at all stages of the project	64
Ensure availability of critical non-software resources according to plan	45

Source: From Dutta, S., Lee, M., and Van Wassenhove, L. Software engineering in Europe: a study of best practices. *IEEE Software*, May/June, 82–90, 1999.

the Distribution domain (which are mostly MIS type) have a very low QA function adoption rate, at only 16 percent.

An analysis of the CMM for Software assessment data available at the SEI reported that the SQA Key Process Area (KPA) was fully satisfied less than 15 percent of the time in maturity level 1 companies.[4] Of course, companies that have a higher maturity satisfy that KPA by definition. A similar analysis of CMMI data at that time found that 0 percent fully satisfied the Process and Product Quality Assurance Process Area. However, meeting the CMMI requirements is slightly more difficult than meeting the CMM for Software requirements.

A large European study indicated that 48 percent of respondents had a QA function overall.[5] The results are presented in Table 4.4. This survey asked about an independent QA function. One can only speculate that had the question not asked about an "independent" QA function, the percentages would have been a bit higher.

For organizations that tend to have better awareness of software engineering, the adoption of this practice is around 50 to 60 percent. For organizations that are not strong in software engineering, the adoption rate can be very low, ranging from 0 percent to the mid-teens. Larger projects are more likely to have a QA function and MIS projects are less likely to have a QA function.

4.2 Metrics

Software metrics are at the core of most good-quality practices. The metrics vary from the basic ones needed to respond to customer problems (i.e., counting post-release defects), to more sophisticated product metrics such as coupling and inheritance metrics to predict quality levels.

Table 4.1 contains the results of a worldwide survey where one of the questions concerned the existence of a metrics program. The percentages are lower than the existence of a QA function. Government (5 percent), Health (8 percent), and Utilities (10 percent) were right at the bottom. The highest adoption of metrics, which was a mere 44 percent of the respondents, was in the Telecommunications industry. In the telecommunications industry, reporting certain metrics is usually part of the supplier contract. Generally, however, one can conclude from this that metrics adoption is rather weak.

A European survey[5] looked at specific types of metrics (see Table 4.5). Here we see that the adoption of basic metrics, such as defect counts, tends to be high. However, other types of metrics, such as size, effort, and testing efficiency, tend to be collected much less often.

One survey[1] found that 26 percent of the respondents collect development metrics, which are then used to measure quality performance. However, 41 percent reported that the metrics they collect are useless or that they collect no data at all. A different survey of attendees at the QAI testing conference in 2003 found that most of the metrics collected by quality-aware organizations are defect-related (e.g., defects categorized by type, severity, and detection).

The results are consistent across surveys. Metrics collection is not frequent; but when it occurs, defect counts is the most likely type of data collected. That metrics are being collected is not an indication that they are being used. Therefore, the use of metrics for decision making is likely very low indeed.

4.3 Testing

There are many different types of testing. For the purpose of evaluating the extent of adoption, there are four clusters: (1) unit testing, (2) beta testing, (3) regression testing, and (4) the rest. We now look at these results.

TABLE 4.5   Percentage of Respondents in a European Survey Who Implemented the Following Measurement Practices

Measurement and the Application of Metrics	*Adoption Percentage*
Record and feedback of estimated versus actual effort into estimation process	55
Maintenance of records and feedback of size into estimation process	21
Collection of statistics on sources of errors and their analysis for cause detection and avoidance	39
Gathering statistics on testing efficiency and their analysis	12
Use of "earned value" project tracking to monitor project progress	35
Comparison of estimated and actual performance levels	46
Logging of post-implementation problem reports and tracking their effective resolution	78
Existence of records from which all current versions and variants of systems can be quickly and accurately reconstructed	73

Source: From Dutta, S., Lee, M., and Van Wassenhove, L. Software engineering in Europe: a study of best practices. *IEEE Software*, May/June, 82–90, 1999.

Unit testing, as shown in Tables 4.2 and 4.3, is used in projects of all sizes and all domains. That unit testing is so universally implemented does not mean that it is being exercised effectively. This issue is discussed further in Section 4.6 on limitations.

Beta testing is more common for the largest systems and less likely for MIS projects. Both of these findings do make sense because running a good beta program is expensive and would make more sense when budgets are large.

The results in Table 4.6 indicate that regression testing is deployed in about half of the projects. Another survey[8] found that 25 percent of the respondents do not perform regression testing. Table 4.7 contains data from an international survey distributed by country. Here we see that almost all projects in India and Japan perform regression testing, and three quarters in Europe and the United States. The results from a European survey in Table 4.8 indicate that regression testing is deployed in only 32 percent of the cases.[5]

**TABLE 4.6 Percentage of Respondents to a Survey that Use the
Following Practices**

Activity	Mean (%)	Median (%)
Functional specification: percentage of functional specification that was complete before team starting coding	55	55
Design specification: percentage of detailed design specification complete before team started coding	20	10
Design review: whether design reviews were performed during development	79	100
Code review: whether code reviews were performed during development	52	100
Early prototyping: percentage of final product's functionality contained in the first prototype	38	40
Daily builds: whether design changes were integrated into the code base and compiled daily	32	0
Regression tests: whether someone ran an integration or regression test when checking code into the build	55	100

Source: From MacCormack, A., Kemerer, C., Cusumano, M., and Crandall, B. Trade-offs between productivity and quality in selecting software development practices. *IEEE Software,* 2003:78–84.

Therefore, we can conclude that in Europe and the United States, between a third and three quarters of the projects have adopted regression testing, with near universal adoption in India and Japan.

The other types of testing — such as function testing, integration testing, system testing, and acceptance testing — are more likely to be adopted by projects that are medium to large. The very small projects (less than 1000 function points) do not have these practices. This is a bit surprising. For example, a 900 function point C program can be close to 100 KLOC in size — which is not a small undertaking. As for distribution by industry type, all industries are equally likely to adopt all of these forms of testing. The data in Table 4.9 indicates that test planning is not rare (57 percent adoption) and acceptance testing is similar, at 56 percent adoption.

4.4 Software Inspections

There is considerable data on the adoption of software inspections. Table 4.6 shows that 79 percent of the respondents had some form of design review, and 52 percent had some form of code review. Similarly, Table

TABLE 4.7 Quality Practices Used across the World

	India	Japan	United States	Europe + Other	Total
Number of Projects	24	27	31	22	104
Architectural specifications (%)	83.3	70.4	54.8	72.7	69.2
Functional specifications (%)	95.8	92.6	74.2	81.8	85.6
Detailed designs (%)	100	85.2	32.3	68.2	69.2
Code generation (%)	62.5	40.7	51.6	54.5	51.9
Design reviews (%)	100	100	77.4	77.3	88.5
Code reviews (%)	95.8	74.1	71	81.8	79.8
Beta testing (%)	66.7	66.7	77.4	81.8	73.1
Pair programming (%)	58.3	22.2	35.5	27.2	35.3
Regression testing on each build (%)	91.7	96.3	71	77.3	83.7

Source: From Cusumano, M., MacCormack, A., Kemerer, C., and Randall, B. Software development worldwide: the state of the practice. *IEEE Software,* 2003:28–34.

TABLE 4.8 Percentage of Respondents in a European Survey that Implemented the Following Software Project Control Practices

Control of the Software Development Process	*Adoption Percentage*
Production of estimates, schedules, and changes only by the project managers who directly control the project resources	76
Obtaining sign-off from all parties before changing plans by the business project manager	57
Procedures for controlling changes to requirements, design, and documentation	64
Procedures for controlling changes to code and specifications	66
Mechanism for performance of regression testing during and after initial implementation	32
Ensuring testing/verification of every function	55

Source: From Dutta, S., Lee, M., and Van Wassenhove, L. Software engineering in Europe: a study of best practices. *IEEE Software,* May/June, 82–90, 1999.

TABLE 4.9 Percentage of Respondents in a European Survey that Implemented the Following Standards and Procedures

Standards and Procedures	Adoption Percentage
Formal assessment of risks, benefits, and viability of projects prior to contractual commitment	73
Periodic reviews of status of each project by management	80
Procedures to ensure that external subcontracted organizations follow a disciplined development process	33
Independent audits (walkthroughs and inspections of design and code) conducted at each major stage	46
Application of common coding standards to each project	75
Documented procedure for estimation of size and for using productivity measures	20
Formal procedure for estimation of effort, schedule, and cost	50
Formal procedure (like review or handover with sign-off) for passing deliverables from one group to another	47
Mechanism to ensure that the systems projects selected for development support organization's business objectives	41
Procedures to ensure that the functionality, strengths, and weaknesses of the system that the software is replacing are reviewed	29
Test planning prior to programming	57
Independent testing conducted by users under the guidance of SQA before system or enhancement goes live	56
Procedure to check that the system configuration passing user acceptance is the same as that implemented	60

Source: From Dutta, S., Lee, M., and Van Wassenhove, L. Software engineering in Europe: a study of best practices. *IEEE Software*, May/June, 82–90, 1999.

4.7 shows around 77 percent adoption of design reviews in the United States and Europe. Code reviews are used in 71 percent of projects in the United States and around 82 percent of projects in Europe.

However, Table 4.7 also indicates universal adoption of design reviews in India and Japan and also universal adoption of code reviews in India. The Japanese adoption of code reviews is comparable to U.S. numbers.

The results in Tables 4.10 and 4.11 shed some light on the numbers above. It can be seen that informal peer reviews and project reviews are

TABLE 4.10   Results from the QAI Survey

"Static Testing" Activities	*Percent*
Formal inspections	19
Project reviews	58
Peer reviews	56
Structured walkthroughs	34
End-user/customer reviews	42
Other	4

Note: The respondents were attendees at the 22nd Annual International Software Testing Conference in 2002.

TABLE 4.11   Results from the QAI Survey

"Static Testing" Activities	*Percent*
Formal inspections	30
Project reviews	56
Structured walkthroughs	43
End-user/customer reviews	61
Other	5

Note: The respondents were attendees at the Annual International Software Testing Conference in 2003.

common, with adoption rates above 50 percent. Walkthroughs are less common, with adoption rates in the 34 to 43 percent range. However, formal inspection adoption is between 19 and 30 percent. This suggests that the respondents to the previous surveys did not differentiate between the informal peer review and the formal inspection, hence explaining the large discrepancy between the two sets of studies. It seems more likely that the adoption rates of formal inspections are below 50 percent.

The data in Table 4.9 indicates that independent audits occur 46 percent of the time.

Tables 4.2 and 4.3 indicate that design reviews and code inspections are most likely on the large projects. Design reviews are common in commercial, systems, and military projects. However, this is more likely an informal review. Code inspections are most likely in military projects.

TABLE 4.12 Percentage of Respondents in a European Survey that Implemented the Following Tools and Technologies

Tools and Technology	Percentage (%)
Usage of tools for tracing forward and backward through requirements, design, and code	29
Usage of a design notation such as SADT	41
Usage of automated testing tools	26
Usage of software tools for tracking and reporting the status of the software/subroutines in the development library	39
Usage of prototyping methods in ensuring the requirements elements of the software	59
Availability of data dictionary for controlling and storing details of all data files and their fields	49
Usage of software tools for project planning, estimation, and scheduling	71

Source: From Dutta, S., Lee, M., and Van Wassenhove, L. Software engineering in Europe: a study of best practices. *IEEE Software*, May/June, 82–90, 1999.

TABLE 4.13 Distribution of Quality-Related Tool Usage Based on a Survey of More than 150 Software Development Organizations

Type of Tool	Percent (%)
Configuration management	52
Software testing	49
Software development metric collection and analysis	26
Software fault monitoring	24
Do not use any SQA tools	26

Source: From Beck, K., Bennatan, E., Evans, D., El Emam, K., Guttman, M., and Marzolf, T. *Software Quality Management Best Practices*, Cutter Consortium, 2003.

4.5 Tools

The most common tools, according to Table 4.12, are those used for project planning and scheduling. Testing tools are used by 26 percent (Table 4.12) to 49 percent (Table 4.13) of the projects. Tools for metrics data collection and analysis are not common at all, being adopted by only 26 percent of the projects (Table 4.13).

Rather surprisingly, only 52 percent of the respondents to the study in Table 4.13 report that they use configuration management tools. One can make a strong case that configuration management tools are fundamental to any project's success.

4.6 Limitations

While this chapter has presented a wealth of information based on benchmarks and surveys worldwide, the numbers have some limitations that should be considered when interpreting the results.

Some of the studies collected data about projects and others collected data about organizations (e.g., the SW-CMM assessment results apply organizationwide). The assumption we make is that if a practice is said to be implemented organizationwide, then it will also be implemented among projects.

The respondents to the surveys discussed here were not indicating how often they were actually using the practices on their projects, only that they did. They also did not indicate how rigorously the practices were followed. For example, some of the surveys on inspection adoption did not differentiate between informal peer reviews and code inspections.

At a broad level, we can divide software projects into two categories: (1) those that are serious about software quality and (2) those that are not. The answers we obtain about adoption of quality practices will depend on which group we survey.

For example, a survey conducted in a conference on software quality will find a large proportion of respondents adopting testing techniques. The same would not be true for a broad survey of the software industry, which will include a large proportion of projects that do not care about quality. Organizations that answer surveys and that participate in process assessments tend to be quality conscious — that is, they care about quality. Therefore, the results presented here will tend to show a higher adoption rate than one would expect to see in all of industrial practice.

We expect that the data presented in this chapter reflects projects that care about quality. If we wish to generalize these results to the entire software industry, then one should interpret the numbers here as upper bounds. The adoption of quality practices across the whole of the software industry is likely lower than the percentages presented here would suggest.

References

1. Beck, K., Bennatan, E., Evans, D., El Emam, K., Guttman, M., and Marzolf, T. *Software Quality Management Best Practices*, Cutter Consortium, 2003.
2. Rubin, H. and Yourdon, E. Industry Canada Worldwide Benchmark Project, Industry Canada, 1995.
3. Jones, C. Variations in software development practices. *IEEE Software*, November/December, 22–27, 2003.
4. Zubrow, D. What process appraisals tell us about QA: an analysis of CMM and CMMI findings. *International Software Quality Conference,* Toronto, October 2003.
5. Dutta, S., Lee, M., and Van Wassenhove, L. Software engineering in Europe: a study of best practices. *IEEE Software*, May/June, 82–90, 1999.
6. MacCormack, A., Kemerer, C., Cusumano, M., and Crandall, B. Trade-offs between productivity and quality in selecting software development practices. *IEEE Software,* 2003:78–84.
7. Cusumano, M., MacCormack, A., Kemerer, C., and Randall, B. Software development worldwide: the state of the practice. *IEEE Software,* 2003: 28–34.
8. Bennatan, E. Software testing — Paying now or paying later. II. Paying (some) later, Agile Project Management Advisory Service — Executive Update, Cutter Consortium, 4(11), 2003.

Chapter 5

A Software
Quality Benchmark

A healthy percentage of software organizations admit to having quality problems. One survey of close to 180 companies[1] revealed that 34 percent had "too many" problems post-release. Another survey of 120 organizations[2] found 33 percent of the respondents confessing that they release software with too many defects. These are the percentages of companies *admitting* that they have quality problems — the true number is probably much higher than that.

This chapter presents the results from a number of international benchmarks and surveys that demonstrate the quality levels of software being shipped today. Quality in these benchmarks is defined as defects found post-release per some unit of size. The two measures of size that we use are KLOC (thousands of lines of code) and function points (FPs).

5.1 Data Sources

We utilize four data sources for our benchmarks: (1) the Industry Canada data set, (2) the Jones data set, (3) the ISBSG data set, and (4) the MIT study data set. These are summarized below.

5.1.1 The Industry Canada Data Set

This was an international survey sponsored by Industry Canada.[3] The survey was conducted by mail. The extensive questionnaires collected considerable data on the processes that the companies were following, as well as performance metrics.

5.1.2 The Jones Data Set

Capers Jones' (ex)company has been performing benchmarking and process assessment studies for almost two decades. In a recent publication he notes that they have collected data from 350 corporations and 50 government organizations in 20 countries.[4] All of their assessments are performed at the project level. Data are collected during group interviews with management and technical staff. A questionnaire included in Jones publication[4] is used as a guide for the interviews. Follow-up phone calls are used to collect further information after the interviews.

5.1.3 The ISBSG Data Set

The ISBSG (International Software Benchmarks and Standards Group) is based in Australia (the Web site is http://www.isbsg.org.au). It collects data about software projects from around the world through local software metrics organizations.

Further descriptive information regarding the projects that were part of the ISBSG benchmark is presented in Appendix B.

5.1.4 The MIT Study Data Set

This worldwide benchmark study was led by MIT and Harvard.[5] An instrument collecting data on project outcomes and practices was administered over the Web. Companies were invited to respond, and a total of 104 responses were obtained. Little information is available about the validation methodology in the published article, but these authors do have a track record of methodologically sound work.

Further descriptive information about the projects that were part of the survey is presented in Appendix B.

5.2 Benchmarks

The data in Table 5.1 illustrates a number of points. First, contemporary software does have a healthy dose of defects in it. Second, across many important business areas, Canadian software quality tends to be lower than its U.S. counterpart. Sometimes, this difference is staggering.

TABLE 5.1   Number of Post-Release Defects per Thousand Lines of Code (KLOC) in Various Industries in the United States and Canada

Business Domain	United States	Canada
Aerospace	2.49	4.8
Finance	3.1	4.2
Software	2.8	2.02
Distribution	2.1	N/A
Telecommunications equipment	1.8	15
Telecommunication services	1.9	8.5

Source: From Rubin, H. and Yourdon, E. Industry Canada Worldwide Benchmark Project, Industry Canada, 1995.

TABLE 5.2   Delivered Defects per Function Point (average) for Different Business Domains

	Small Projects		Medium Projects		Large Projects	
Business Domain	Average	Best	Average	Best	Average	Best
MIS	0.15	0.025	0.588	0.066	1.062	0.27
Systems software	0.25	0.013	0.44	0.08	0.726	0.15
Commercial	0.25	0.013	0.495	0.08	0.792	0.208
Military	0.263	0.013	0.518	0.04	0.816	0.175

Note: The domains are defined in Appendix A).[4] For MIS and commercial projects, a small project is 100 FP, a medium project is 1000 FP, and a large project is 10,000 FP. For systems software and military projects, a small project is 1000 FP, a medium project is 10,000 FP, and a large project is 100000 FP. The backfiring table for converting these numbers to defects per KLOC is included in Appendix D.

Now consider an example to illustrate the implications of these numbers. One would expect a 29-million LOC operating system built in the United States to have more than 81,000 post-release defects!!

An examination of the data in Table 5.2 indicates that, across all business domains, there tend to be more defects per unit of size for larger projects than for smaller projects. Also, the table indicates that commercial and MIS software tends to have more defects than the other domains.

Table 5.3 shows that new development and enhancement releases tend to have rather similar defect densities. Here we display both the median and the mean because the distribution of defect density is quite skewed.

TABLE 5.3   Defect Density Values by Development Type of the Project

Development Type	Median Defect Density	Mean Defect Density
New development	0.0179	0.1022
Enhancement	0.0182	0.0876
Redevelopment	0.0203	0.0395

Note: Defect density is defined as defects per Function Point. This is derived from the ISBSG data set. The backfiring table for converting these numbers to defects per KLOC is included in Appendix D.

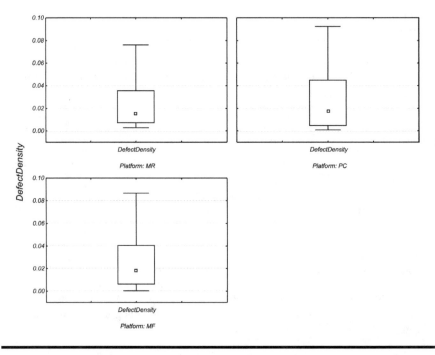

FIGURE 5.1   Box-and-whisker plots showing the distribution of defect density by platforms. This is derived from the ISBSG data set. MR: mid-range; PC: personal computer; MF: mainframe.

Figure 5.1 depicts the variation for each of three (target) platforms. While the median defect density is more or less the same across the platforms (also see Table 5.4), the variability is highest with PC applications. This means that quality is less predictable with PC applications than with mainframe and mid-range applications. Also, the maximum defect density is highest with PC applications.

TABLE 5.4 Defect Density Values by Deployment Platform

Development Type	Median Defect Density	Mean Defect Density
Mainframe	0.0179	0.0649
Midrange	0.0157	0.1755
PC	0.0173	0.0727

Note: Defect density is defined as defects per Function Point. This is derived from the ISBSG data set. The backfiring table for converting these numbers to defects per KLOC is included in Appendix D.

TABLE 5.5 Defect Density of ISBSG Projects by Their Business Domains

Domain	Median Defect Density	Median Defect Density
Sales	0.0165	0.032
Financial (excluding banking)	0.029	0.096
Insurance	0.0175	0.0407
Accounting	0.0171	0.0227
Inventory	0.0178	0.1456
Banking	0.0158	0.0216
Manufacturing	0.0118	0.1471
Telecommunications	0.0176	0.0501
Marketing	0.0322	0.1477
Legal	0.0206	0.0548
Engineering	0.0225	0.2295
Personnel	0.0218	0.0259

Note: Domains with less than five observations are not shown. Defect density is defined as defects per Function Point. The backfiring table for converting these numbers to defects per KLOC is included in Appendix D.

Table 5.5 indicates that manufacturing and banking tend to have the lowest defect density and that marketing applications tend to have the highest defect density.

The ISBSG data set reveals that smaller projects tend to have a higher defect density. The smallest third had 0.0277 defects per FP, while the largest third had 0.0130 defects per FP. This is contradictory to the previous results from the Jones data set. Such contradictions make it difficult to

TABLE 5.6   Median Defect Density for Software Projects across the World from the MIT Study

	India	Japan	United States	Europe and Other	Total
Number of projects	24	27	31	22	104
Defect density	0.263	0.02	0.4	0.225	0.15

Note: The defect density is defined as the median number of defects found within 12 months post-release per KLOC. The results are categorized by country and region. The total is the median of the total data set.

Source: From Cusumano, M., MacCormack, A., Kemerer, C., and Randall, B. Software development worldwide: the state of the practice. *IEEE Software*, pp. 28–34, 2003.

draw strong conclusions about whether or not larger projects have higher quality. Larger projects tend to have better disciplines and practices. However, because of their size, larger software will have more defects in it. Whether the increased defects are adequately addressed by the better practices will depend on how rigorously these practices are applied. One can argue that the more mature a large project is, the lower its defect density. This is consistent with the benchmarks in that the Jones data set relied on estimated defect density when actual numbers were not available — so that data set comes from organizations with a wide spectrum of maturity. The ISBSG data set used data provided by the projects — hence, only projects that are more mature will have that data to report upon. Therefore, the ISBSG data set tended to have more mature projects.

The results in Table 5.6 are the most recently reported but they do provide comparative values across different regions of the world. The first thing to note is that the quality of Indian, Japanese, and European software is higher than that of the United States. The Japanese results are quite startling in terms of their low defect density. The Indian results, demonstrating higher quality compared to that in the United States, are likely to fuel the offshore outsourcing debate.

An examination of the descriptive summary of the MIT data (in the appendix) does not indicate substantive differences in the types of projects between the United States and India to explain the quality differences. One other explanation is that the Indian software companies that did respond tended to have better software quality practices. This is plausible, given that the October 2002 update of high maturity organizations (published by the Software Engineering Institute) notes that there were 50 SW-CMM Level 5 organizations in India whereas there were 20 in the United States. To the extent that more of those high maturity Indian companies responded, then this would explain the quality differences.

5.3 Summary

These benchmarks demonstrate an important point: that contemporary software has many defects in it. Note that organizations that have reported defect data are the ones that are most likely doing well. That is, they are not representative of the software engineering industry; rather, they are mostly the organizations that have the best quality levels or that care enough about quality to actually collect some data about it. The real situation in the software industry is worse than alluded to by these numbers.

The positive side of this is that, given that the bar is so low, it is not tremendously difficult for any single organization to improve its quality and be a leader in its industry. This, as we shall demonstrate, can have substantial benefits for the software vendor as well as the vendor's customers.

References

1. Bennatan, E. Software testing — Paying now or paying later. II. Paying (some) later, Agile Project Management Advisory Service — Executive Update, Cutter Consortium, 4(11), 2003.
2. Beck, K., Bennatan, E., Evans, D., El Emam, K., Guttman, M., and Marzolf, T. *Software Quality Management Best Practices*, Cutter Consortium, 2003.
3. Rubin, H. and Yourdon, E. Industry Canada Worldwide Benchmark Project, Industry Canada, 1995.
4. Jones, C. *Software Assessments, Benchmarks, and Best Practices*, Addison-Wesley, 2000.
5. Cusumano, M., MacCormack, A., Kemerer, C., and Randall, B. Software development worldwide: the state of the practice. *IEEE Software,* pp. 28–34, 2003.

Chapter 6

Quality and the Cost of Ownership

This chapter presents a model for calculating the relationship between software quality and the cost of ownership of software. Through a number of examples, we demonstrate that low-quality software can be quite expensive for the customer.

6.1 A Definition of Customer Costs

When software is purchased, customer costs consist of three elements:

1. *Pre-purchase costs* constitute the resources expended by the customer to investigate different software companies and products.
2. *Installation costs* constitute the resources invested in installing and verifying the operation of new software beyond that which is covered in the purchase contract (i.e., as part of the purchase price).
3. *Post-purchase costs* constitute the resources to deal with software failures, including consultants and the maintenance of redundant or parallel systems.

For our purposes, we focus mainly on the latter two cost categories as being the most relevant. Both cost categories increase when there are defects in the software.

Installation defects typically are due to interface problems with legacy systems or interoperability with preinstalled software. For commercial (shrink-wrap) software, installation problems are usually minimal. However, if there are problems during installation, the customer bears the cost of trying to figure out the problem and making support calls to the vendor. For customized software, there are greater chances of installation difficulties. Dealing with them may entail expenditures on consultants and third-party integrators. Additional cost components here are those of lost productivity due to the software not being installed on time, and lost sales or revenue due to the unavailability of an operational system.

Post-purchase costs occur because the customer has to deal with failures of the software or lower performance than expected. This entails interacting with the vendor to describe and recreate the problem, and implementing workaround procedures (which may be inefficient) while waiting for the fix. Bugs may result in the loss of data and the need to reenter them, and may result in capital costs being incurred due to early retirement of new but ineffective systems. Another cost of failures is that of operating redundant or parallel systems at the same time as the new software until the new software is fully functional with no quality problems.

Also, vendors regularly send patches to their customer to fix newly discovered problems. It is quite common for the customer not to install the patches out of fear that the patches will cause more or new problems. Therefore, latent defects in the software can affect customers even if fixes exist and the customer has the fixes. In fact, the customer may be prepared to continue suffering the financial consequences of a buggy product for a long time to avoid taking the risk of installing a patch.

If the customer decides to install the patch, additional costs would be incurred to set up a test system and perform an acceptance test of the newly patched system before deploying it. If the acceptance test passes, then deploying the new patched system includes backing up all the data and switching over. If there are problems during the switch-over, the system must be rolled back. Because typically switchovers must be performed outside regular work hours, the systems staff must be paid overtime to complete this.

These costs tend to be different across enterprises depending on whether the customer company is small or large. Small companies tend to incur relatively larger costs due to software defects because[1]:

- ■ Smaller companies are less likely to have internal support staff that can help troubleshoot and correct errors. This means that the customer must go back to the vendor, which takes longer. The consequence is that the disruptive effects of defects last longer.

■ Larger corporations tend to get higher priority from the software vendors. Therefore, their requests for fixes, patches, and workarounds get more immediate attention than smaller companies. Also, large companies are more likely to have internal support staff (or a help desk) that can solve many problems right away without calling the vendor. Therefore, the disruptions from discovering problems are minimized.

For example, in the manufacturing sector it has been estimated that the software defect costs per employee vary from U.S.$1466.1 to U.S.$2141.4 for small companies (less than 500 employees), and from U.S.$128.9 to U.S.$277.8 for large companies (more than 500 employees).[1] For a 100-person company, that translates to U.S.$146,614 to U.S.$214,138; and for a 10,000-employee company, that makes U.S.$1,289,167 to U.S.$2,777,868 per year.

6.2 Savings from Higher-Quality Software

We can derive a model to estimate the savings to the customer from purchasing higher-quality software. The scenario is that of a customer choosing between two products from two vendors. The products are to perform the same functions.

To develop a model that is actionable and where sufficient benchmark data is available that can be used, certain assumptions should be made. The approach that we take is to make assumptions that are *conservative*. That means we will make assumptions that result in the estimate of savings from better quality being underestimated rather than being exaggerated. This way, we develop a *lower bound model*.

The installation and post-purchase costs for a customer who has bought a software product are given by:

$$\text{Customer Cost} = Q \times S \times C \times P \qquad (6.1)$$

where:

Q = The quality of the product defined in terms of defect density. Defect density is total defects found by all customers after release per one thousand lines of code or Function Points (or some other size measure).

S = This is the size of the product in thousand lines of code or Function Points (or some other size measure).

C = The cost per defect for the customer. This is due to installation and post-purchase problems.

P = The proportion of defects that the customer finds. It is defined as the fraction of all of the defects in the software that a single customer is likely to find. For example, if it is 0.01, it means that any single customer is likely to experience 1 percent of all the detectable defects in the software.

Let us assume that we have two software products, A and B, that have the same functionality (i.e., say the Function Points count is the same). Let us also assume that A has higher quality than B (i.e., it has a lower defect density). These two products are of the same size and will be used in the same way. A customer can choose between these two products. The percentage cost savings to the customer from using product A as opposed to product B would be:

$$\text{Percentage Savings} = \frac{\left[\text{Customer Cost}_B\right] - \left[\text{Customer Cost}_A\right]}{\left[\text{Customer Cost}_B\right]} \times 100 \quad (6.2)$$

For example, if the percentage saving is 20 percent, then this means that the costs incurred by the customer due to quality problems in product A (the installation and post-purchase costs) would be 20 percent less than that of owning product B.

We can make the assumption that the sizes for A and B are the same because we are talking about the same system functionality. Therefore, the percentage savings equation becomes:

$$\text{Percentage Savings} = \frac{\left[Q_B \times C_B \times P_B\right] - \left[Q_A \times C_A \times P_A\right]}{\left[Q_B \times C_B \times P_B\right]} \times 100 \quad (6.3)$$

We can simplify this to:

$$\text{Percentage Savings} = \left(1 - \frac{\left[Q_A \times C_A \times P_A\right]}{\left[Q_B \times C_B \times P_B\right]}\right) \times 100 \quad (6.4)$$

Let:

P_A = the proportion of defects that the customer finds in program A
P_B = the proportion of defects that the customer finds in program B

And, because B has more defects than A, we would also expect that:

$$P_B > P_A \quad (6.5)$$

Then, it is clear that:

$$\left(1 - \frac{\left[Q_A \times C_A\right]}{\left[Q_B \times C_B\right]}\right) < \left(1 - \frac{\left[Q_A \times C_A \times P_A\right]}{\left[Q_B \times C_B \times P_B\right]}\right) \tag{6.6}$$

Therefore, if we use the following equation, we are actually calculating a *lower bound* on the percentage saving:

$$\text{Percentage Savings} = \left(1 - \frac{Q_A \times C_A}{Q_B \times C_B}\right) \times 100 \tag{6.7}$$

The C component in the above equation (cost per defect) reflects organizational costs due to defects. Therefore, one can argue that the cost per defect will be the same for both products A and B. However, we show below that even if a new product has close to zero defects, the costs of the better product still do not reach zero.

The cost incurred by the customer due to defects has two elements:

1. Mitigation costs, which are the costs that the customers incur in response to defects actually manifesting themselves
2. Avoidance costs such as installation costs and redundant system costs

There is evidence that the mitigation costs of the customers are linearly proportional to the reduction in defects.[1] This means that as the number of defects detected decreases, the customer costs decrease proportionally.

However, the avoidance costs decrease nonlinearly with defects.[1] In fact, in many instances, the benefits of reduced defects do not really accrue until the defect counts approach zero. For example, redundant systems must be kept in place even if one defect remains because one defect is sufficient to bring down the whole system, which would then require the redundant system to kick in. Similarly, some of the customer costs will not disappear even if the software did have zero defects. For example, there will always be installation costs even for perfect software because some of the legacy applications that the new software integrates with might have defects that can become exposed during installation.

For the avoidance costs we make the conservative assumption that a reduction in defects will have no impact on the customer because in most cases it is unlikely that the true defect density will approach zero. The only component that can be reduced due to better-quality software is the mitigation component.

Based on the recent data collected by NIST,[1] we can make another conservative assumption that 75 percent of the post-purchase customer costs are mitigation costs, and the remaining 25 percent are avoidance costs. This means that if the defect content of the software went all the way to zero, 25 percent of the current post-purchase costs would still be incurred.

To demonstrate the conservatism in this assumption, the NIST report notes that the cost per defect in the manufacturing sector is, on average, U.S.$4,018,588. The total of installation, acceptance, maintenance, and redundant system costs per firm (the avoidance costs) is U.S.$258,213. If, on average, a firm experiencing defects has 40 major ones per year, then the mitigation costs can actually be quite large compared to avoidance costs according to these numbers.

Therefore, if we say that 75 percent of customer costs are mitigation costs that decrease proportionally to defect reduction, then the above equation becomes:

$$\text{Percentage Savings} = \frac{Q_B - Q_A}{Q_B} \times 100 \times 0.75 = \left(1 - \frac{Q_A}{Q_B}\right) \times 75 \quad (6.8)$$

which gives a lower bound on the post-purchase cost savings from improved quality.

There are two interesting things to note about Equation (6.8). First, in practice, it is quite easy to get comparative values for Q_A and Q_B. Even if Q_A and Q_B are not readily available, there are reliable ways to estimate their ratio using black-box testing techniques. Therefore, it provides us with a very actionable model for evaluating the customer cost. Second, the excessive conservatism that we emphasized in deriving our model, as you will see, does not dilute the strong conclusions that can be drawn about the cost of quality to the customer.

A purchasing decision is complex and many factors enter into making it, such as financial and technical. However, given the direct relationship between quality and customer cost, a consideration of quality may very well influence the ultimate decision to buy. We now look at a number of examples to illustrate the benefit of better-quality software from the customer perspective using benchmark data.

6.3 Benchmarking Customer Costs

Tables 6.1 through 6.3 are based on published data and illustrate the savings to the customer under a diverse set of scenarios. The savings are calculated according to Equation (6.8).

TABLE 6.1 Percentage Reduction in Installation and Post-Purchase Ownership Costs due to Improved Quality from the Customer's Perspective

	ML1	ML2	ML3	ML4	ML5
ML1		12.6%	27.7%	52.2%	64.5%
ML2			18%	47.6%	62.4%
ML3				38.8%	58.3%
ML4					40.5%
ML5					

Note: Improved quality is measured in terms of higher SW-CMM maturity.

6.3.1 SW-CMM Example

Jones[3] has published the defect density of software from companies at different maturity levels as measured on the Capability Maturity Model for Software. If we consider the average values, we can construct Table 6.1, which shows the reduction in the customer's cost as the maturity of the supplier increases. The rows are the maturity levels of the low-maturity supplier and the columns are the maturity levels of the higher maturity supplier. The cells are the savings due to moving from the lower maturity supplier to the higher-maturity supplier.

For example, software from companies at ML3 (CMM Maturity Level 3) is 27.7 percent cheaper from the customer's perspective compared to software from an ML1 company. One can also see that there are dramatic reductions in the customer cost as the maturity of the supplier reaches the higher levels.

6.3.2 Customer Savings by Industry, Country, and Platform

We can also compare the customer cost when buying software from average companies in their domain versus best-in-class ones. Jones[2] identifies delivered defects per Function Point for average and best-in-class companies in a number of different business domains. Best-in-class are the top performers in their domain (defined as the top 10 percent).

Using those numbers we can determine the cost savings to a customer from buying software from an average company compared to a best-in-class company. These results are shown in Table 6.2. As is obvious, there are quite dramatic benefits to the customer from buying software from a

TABLE 6.2 Percentage of Customer Installation and Post-Purchase Cost Reduction between the Average and Best-in-Class Companies in Each Business Domain at the Three Project Sizes

	Small Projects (%)	Medium Projects (%)	Large Projects (%)
MIS	62.5	66.6	55.9
Systems software	71.1	61.4	59.5
Commercial	71.1	62.9	55.3
Military	71.3	69.2	58.9

Note: See Appendix A for definitions of these domains. For MIS and commercial projects, a small project is 100 FP, a medium project is 1000 FP, and a large project is 10,000 FP. For systems software and military projects, a small project is 1000 FP, a medium project is 10,000 FP, and a large project is 100,000 FP.

Source: From Jones, C. *Software Assessments, Benchmarks, and Best Practices,* Addison-Wesley, 2000.

TABLE 6.3 Installation and Post-Purchase Cost Savings to the Customer in terms of Buying Software from the Best Performers versus Average and Worst Performers within Each Country

	Best-in-Class versus Average Performers (%)	Best-in-Class versus Worst Performers (%)
Australia	53.25	69.75
Canada	66	69.75
India	72	74.25
Japan	63.75	74.25
Netherlands	60	69
United Kingdom	60.75	74.25
United States	52.5	70.5

Note: This means that, for example, if an Australian customer buys software from a company that delivers best-in-class projects, then their post-purchase costs would be about 70 percent cheaper compared to if they buy it from a worst performer and over 50 percent better compared to if they buy it from an average performer.

best-in-class company that delivers high-quality software. The savings in ownership costs can be quite large compared to average producers (assuming a bell curve, one can make the reasonable assumption that at least half of the vendors in each category are at or below average).

Based on defect density data collected during the most recent ISBSG benchmark (see Appendix B for a descriptive summary of this data set), we can evaluate the difference to the customer in acquiring software from best-in-class companies (in the top 10 percent as measured by delivered defect density) and average performers. We also compare best-in-class to worst performers (bottom 10 percent as measured by delivered defect density).

The within country data is presented in Table 6.3. Note that one cannot do country-by-country comparisons using these summaries. However, this indicates within each country the difference to the customer in buying software from the best performers.

The next summary shows the results based on the business domain for which the software is being built. This is shown in Table 6.4. And the final summary compares the savings within target platforms, as shown in Table 6.5.

6.4 Discussion

The data in this chapter, especially taking into account the conservatism in the assumptions made, provides compelling evidence that substantial reductions in post-purchase costs can be gained by focusing on higher-quality suppliers. In fact, one would contend that in many cases the savings would exceed the actual initial and annual licensing costs of the software.

To illustrate, let us consider a 100-employee U.S. company in the manufacturing sector (automotive) whose total annual company costs associated with software defects in CAD/CAM/CAE or PDM software is $146,614. Let us say that this software is purchased from an average company (i.e., one who produces average quality software). Now, if the vendor had bought the software from a best-in-class vendor (savings of at least 52.5 percent in defect costs), the three-year present value of the savings, assuming a 5 percent discount rate, is $209,614. This saving comes about from switching suppliers from an average one to a best-in-class one that can deliver higher-quality software.

A more general view is given in Figure 6.1 and Figure 6.2 where we plot the savings over three years for small and large companies, respectively. These plots assume that each company purchases five software products to run their business (i.e., we aggregate the savings across five

TABLE 6.4 Installation and Post-Purchase Cost Savings to the Customer in terms of Buying Software from the Best Performers versus Average and Worst Performers within Each Business Area

	Best-in-Class versus Average Performers (%)	Best-in-Class versus Worst Performers (%)
Sales	51.75	63.75
Financial (excluding banking)	65.25	74.25
Insurance	49.5	68.25
Accounting	51.75	63
Inventory	34.5	73.5
Banking	63.75	70.5
Manufacturing	61.5	74.25
Telecommunications	69	73.5
Marketing	64.5	74.25
Legal	54	72
Engineering	65.25	74.25

Note: This means that, for example, if a customer buys sales software from a company that delivers best-in-class projects, then their post-purchase costs would be over 60 percent cheaper compared to if they buy it from a worst performer and over 50 percent better compared to if they buy it from an average performer.

TABLE 6.5 Installation and Post-Purchase Cost Savings to the Customer in terms of Buying Software from the Best Performers versus Average and Worst Performers within each Target Platform

	Best-in-Class versus Average Performers (%)	Best-in-Class versus Worst Performers (%)
Mainframe computers	64.5	73.5
Mid-range computers	53.25	71.25
PCs	63.75	74.25

Note: This means that, for example, if a mainframe customer buys software from a company that delivers best-in-class projects, then their post-purchase costs would be over 70 percent cheaper compared to buying it from a worst performer and around 64 percent better compared to buying it from an average performer.

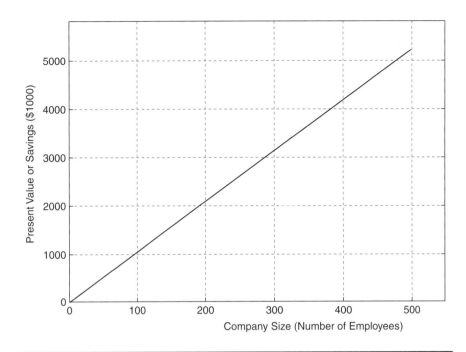

FIGURE 6.1 An example of the benefits from buying five software products from a best-in-class supplier compared to an average supplier. This shows present value of savings over three years for a U.S.-based company in the manufacturing sector assuming a 5 percent discount rate over three years. This graph assumes only small companies up to 500 employees. Some of the values used to perform this computation were obtained from NIST.

We make similar assumptions to produce this plot as the Department of Commerce report did when generalizing from their sample to the overall U.S. economy.[1] However, that report and all of its estimates assumed that the customer is using a single product (i.e., their quality estimates were too low). In our analysis we make the more realistic assumption that customers will have multiple software products and each contributes to the overall cost of low quality.

products). If the purchases were greater than five, then of course the savings would be larger.

While vendors use various lock-in mechanisms to make it more expensive for a customer to switch to a different product, the users of software should consider the savings from moving to a product with fewer defects when calculating their switching costs. This would at least place increased pressure on vendors to improve their quality.

Two concrete actions that a customer can take to ensure that she is buying a higher-quality product are to:

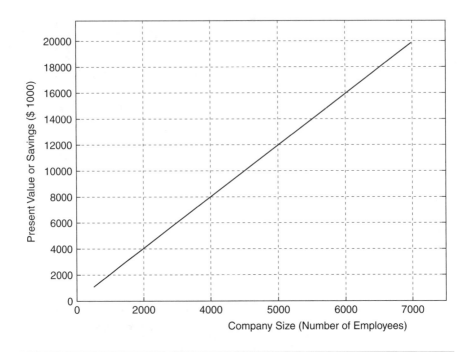

FIGURE 6.2   An example of the benefits from buying five software products from a best-in-class supplier compared to an average supplier. This shows present value of savings over three years for a U.S. based company in the manufacturing sector assuming a 5 percent discount rate over three years. This graph assumes only large companies with greater than 500 employees. Some of the values used to perform this computation were obtained from NIST.

We make similar assumptions to produce this plot as the Department of Commerce report did when generalizing from their sample to the overall U.S. economy.[1] However, that report and all of its estimates assumed that the customer is using a single product (i.e., their quality estimates were too low). In our analysis we make the more realistic assumption that customers will have multiple software products and each contributes to the overall cost of low quality.

1. Evaluate the maturity of the vendors from which she buys software
2. Evaluate the software product itself

Organizations that are more mature tend to employ more good software engineering practices.[4] There is accumulating evidence that higher-maturity organizations produce higher-quality software.[5] Therefore, it would pay to seek higher-maturity suppliers and demand that existing suppliers invest in improving their maturity levels.

References

1. NIST. The Economic Impacts of Inadequate Infrastructure for Software Testing, National Institute of Standards and Technology, U.S. Department of Commerce, 2002.
2. Jones, C. *Software Assessments, Benchmarks, and Best Practices*, Addison-Wesley, 2000.
3. Jones, C. The economics of software process improvements, in *Elements of Software Process Assessment and Improvement*, El Emam, K. and Madhavji, N. (Eds.). IEEE CS Press, 1999.
4. El Emam, K. and Madhavji, N. *Elements of Software Process Assessment and Improvement*, IEEE CS Press, 1999.
5. El Emam, K. and Goldenson, D. An empirical review of software process assessments, *Advances in Computers*, 53:319–423, 2000.

Chapter 7

Quality and the Cost to Developers

It is almost an axiom that higher software quality benefits the developers of software. While we explore that in a bit more depth later on, in this chapter we try to develop an understanding of the economics of software projects by looking at cost distributions and how the cost distributions are affected by quality improvements.

7.1 Project Costs

Figure 7.1 shows a typical breakdown of software project costs. This breakdown covers the total life cycle of a software product from initiation to retirement. We consider the development (pre-release) activities separately from the maintenance (post-release).

In many organizations, maintenance consumes a significant portion of the IT budget.[1] For example, as a percentage of total budget, maintenance has been estimated to consume 40 percent,[2] between 40 and 70 percent,[3] 35 percent,[4] and 55 percent.[5]

Every project has fixed and overhead costs. These include things such as rent, furniture, and electricity bills. Typically, these costs are a small fraction of total project costs. The fixed and overhead costs apply across the whole project, whether it is pre-release or post-release.

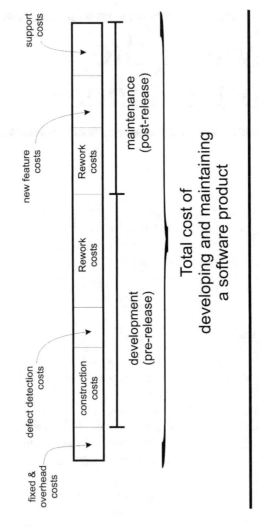

fixed & overhead costs

defect detection costs

construction costs

Rework costs

development (pre-release)

new feature costs

Rework costs

support costs

maintenance (post-release)

Total cost of developing and maintaining a software product

FIGURE 7.1   A breakdown of software project costs.

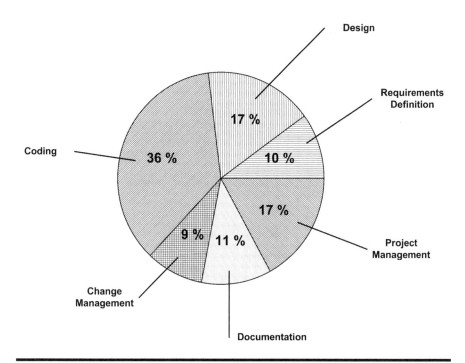

FIGURE 7.2 **The distribution of costs across the main activities that make up software construction during development for MIS projects.** *(Source:* **From Jones, C.** *Estimating Software Costs.* **McGraw-Hill, 1998.)**

7.1.1 Distribution of Pre-Release Costs

Construction costs consist of the effort associated with the actual software development activities, such as requirements analysis, design, and coding. The distribution of construction costs for MIS projects is shown in Figure 7.2. Here we see the percentage of effort devoted to each of the main activities that make up construction. Figures 7.3, 7.4, and 7.5 show the same distribution for systems projects, commercial projects, and military projects, respectively. A definition of these application domains is provided in Appendix A.

As the pie charts show, coding takes up much of the construction costs. This is followed by design and project management. It should be noted that the averages in these figures are for 1000-Function Point projects (around 100 KLOC in a language such as C). One would expect less effort on design and project management for smaller projects, as well as a larger emphasis on coding in smaller projects.

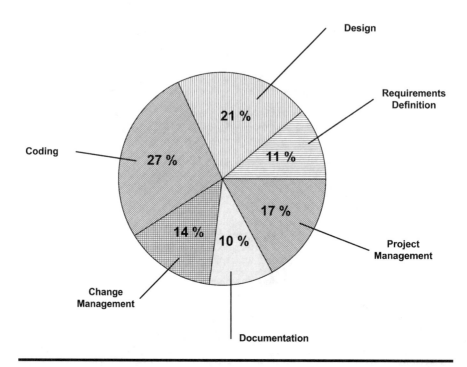

FIGURE 7.3   The distribution of costs across the main activities that make up software construction during development for systems projects. (*Source:* From Jones, C. *Estimating Software Costs.* McGraw-Hill, 1998.)

Defect detection costs comprise the effort to look for defects introduced during construction. Defect detection includes activities such as inspections (peer reviews), testing, and root cause analysis. One estimate puts testing as consuming between 22 and 36 percent of development costs.[6] Other studies suggest that over half, and in some instances approaching 90 percent, of total development effort is spent on testing for a wide variety of application domains.[7-9] As can be gathered, the percentage of effort devoted to testing varies widely across the industry.

Rework costs are all costs to fix defects. Pre-release rework is due to fixing defects found during inspections and testing, as well as other defect detection activities before the product is released. A large portion of effort is spent on fixing defects that have been discovered. These fixes can occur at various stages of a project (for example, during inspections), but mostly take place during testing. One published report notes that 44 percent of total development project costs is rework.[10] Other data shows ranges of rework from 20 percent to as high as 80 percent.[11]

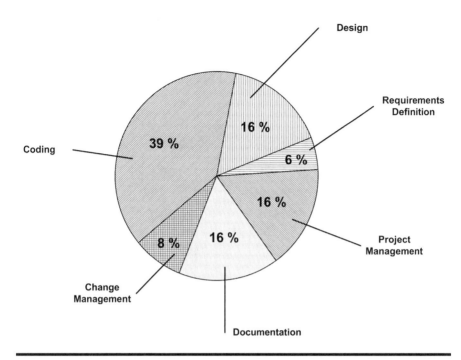

FIGURE 7.4 The distribution of costs across the main activities that make up software construction during development for commercial projects. (*Source:* From Jones, C. *Estimating Software Costs.* McGraw-Hill, 1998.)

Rework costs are distributed across all pre-release activities but tend to concentrate around coding in most projects.

7.1.2 Distribution of Post-Release Costs

Post-release rework is due to fixing defects that were detected largely by customers. However, a minority of defects will be found through internal testing even after a product is released. After a product is released, further effort is spent adding new features and porting the application.

There are two ways to measure post-release rework:

1. As effort spent on correcting defects or "corrective maintenance"
2. As the number of changes that are corrective in nature

These are both discussed below.

During post-release, one study estimated that 24 percent of maintenance resources is consumed by testing.[12] The total effort spent on rework

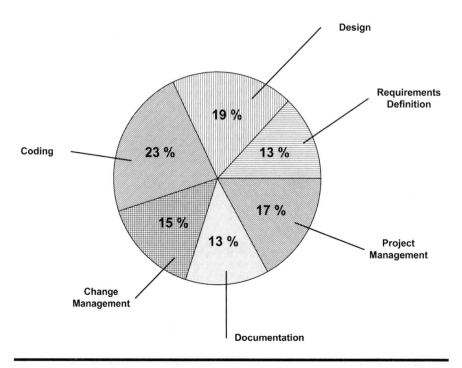

FIGURE 7.5 **The distribution of costs across the main activities that make up software construction during development for military projects. (*Source:* From Jones, C. *Estimating Software Costs*. McGraw-Hill, 1998.)**

varies, for example, 14 percent,[12] 26 percent,[2] 17.4 percent,[3] 17 percent (a study by Ball[5]), 16 percent (a study by Dekleva[5]), and 21 percent.[5] One study that utilized direct observation and measurement of maintainers' work practices estimated that they spend, on average, 57 percent of their time fixing bugs.[13] Overall, Canadian software companies spend 35 percent of their maintenance resources on fixing bugs, versus 28 percent of maintenance resources in the United States.[14]

There have been studies that look at the proportion of changes that are of a corrective nature. One found that 43 percent of the post-release changes were corrective for a real-time system, up to 74 percent of the changes were to fix bugs in the Linux kernel, and up to 68 percent of the changes were to fix bugs in the GCC compiler.[15] An examination of the changes for a large real-time system found that up to 45 percent of the maintenance change requests had to do with fixing defects.[16]

There are also the costs associated with running a support function. Sidebar 7.1 provides a more detailed discussion of the economics of the support function.

▼

SIDEBAR 7.1   Understanding Support Costs and Benefits

It is estimated that software companies spend, on average, a little over 8 percent of their revenues on support activities.[1] These costs exclude the defect fix costs, which are usually taken care of by the development organization. The average proportion of staff employed in the support function is 15 percent of total headcount.[2]

Some organizations I work with generate a tidy revenue from the support organization. One company I know generates about one third of its revenue from the support function. A recent survey reports that support can contribute 30 to 40 percent of an organization's revenues.[1]

This can be achieved by having separate support and maintenance contracts with customers. There are a number of models that can be used for support contracts:

■ A per-incident model whereby the customer pays a flat fee for each support incident, irrespective of how long it took to resolve it.

■ A per-minute model whereby the customer pays for the amount of time it took to process the support request

■ An annual fee contract, irrespective of the number of support incidents and how long they take

The per-minute model tends to be less popular in practice. For corporate customers, the annual fee is most popular, whereas for personal or individual users, the fee per incident model is most popular. One possible explanation for this is that the cost per support incident tends to decrease as the number of seats sold increases. Therefore, it is more profitable to have an annual fee based model for large customers.

There is a relative reduction in the number of support incidents as the number of seats sold increases. The number of seats refers to the number of actual users of the software. Clearly, enterprise licenses will have many more seats than individual licenses, for example.

Support contracts are priced to exceed the expected cost of the support organization, and a sales staff is employed to maximize the annual renewal of these contracts. For annual plans, the most common pricing model is to have support as a percentage of the list price of a software product. It is common to charge between 15 and 20 percent of the list price for support.[1]

It is reported that enterprise customers are less likely to purchase annual support contracts for lower-priced products, but much more likely to purchase support contracts for expensive software.[1] Once a support contract is purchased, the renewal rate approaches 95 percent for the high-end software and a respectable 75 percent for low-end software.[1] This means that it is very important to make the sale of a support contract with the initial purchase of the software. In some instances, for high-end enterprise software, the first year support contract is mandatory as part of the offering.

In practice, the most virulent field defects will occur soon after a release and will have to be fixed anyway because they will affect many customers. After a certain period, the support costs for the organization should decline. The total value of the warranty contracts must exceed the costs of the support organization for that initial post-release period.

As an illustration, let us say that most defects are reported in the first two months after release, and that the support organization cost for two months is $X. If the warranty contracts are annual, the total value of the support contracts sold should exceed kX, where k is the number of major releases per year.

To minimize warranty costs, it is important to have good user documentation and clear help systems. Also, the installation should be very simple and as automated as possible. In many cases, a nontrivial portion of support calls are related to misunderstandings and problems with installation and setting up. For example, one organization incurred considerable support costs because the serial number for installing the software on their packaging was not obvious to find. Soon after release, a large number of support calls came in asking about obtaining a serial number. This was an avoidable cost.

References

1. ASP. Trends in Fee-Based Support, The Association of Support Professionals, 2000.
2. ASP. Technical Support Cost Ratios, The Association of Support Professionals, 2000.

▲

7.1.3 Breakdown of Rework Costs

Rework costs can be further itemized as follows:

- *The effort to recreate the problem.* This is relevant primarily for problems reported by users, where it can take some effort to first find out what the user did and the user's configuration, and then additional effort to set up a similar configuration to recreate the reported problem and confirm its existence.
- *Trace from observed failure to the defect.* This is relevant for problems reported by customers and failures observed during testing. It could take some time to trace from the symptoms that are observed to the actual defects in the code that need to be fixed. This tracing can be manual or aided by debuggers.

- *Implement a fix.* The fix for a particular failure may involve making changes to multiple modules or components. It may involve a redesign of part of the system that is not localized.
- *After making the fix, test cases must be written to test for that particular failure.* The test case is to ensure that the fix is correct, and the test cases go into the regression test suite. The regression test suite ensures that the problem does not occur again inadvertently due to future changes.
- *The regression test suite is then rerun.* Retesting may involve the setup of special hardware or databases, and can be quite expensive.
- Once the fix has passed regression testing, the change usually must be documented or documentation must be updated.
- The fix, alone or perhaps along with other fixes, is packaged into an emergency release, a service release, or a full release and shipped to the appropriate customers. If the product has not been released yet, then special packaging costs for the fix will not be incurred.

The first two items constitute what is known as isolation effort when making a change. One study estimated that 26 percent of the effort to correct defects is spent on isolation.[12]

7.2 The Payoff from Cost Reductions

Software quality practices can lower project costs. If we can reduce the effort for any of the activities depicted in Figure 7.1, then project costs would decrease. Given that a large percentage of total life-cycle costs is rework, reducing rework costs is the best way to reduce project costs. There are many ways to reduce rework costs that are very effective. Two broad approaches are:

1. Reduce the number of defects that are actually introduced into the software.
2. Improve the way defects are detected in the software.

It should be noted that if we managed to eliminate all defects in a software product, the rework costs might go down to zero. However, the defect detection costs would never go down to zero. For example, when software is tested, even if no defects are found, there is a cost incurred for test planning, writing tests, managing the test process, executing tests, and recording the results of testing.

We can also reduce project costs by reducing construction and new feature costs. This can be achieved, for example, through code generation tools and other forms of automation.

In this section we present, at a conceptual level, how the payoff from cost reductions comes about. Let us first consider the payoff from reuse.

In Figure 7.6 we can see the breakdown of project costs without reuse and the breakdown after reuse. It is expected that construction costs will decrease after reuse.[17]

The project that develops the reusable components the first time will have to make an investment. Writing reusable code costs more than code that will not be reused. A subsequent project that is reusing code also must make some investment, albeit a smaller one. This smaller cost involves the effort to identify the code that should be reused, the licensing costs of tools that are required to reuse, and the effort that may be required to wrap and document new interfaces. However, given that code is not being developed from scratch, the overall savings in construction result in an overall reduction in project cost (i.e., overall project cost savings).

In addition, there is evidence that reuse of existing artifacts can improve quality.[18] Reused object-oriented classes tend to have a lower defect density than classes that were new or reused with modification.[19] In general, it was found that reuse reduced the amount of rework. This quality practice, through improving pre-release quality, reduces rework and hence increases overall productivity.

Figure 7.7 illustrates the payoff from techniques that reduce rework. Most of these are defect detection techniques. Here there is an initial investment in defect detection. Therefore, defect detection costs increase, while rework costs before and after release decrease considerably. Hence, the pre- and post-release project cost would be smaller than for the initial project.

When we evaluate ROI, we essentially look at the trade-off between the amount that is invested versus the project savings.

7.3 Reducing Rework Costs

Rework, as the name suggests, involves doing work again. It describes fixing defects in software projects. The cost of rework rises as one moves into later phases of a project. Figure 7.8 illustrates this rise in the cost of fixing defects. The figure assumes that the software had a design defect. The cost of fixing the design defect during design is relatively low. If the defect escapes into coding, then the costs escalate. If the defect slips further into testing and later into release, and is found by the customer, the correction costs can be considerable. Therefore, it is much cheaper

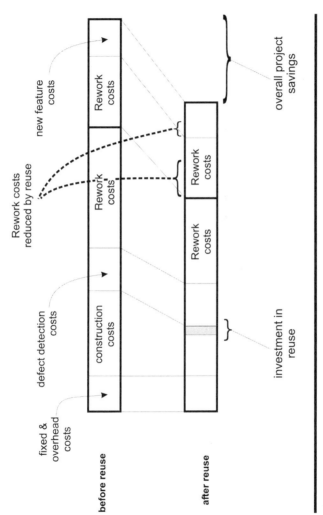

FIGURE 7.6   Illustration of the payoff from increased reuse.

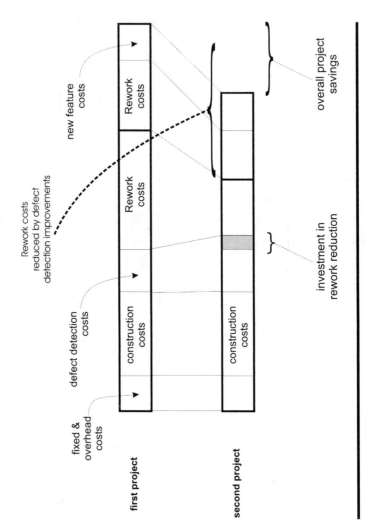

FIGURE 7.7 Illustration of the payoff from better defect detection techniques.

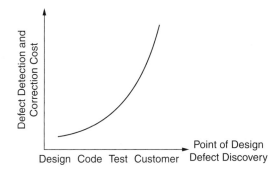

FIGURE 7.8 The increasing costs of fixing a design defect.

to find and correct defects as early as possible when their costs are relatively low.

There are many examples in the literature of the increasing costs of finding defects later in the life cycle. Khoshgoftaar[20] cites a case in a telecommunications company where the cost of a post-release defect was 200 times larger than finding and fixing the defect pre-release. Another telecommunications system project costs a post-release fix as high as 880 times more expensive than when done earlier in a project[21] Further data from other domains shows cost increases per defect greater than 100 times from before to after release[11] for severe defects. One study of a large real-time switching system found that fixing inspection defects was much easier than fixing defects found during testing.[16]

To find a defect as early as possible in the project, various defect detection activities are employed. Figure 7.9 shows an example of a defect detection life cycle throughout a project. Here, both design and code inspections are used to detect defects. Detecting defects during inspections is much cheaper than detecting them in testing or having them be detected by the customer.

Defects in the requirements, architecture, and design documents enter the design inspection process. Effort is spent during the design inspection to find and fix these defects. Some of the fixes will be bad and will introduce more defects. The *bad fix ratio* tells us how many of the fixes that are made will introduce another defect. For example, if this is 10 percent, then one in ten fixes will not be done properly and will introduce another defect. One study found that 27 percent of the correction effort during software maintenance was devoted to bad fixes.[12] Other studies report 17 percent bad fixes in inspections,[22] 5 percent in code inspections, 3 percent in design inspections, and 5 percent in testing.[6]

A design inspection will not capture all defects, so there will be escapes. The number of requirements and design defects detected during the

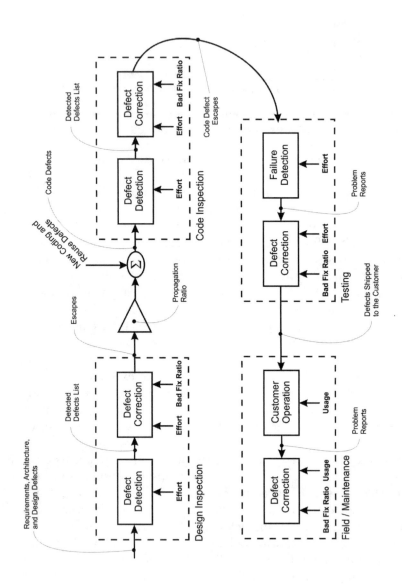

FIGURE 7.9 The defect detection life cycle. Although there is only one testing phase shown, in practice there are many types of testing and testing is performed over multiple phases.

inspection will depend on how well the inspection process is optimized. Escapes occur because there are certain types of defects that a design inspection is not really capable of detecting; and even for those defects that are targeted by the inspection, the inspection process rarely achieves 100 percent perfection. In fact, as shown in Appendix C, the average effectiveness for design and code inspections is 57 percent (i.e., they will find 57 percent of the defects in the design and code, respectively).

An escaped design defect can propagate into more than one coding defect. This is captured by the *propagation ratio* (PR). Usually, this is due to an incorrect assumption made at the design stage that leads to many instances of defects in the implementation, for example, assumptions about the capabilities of an external component.

Further defects will be added to the software during coding. Also, reused code either from third parties as a component or from an earlier release or project will also have defects in it.

Code inspections behave in a manner that is similar to design inspections. After code inspections, the escapes go through testing. Note that there is no propagation ratio for code defects and no new defects are introduced after testing except due to bad fixes.

Testing identifies failures and these are documented as PRs. Programmers then trace from the PRs to defects and fix these. Testing can introduce defects due to bad fixes. Defects that escape testing go into the field where customers discover them. Customers report failures that are documented as PRs, and these then make their way to the development organization for fixing.

One of the major drivers for pre-release defect detection effectiveness (i.e., how well these activities can find defects) is the effort spent on defect detection. The more effort spent on defect detection, the more defects will be found. The relationship is illustrated in Figure 7.10. The

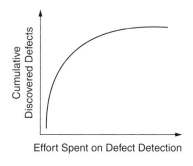

FIGURE 7.10   Relationship between effort spent on pre-release defect detection activities and defects found.

rate at which defects are found tends to plateau because most easy defects are found early and the harder defects remain. Harder defects require more effort to find. In the case of inspections, inspector fatigue results in defect detection slowing down after a certain period of time (around two hours of reviewing time per inspector).

The implication is that there is a trade-off between spending large amounts of effort detecting defects and having defects escape to the customer. For some applications, the trade-off is clear. For example, with safety-critical systems, whatever effort is required to eliminate detected field defects will be spent. But for most projects, this is a business decision. Similarly, if any of the defect detection activities is skipped, then the escapes will increase and the number of defects making it to the field will also increase.

Escapes from testing go to the customer. Post-release defects originate primarily from PRs from external customers. External customer PRs are driven largely by usage, but sometimes there are internal customers who generate PRs, and testing of changes and fixes also identify defects.

References

1. Harrison. W. and Cook, C. Insights into improving the maintenance process through software measurement. *International Conference on Software Maintenance,* 1990.
2. Krogstie, J. and Solvberg, A. Software maintenance in Norway: a survey investigation. *International Conference on Software Maintenance,* 1994.
3. Lientz, B., Swanson, E., and Tompkins, G. Characteristics of application software maintenance. *Communications of the ACM,* 21(6):466–471, 1978.
4. Nosek, J. and Palvia, P. Software maintenance management: changes in the last decade. *Journal of Software Maintenance: Research and Practice,* 2:157–174, 1990.
5. Abran, A. and Nguyenkim, H. Analysis of maintenance work categories through measurement. *IEEE Conference on Software Maintenance,* 1991.
6. Jones, C. *Estimating Software Costs.* McGraw-Hill, 1998.
7. Beizer, B. *Software Testing Techniques.* International Thomson Computer Press, 1990.
8. Hailpern, B. and Santhanam, P. Software debugging, testing, and verification. *IBM Systems Journal,* 41(1):2002.
9. Jones, C. *Software Assessments, Benchmarks, and Best Practices:* Addison-Wesley, 2000.
10. Wheeler, D., Brykczynski, B., and Meeson, R. An introduction to software inspections, in Wheeler, D., Brykczynski, B., Meeson, R. (Eds.), *Software Inspection: An Industry Best Practice.* IEEE Computer Society Press, 1996.

11. Shull, F., Basili, V., Boehm, B., Brown, A.W., Costa, P., Lindvall, M., et al. What we have learned about fighting defects. *Proceedings of the Eighth IEEE Symposium on Software Metrics,* 2002.

12. Basili, V., Briand, L., Condon, S., Kim, Y., Melo, W., and Valet, J. Understanding and predicting the process of software maintenance releases. *Eighteenth International Conference on Software Engineering;* 1996.

13. Singer, J., Lethbridge, T., and Vinson, N. An Examination of Software Engineering Work Practices. National Research Council of Canada, Ottawa. pp. 1–12, 1997.

14. Rubin, H. and Yourdon. E. Industry Canada Worldwide Benchmark Project, Industry Canada, 1995.

15. Schach, S., Jin, B., Yu, L., Heller, G., and Offutt, J. Determining the distribution of maintenance categories: survey versus measurement. *Empirical Software Engineering,* 8:351–366, 2003.

16. Mockus, A. and Votta, L. Identifying reasons for software changes using historic databases. *International Conference on Software Maintenance,* 2000.

17. Poulin, J. *Measuring Software Reuse: Principles, Practices, and Economic Models,* Addison-Wesley, 1997.

18. Thomas, W., Delis, A., and Basili, V. An evaluation of Ada source code reuse. *Ada-Europe International Conference,* 1992.

19. Basili, V., Briand, L., and Melo, W. How reuse influences productivity in object-oriented systems. *Communications of the ACM,* 39(10):104–116, 1996.

20. Khoshgoftaar, T., Allen, E., Jones, W., and Hudepohl, J. Return on investment of software quality predictions. *IEEE Workshop on Application-Specific Software Engineering Technology,* 1998.

21. Baziuk, W. BNR/Nortel path to improve product quality, reliability, and customer satisfaction. *Sixth International Symposium on Software Reliability Engineering (ISSRE95),* 1995.

22. Fagan, M. Advances in software inspections. *IEEE Transactions on Software Engineering,* 12(7):744–751, 1986.

Chapter 8

Quality and Profitability

The amount of money invested in improving software quality is a business decision. One way to inform this decision is to consider how quality and profit are related. An argument can be made that the appropriate investment in quality is the amount that will maximize profit. We explore this idea further in this chapter and describe how to operationalize it.

8.1 Product Positioning

An approach to determine the appropriate investment in software quality is to look at the quality that is expected by the customer base of your product and what price you can charge for it. This is illustrated in the product positioning matrix in Table 8.1.

If the customers bear some of the share of the cost associated with the lack of quality of a product, this will influence the price they are willing to pay. One would expect price and quantity of sales to peak when the costs incurred by the customer are minimized.

For example, for a new entrant in a market, it may be better to follow a market penetration strategy. If customers are price sensitive, then a medium-quality/low-price strategy may be followed. For mission-critical systems, customers expect high quality and they would normally expect to pay a premium for that quality.

Strategies to the right of and below the diagonal are recommended. Strategies to the left of and above the diagonal generally result in loss of market share.

TABLE 8.1 Product Positioning Matrix

		Quality		
		Low	Medium	High
Price	High	Price skimming	High price strategy	High end
	Medium	Low quality	Mid-range	Market penetration
	Low	Low end	Competitive pricing	Price war

8.2 Revenue and Quality

We start by making the assumption that sales are a function of quality. This means that as a company makes a better-quality product, more copies will be sold. One of the reviewers of this book provided me with some counter-examples whereby a product was selling well even though it was known to have many serious bugs. However, in that case, the vendor produced multiple releases in succession, each incrementally improving its quality.

Given the current state of software quality, one can charge a premium for having quality products. Thus, the price can be a bit higher. We also assume that the relationship between revenue and quality is monotonic. Revenue is defined as the multiplication of the price and the quantity sold.

Indefinite increases in quality will not result in indefinite increases in revenue. At some point, revenue will plateau. Possible reasons include:

■ You cannot increase the price anymore because customers will not pay that much.
■ The cost of quality has become too high.

The relationship between revenue and quality can therefore be depicted as in Figure 8.1.

Figure 8.2 depicts the general dynamics that affect revenue. A product with many defects will result in less usage (i.e., fewer buyers or those who buy cannot continue to use the product). Low usage means low revenue. It also means lower post-release costs, as the number of PRs will decrease (because PRs are driven, at least partially, by usage). The fewer defects discovered ensure that post-release costs remain low.

The scenario described above is a state of equilibrium for a low-quality product. This equilibrium is that of low revenue. To the extent that the organization can sustain low revenue, this can continue for quite some time.

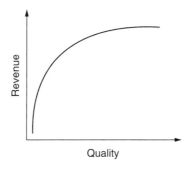

FIGURE 8.1   Relationship between quality and revenue.

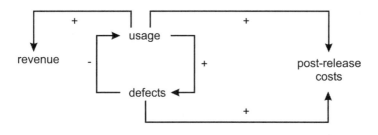

FIGURE 8.2   Dynamics affecting revenue.

Another scenario is that of the high-quality product, which results in higher usage. More usage means more revenues, but also more defects being discovered. The higher usage and defects mean that the post-release costs will increase. Again, this scenario is a state of equilibrium for high-quality products because the revenue will offset the higher post-release costs. To the extent that the organization can invest in quality, revenue would remain high.

8.3 Quality and Profit

If we can keep reducing the development cost by investing in quality, does this mean that one can potentially be very profitable by investing in quality indefinitely? No, this is not the case.

Most software companies have such poor practices that investments in quality will reduce pre-release costs, just as this book describes. However, at a certain point, additional investments in quality become very expensive and have diminishing returns. Very few companies are at that level.

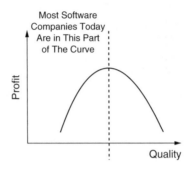

FIGURE 8.3   Relationship between quality and profit.

For example, the project that develops the on-board flight software for the Space Shuttle is at Maturity Level 5 (ML5) on the SW-CMM. This project invests heavily in quality and staff are continuously evaluating and adopting new quality improvement techniques. In one recent article,[1] it was reported that 17 percent of inspections result in a reinspection. This means that the inspection moderator decided that the defects were too important and that the code needed to be reviewed again after the discovered defects are corrected. Out of these reinspections, 65 percent did not find any new defects.

The above example illustrates that there does come a point where the costs of quality improvement become very high, and eventually the potential benefits will not be worth the costs. Except for a few high-maturity organizations in the world, this does not apply. However, this observation allows us to develop a model of profit. We define profit as:

$$\text{Profit} = \left[\text{Revenue}\right] - \left[\text{PreRelease Costs}\right] - \left[\text{PostRelease Costs}\right] \quad (8.1)$$

The relationship between quality and profit is shown in Figure 8.3. Here we see an optimal quality level that maximizes profit. It is probably safe to say that most software companies today have not reached the optimal point yet. However, this diagram illustrates the progression that one would expect to see.

8.4 Improving Productivity

Given that most software companies have not reached their optimal levels of quality, what actions should they take? As a starting point, companies should invest in quality improvement to reach the optimal level. This means that practices that are known to reduce rework should be a primary focus of investment.

FIGURE 8.4   Impact of reducing post-release costs on profit.

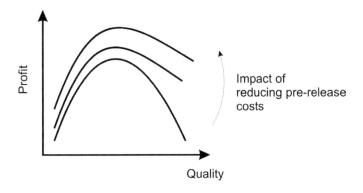

FIGURE 8.5   Impact of reducing pre-release costs on profit.

There are practices that will directly improve productivity, but not necessarily reduce the amount of rework. For example, there are tools that help developers navigate through source code, cross-referencing variables and functions, and identifying uses and used-by relationships among functions. This kind of information can speed up making changes to code because developers spend a large percentage of their time looking for code that they think is related to their current task. Additional practices such as automating regression testing can improve overall productivity.

As Figure 8.4 shows, investment in improving the efficiency of post-release activities results in higher profits for organizations that have not yet reached the optimal point. Today, therefore, for most software companies that have not reached optimal quality, improving the productivity of maintenance activities would be the optimal strategy. As shown in Figure 8.5, investment in improving the productivity of pre-release activities has a relatively much smaller impact on profitability.

Therefore, the second action that software firms should take is to improve the productivity of maintenance.

The above argument highlights an important point: that it is not the best strategy for contemporary software companies to invest during development (i.e., pre-release) in practices and tools that do not improve quality directly, including any forward-engineering tools. For example, investing in new design or requirements methodologies that will not necessarily improve quality is not the optimal choice for most software companies.

References

1. Barnard, J., El Emam, K., and Zubrow, D. Using capture-recapture models for the reinspection decision. *Software Quality Professionals*, 5(2): 11–20, 2003.

Chapter 9

Calculating Return-On-Investment

From a developer's perspective, there are two types of benefits that can accrue from the implementation of software quality practices: (1) money and (2) time. A financial ROI looks at cost savings and the schedule ROI looks at schedule savings.

9.1 Cost Savings

Costs and direct financial ROI can be expressed in terms of effort because this is the largest cost item on a software project. It is trivial to convert effort into dollars. We therefore use effort and dollars interchangeably.

There are a number of different models that can be used to evaluate financial ROI for software quality, and we explore two of them. The first is the most common ROI model; this model is not appropriate because it does not accurately account for the benefits of investments in software projects. This does not mean that that model is not useful (for example, accountants and CFOs that I speak with do prefer the traditional model of ROI), only that it is not emphasized in the calculations herein.

Subsequently presented is the second model, which I argue is much more appropriate. The models here are presented at a rather conceptual level, and this chapter also looks at ROI at the project level rather than

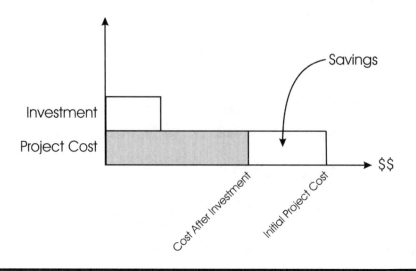

FIGURE 9.1   Definitions of ROI concepts.

at the enterprise level. ROI at the enterprise level (or across multiple projects) requires a slightly different approach, which is addressed later on.

The detailed equations, models, and justifications for the ROI model are presented in Appendix E. This chapter provides highlights and explains the model at a higher level.

Consider the diagram in Figure 9.1. This has cost on the *x*-axis and the categories of dollars spent on the *y*-axis. The lower bar shows the cost of a software project. The top bar shows the cost of an investment in the project. The investment may be in any software quality practice.

After the investment in the project, the project cost goes down because of reduced rework. So now the shaded area is the new project cost. The savings are marked in the figure. The question is whether or not that investment was worth the savings.

The most common ROI model, and the one that has been used more often than not in software engineering, is shown below:

$$\mathrm{ROI}_1 = \frac{\mathrm{Cost\ Saved - Investment}}{\mathrm{Investment}} \tag{9.1}$$

This ROI model gives how much the savings gained from the project were compared to the initial investment. Let us look at a couple of examples to show how this model works.

Let us assume that we have a software project that costs $1000. This is the total cost for the project. In Figure 9.2 we have an example of a specific investment — the investment was of $10. The investment was in

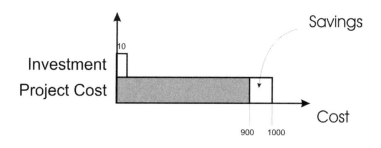

FIGURE 9.2   Example of investment A.

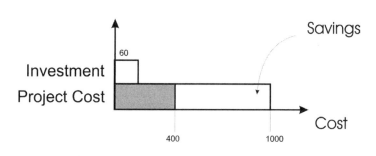

FIGURE 9.3   Example of investment B.

some techniques to improve the development processes and the quality of the product. The benefits gained were a reduction in the total project cost to $900. According to the traditional ROI model, the ROI for this investment is:

$$ROI_1 = \frac{100 - 10}{10} = 9 \qquad (9.2)$$

If we translate this into a percentage, then the ROI is 900 percent: We invested $10 and saved $90.

Now consider the second project in Figure 9.3. If you perform the same calculations for project B, you will see that the ROI for project B is also 900 percent. However, the savings for project B were dramatic: six times more savings than for project A ($540 versus $90). However, the ROI is exactly the same. By most accounts, one would much prefer to have the benefits of a project B and the ROI should reflect that.

Therefore, we do not use the traditional ROI calculations. Rather, we formulate an alternative model that is based on Kusumoto's work.[1] The model is given as follows:

$$\text{ROI}_2 = \frac{\text{Costs Saved} - \text{Investment}}{\text{Original Cost}} \qquad (9.3)$$

This ROI model tracks the benefits of investments very well. It is inter-preted as the overall project savings from the investment (i.e., how much money is saved during the project from the investment).

For project A, the ROI is then calculated as:

$$\text{ROI}_2 = \frac{100 - 10}{1000} = 0.09 \qquad (9.4)$$

This means that in project A, the investment only saved 9 percent of the overall project cost. Now for project B we have:

$$\text{ROI}_2 = \frac{600 - 60}{1000} = 0.54 \qquad (9.5)$$

Therefore, project B had a savings of 54% from its original cost.

To make this realistic, if the original project cost was $1 million, then after investment B of $60,000, the project would cost $400,000, a $600,000 reduction. After deducting the investment itself, this is a savings of 54 percent.

Kusumoto's basic model has been expanded and used to evaluate the benefits of various software engineering technologies, such as inspections and risk assessment.[2-4] In essence, this model has received acceptance in the software engineering scientific community as a valid way to evaluate ROI.

In practice, one of the major differences between ROI_1 and ROI_2 is that the former tends to have larger values. This is a consequence of the fact that the two models really are measuring different things. The former is a traditional measure of ROI, whereas the latter is a measure of savings.

9.2 Schedule Benefits

If software quality actions are taken to reduce the development cost, then this will also lead to a reduction in development schedule. We can easily calculate the reductions in the development schedule as a consequence of reductions in overall effort. This section outlines the schedule benefits of quality improvements. In doing so, it uses the schedule estimation model from COCOMO II.[5]

It is instructive to understand the relationship between project size and schedule as expressed in the COCOMO II model. This is illustrated in Figure 9.4. Here we see economies of scale for project schedule. This means that as the project size increases, the schedule does not increase as fast. The three lines indicate the schedule for projects employing different levels of practices. The lower risk and good practice projects tend to have a shorter schedule.

Another way to formulate the ROI model in Equation (9.3), which will prove handy, is:

$$\text{ROI}_2 = \frac{\text{Original Cost} - \text{New Cost}}{\text{Original Cost}} \qquad (9.6)$$

The New Cost is defined as the total cost of the project after implementing the quality improvement practices or tools. This includes the cost of the investment itself. Let us look at some examples. For project A we have:

$$\text{ROI}_2 = \frac{1000 - 910}{1000} = 0.09 \qquad (9.7)$$

This means that in project A, the investment only saved 9 percent of the overall project cost. Now for project B we have:

$$\text{ROI}_2 = \frac{1000 - 460}{1000} = 0.54 \qquad (9.8)$$

We can then formulate the New Cost as follows:

$$\text{New Cost} = \text{Original Cost} \times \left(1 - \text{ROI}_2\right) \qquad (9.9)$$

Now the schedule reduction (SCEDRED) is formulated as a fraction (or percentage) of the original schedule as follows:

$$\text{SCEDRED} = \frac{\text{Original Schedule} - \text{New Schedule}}{\text{Original Schedule}} \qquad (9.10)$$

By substituting the COCOMO II equation for schedule, we now have:

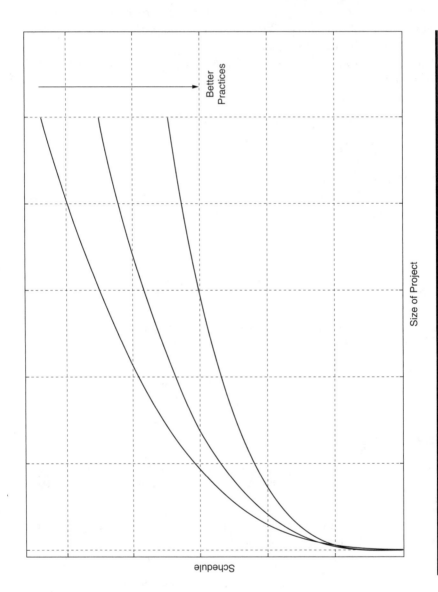

FIGURE 9.4 **Relationship between project size and schedule in COCOMO II.**

TABLE 9.1 Definition of the Five Scale Factors Required for Computing Schedule Reduction

Scale Factor	Definition
Precedentedness (PREC)	If a product is similar to several previously developed projects, then the precedentedness is high
Development flexibility (FLEX)	The extent to which there are flexibilities with respect to preestablished requirements and interfaces
Architecture/risk resolution (RESL)	The extent to which design reviews are performed as well as other risk mitigating factors
Team cohesion (TEAM)	Accounts for the sources of project turbulence and entropy because of difficulties in synchronizing the project's stakeholders, users, customers, developers, maintainers, and interfaces
Process maturity (PMAT)	Maturity as measured by the SW-CMM or its equivalent

Note: The exact way to measure these Scale Factors is described in Appendix F.

$$\text{SCEDRED} = \frac{PM_{\text{Original}}^{\left(0.28+\left(0.002\times\sum_{j=1}^{5} SF_j\right)\right)} - PM_{\text{New}}^{\left(0.28+\left(0.002\times\sum_{j=1}^{5} SF_j\right)\right)}}{PM_{\text{Original}}^{\left(0.28+\left(0.002\times\sum_{j=1}^{5} SF_j\right)\right)}} \qquad (9.11)$$

where:

PM_{Original} = The original effort for the project in person-months
PM_{New} = the new effort for the project (after implementing quality practices) in person-months
SF_j = a series of five Scale Factors used to adjust the schedule (precedentedness, development flexibility, architecture/risk resolution, team cohesion, and process maturity). These are summarized in Table 9.1.

Now, by making appropriate substitutions, we have:

$$\text{SCEDRED} = \frac{PM_{\text{Original}}^{\left(0.28+\left(0.002\times\sum_{j=1}^{5} SF_j\right)\right)} - \left[PM_{\text{Original}}^{\left(0.28+\left(0.002\times\sum_{j=1}^{5} SF_j\right)\right)} \times \left(1-\text{ROI}_2\right)^{0.28+\left(0.002\times\sum_{j=1}^{5} SF_j\right)}\right]}{PM_{\text{Original}}^{\left(0.28+\left(0.002\times\sum_{j=1}^{5} SF_j\right)\right)}} \qquad (9.11a)$$

which simplifies to:

$$\text{SCEDRED} = 1 - \left(1 - \text{ROI}_2\right)^{0.28+\left(0.002\times\sum_{j=1}^{5} SF_j\right)} \tag{9.12}$$

Equation (9.12) expresses the schedule reduction directly in terms of the financial ROI.

The relationship between cost savings and schedule reduction is shown in Figure 9.5. As can be seen, the schedule benefits tend to be at smaller proportions than the cost benefits. Nevertheless, shaving off 10 percent or even 5 percent of your schedule can have nontrivial consequences on customer relationships and market positioning.

9.3 The ROI Evaluation Process

The ROI evaluation presented here focuses on the project as the unit of analysis. Extrapolating these project results to an enterprise level is discussed later on; but for now, just note that an enterprise ROI analysis consists of aggregating the ROI analyses performed for all of the projects within the enterprise.

The first activity in performing an ROI evaluation is to establish a baseline for the project. A baseline consists of two things:

1. A process model of the defect detection life cycle of the project
2. Data characterizing the activities of the defect detection life cycle

These two steps are discussed further below.

Once a baseline is established, the equations and models presented in this book can be used to calculate the ROI values.

9.3.1 Developing a Process Model

The type of process model is rather simple. This process model documents the series of activities throughout the project life cycle that eliminate defects. It is important to have a good understanding of this series because that is the basis for deriving the ROI equations.

Let us take a basic software project. Figure 9.6 shows the defect detection life cycle for that project. Here we have only one activity to detect defects before the product is released — namely, acceptance testing.

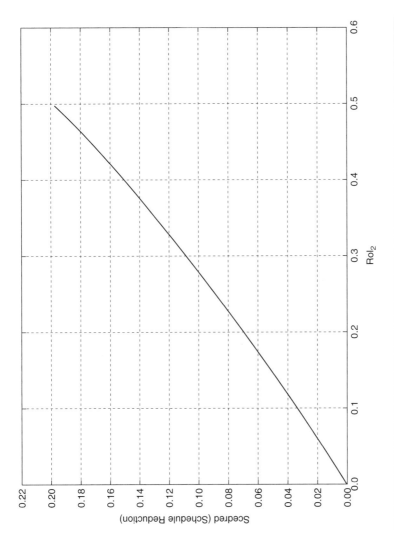

FIGURE 9.5 The relationship between cost savings and schedule reduction for up to 50 percent cost savings. The assumption made for plotting this graph was that all Scale Factors were at their nominal values.

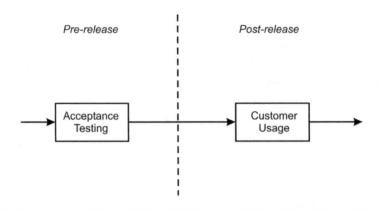

FIGURE 9.6 A basic defect detection life cycle consists of one phase of testing and then customer usage.

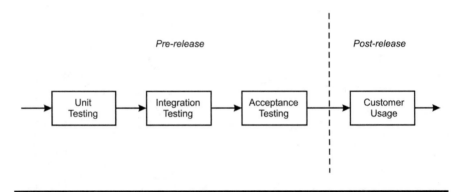

FIGURE 9.7 A more comprehensive defect detection life cycle that has multiple phases of testing but no inspections.

The defects that escape from acceptance testing will go to the customer and will be detected through customer usage.

A more complete model is shown in Figure 9.7. Here we have a typical defect detection life cycle that depends largely on testing to find defects.

Now that we understood the defect detection life cycle before introducing any quality practices, it is necessary to extend the model to take into account the new quality practices that will be added. These activities can be tools as well as processes. For example, if we wish to add code inspections after unit testing, then the desired defect detection life cycle is illustrated in Figure 9.8.

The ROI models that were defined work by comparing the cost structure of the defect detection life cycle *before* introducing a new quality practice with the cost structure of the life cycle *after* introducing the practice. There-

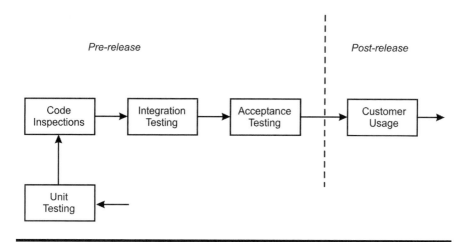

FIGURE 9.8 **A defect detection life cycle after adding code inspections.**

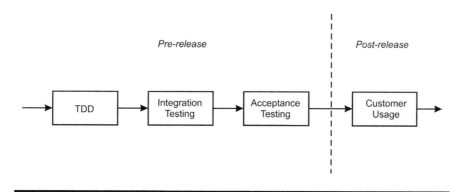

FIGURE 9.9 **A defect detection life cycle where traditional (test last) unit testing is replaced by Test-driven development (TDD).**

fore, when computing the ROI of code inspections, we would compare the cost structure of Figure 9.8 to the cost structure of Figure 9.7.

If the defect detection life cycle were different than that shown in Figure 9.7 and Figure 9.8, then we would get different ROI results for code inspections. Therefore, the ROI results depend on the defect detection life cycles that are being looked at.

There is one further consideration. Sometimes, we do not wish to add a new defect detection activity, but rather we wish to replace an existing activity. Consider Figure 9.9, where we replaced the regular unit testing activity with Test Driven Development (i.e., test first). In such a case, we would be comparing the model in Figure 9.9 with the model in Figure 9.7 to compute the ROI.

9.3.2 Data Characterization

The second step is to characterize the activities in the model. Characterization means determining the following values for each of the activities in the model:

- The effectiveness of the activity: the proportion of defects that this activity can detect.
- The cost to find and fix a single defect using that activity. The cost can be in terms of effort or in terms of dollars.

Two restrictions are placed on that for simplification:

1. It is not necessary to characterize any post-release activity.
2. It is not necessary to characterize any activity before the activity for which you wish to calculate the ROI. (For example, if the project performed design reviews and the focus was only on evaluating TDD in Figure 9.9, then we do not need to characterize design reviews. This reduces the amount of data that needs to be collected and results in good ROI estimates in most situations.

But where do you get this data?

There are three ways to get this kind of data:

1. If the organization has a measurement program, then it may be possible to collect this data by mining existing metrics databases within the organization. Typically, a Software Quality Assurance group would be the owner of such data.
2. If there is no measurement program, then international benchmark data can be used. Benchmark databases consist of data from many projects all over the world. For many instances, they provide reasonable and defensible averages that can be used for ROI evaluation. For example, the data in the appendix, which is effectively a benchmark, tells us that, on average, code inspections detect 57 percent of the defects in the code.
3. For new quality practices, such as using new tools, it would be useful to contact the vendor and ask for the effectiveness and cost data. If the vendor is not forthcoming with this data or does not have such data, then try to interview existing customers or members of a user group to get some idea of effectiveness and cost per defect.

It is generally a good idea to perform a sensitivity analysis on the ROI results. A sensitivity analysis changes one or more variable(s) at a time to see the effect on the ROI. Depending on the quality of the data that is used in the ROI model, one can focus on the most uncertain or suspicious variables. For example, it is expected that vendors will exaggerate the benefits of their tools. Therefore, there is a lot of uncertainty associated with that variable, and a sensitivity analysis should be performed on it.

If it is found that the ROI calculations are very sensitive to specific variables, extra effort should be expended to ensure that the values used are as accurate as possible. Alternatively, a range of plausible values characterizing the maximum and minimum should be used for the uncertain variables and the ROI results presented in terms of a range rather than a single value. Some examples are given in Chapter 10.

9.4 Discounting

Because most of the returns from quality practices are due to a reduction in rework, there is a time lag between the investment and the returns. For example, we want to implement code inspections on a two-year development project. Out-of-pocket expenses will include training on inspections and some consulting in the first year. The reduction in rework will occur mostly during testing, which will likely occur in the second year. This is illustrated in Figure 9.10. Management must wait two years for the savings to be accounted for.

The value of money changes over time. For example, $1000 today will not be worth that much in two years' time. *Discounting* is the mechanism whereby we can account for the time value of money.

If the investment is $100,000 and is made at the beginning of the first year. The return is $1 million at the end of the second year. Does that make a 10:1 benefit-cost ratio? No, because the $1 million in two years cannot be compared directly to $100,000 today.

Let us assume that the $1 million in two years is worth much less in today's terms. Because $100,000 is being spent now, the investment and return must be made equal in terms of time. One way to do this is to discount the $1 million to calculate its value today. It turns out that $1 million in two years is worth $907,029 today. This means that if you put $907,029 in the bank today and that accumulates interest at 5 percent per year, then it would be worth $1 million in two years.

Discounting future benefits allows us to be indifferent between a benefit (or cost) received now and a benefit received later.

The equation for computing the Present Value of a future cost or benefit is:

$$P = \frac{F}{\left(1 + I\right)^n} \qquad (9.13)$$

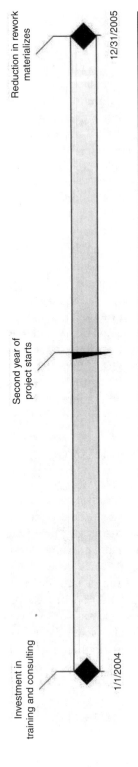

FIGURE 9.10 Timeline showing the point of investment and point when returns materialize for a two-year project that started at the beginning of 2004.

where:
P = Present value
F = Future value
I = Discount rate
N = Number of years

The term:

$$\frac{1}{(1+I)^n} \qquad (9.14)$$

is called the Discount Factor. The formula in Equation (9.14) assumes that the costs or benefits (the future value) occur as a lump sum at the end of the year. The formula for the mid-year Discount Factor is:

$$\frac{1}{(1+I)^{n-0.5}} \qquad (9.15)$$

And the formula for the Discount Factor when the costs or benefits occur as a lump sum at the beginning of the year:

$$\frac{1}{(1+I)^{n-1}} \qquad (9.16)$$

The discount rate can be obtained from the finance department in your organization. It will be based on what one can get in interest when one puts the money in a safe investment (e.g., GICs or government bonds). It also takes into account the inflation rate.

Let us take a simple hypothetical example to make this concrete. We have a two-year development project. The cost of introducing code inspections is $30,000, including training and consulting. These costs will be incurred at the *beginning* of the first year (i.e., now) and therefore they are not discounted. The savings for the project will be $250,000, accounted for as a lump sum at the end of the second year. These will be discounted by 0.907.

The resulting calculations are shown in Table 9.2. Here we see that the savings in today's terms are worth $226,750. Therefore, the benefits to costs ratio is just over 7.5 times (this is the ratio of the discounted values):

TABLE 9.2 ROI Calculation Table for a Hypothetical Two-Year Project

Year	Costs	Savings	Discount Factor	Discounted Costs	Discounted Savings
1	$30,000		0.952	$30,000	
2		$250,000	0.907		$226,750
Total				$30,000	$226,750

$$\text{Benefits to Cost Ratio} = \frac{\text{Discounted Savings}}{\text{Discounted Costs}} \qquad (9.17)$$

This tabular format will be used to present the ROI calculations in the next chapter.

9.5 Uncertainty and Sensitivity Analysis

Sensitivity analysis is useful when there is some uncertainty in variables that are used to calculate ROI. For example, if we get some data from a tool vendor, then it would be prudent to attach a lot of uncertainty to those values when calculating ROI.

By designating a variable as uncertain, we can assign it a range of possible values rather than a single value. This means that the ROI calculations will be a range of values rather than a single value.

For example, if a vendor told us that its tool could find 40 percent of the defects in the code, we can evaluate ROI at 10, 20, 30, 35, and 40 percent. This way we can see how sensitive our ROI results are to this particular number.

If we find that, for example, the ROI was still respectable at 10 percent, then it may be worthwhile to deploy that tool on the project. One can argue that if the ROI is still good after we reduce the vendor's claims by three quarters, then there is a good chance that a decent ROI will be attained even if the vendor is only slightly accurate.

If the ROI turns negative at 35 percent, for example, then there is a very high likelihood that the benefits will not materialize and we should reconsider the tool purchase. In this case we can see that if the vendor's claims are even slightly wrong, the ROI will not be good enough. The chances that a vendor's claims are slightly wrong are quite high.

If the ROI starts becoming unattractive at 20 percent, for example, then we should dig deeper into that number and ask the vendor for evidence and data demonstrating the 40 percent effectiveness claims. If we convince ourselves that the effectiveness will not approach 20 percent, then it would be worthwhile to deploy the tool from an ROI perspective.

A basic sensitivity analysis would vary only one variable at a time and see what the effect on the final ROI calculations are. If there are many variables that are uncertain, then a multi-way sensitivity analysis can be performed whereby combinations of values can be examined. For example, if the vendor also told us that the cost to find and fix a defect using their tool is, on average, two hours, we can translate this to, say, $100 of labor. But because this claim is likely to be on the low side, we may want to vary that to $150 and $200. Now we wish to look at combinations of effectiveness and cost values. Modern sensitivity analysis tools will allow us to do this and explore the combinations of conditions that would make the tool unattractive. For example, we may find that if the effectiveness dipped below 20 percent and the cost per defect was higher than $120, then the ROI would no longer be sufficiently high to make the tool purchase worthwhile.

If we tried to identify that minimal set of acceptable values by doing a sensitivity analysis on each variable alone, we would not get the right information. Therefore, it is best to perform a multi-way sensitivity analysis.

When there are many uncertain variables, it is useful to rank them in terms of their influence on the final ROI values and then focus the effort on the top two or three variables. In many cases it is not worth the effort to focus on variables that have the least influence on ROI. For the most influential variables, one should try to collect better data on the variables and spend more time exploring their interactions to find the minimal acceptable combination of values that would generate a positive ROI.

9.6 Subjective Distributions

Rather than treating uncertain values as a range, we can assign a statistical distribution to these values. The problem with using a simple range is that it effectively treats each possible value within that range as equally likely. If we revisit our cost per defect for the tool example, we assume that the likelihood that the cost will be $100 is the same as the likelihood that the cost will be $150.

In reality, we would probably expect that $150 is closer to the truth, and the extreme values are $100 and $200. The extreme values are less likely. This can be represented as a triangular distribution as shown in Figure 9.11. Here we assume that the $150 value is the most likely value for the cost per defect and can incorporate that information in our ROI model.

When little is known about the shape of the actual distribution of a phenomenon, there is no compelling reason to use a distribution more

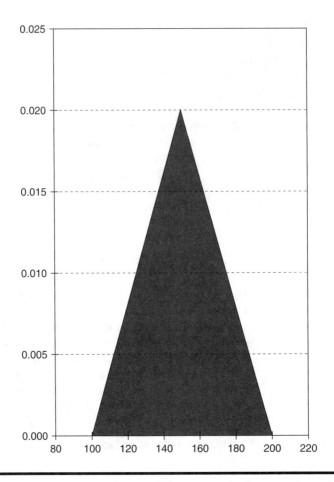

FIGURE 9.11 **A triangular distribution for the cost per defect of a tool. The most likely value in this distribution is $150, with the $100 value quoted by the vendor at the low end. The properties of the triangular distribution are discussed at length elsewhere.[6]**

complex than the triangular one.[7] We therefore use that distribution and use subjective information based on best judgment to decide on the minimum, maximum, and most likely values. In practice, this approach provides very useful results that are quite actionable and has worked well in practice for quite some time.

When a triangular distribution is used for the uncertain variables, then a Monte Carlo simulation is performed on the ROI model to sample from the distributions and calculate the ROI for each iteration. Usually one performs 1000 or 5000 iterations for the simulation. The resulting ROI is no longer a single value or a range, but rather an ROI distribution.

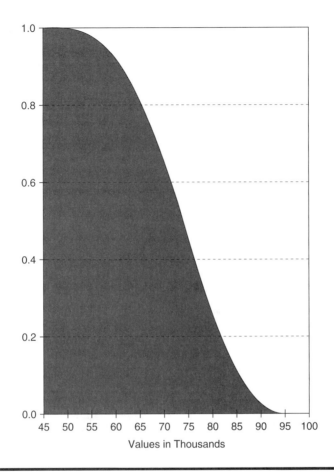

FIGURE 9.12   An example ROI distribution (cumulative descending) in 1000s of dollars for a hypothetical project. The y-axis is a probability.

An example distribution of ROI is shown in Figure 9.12. This is a cumulative descending distribution. The *x*-axis is the ROI and the *y*-axis is a probability. This probability is that of getting an ROI as large as the one on the *x*-axis or larger. For example, if the organization that is doing an ROI is very conservative and does not wish to make investments unless there is a high certainty about the benefits, then it might choose a threshold probability of 0.9 for a return of $60,000. This means that if the probability of getting a return of $40,000 (or higher) is 0.9, then this organization will make the investment. In Figure 9.12, the probability of having an ROI of $60,000 is actually greater than 0.9, and therefore this organization would be willing to take the risk and invest.

The advantage of this approach is that it can be customized to the level of risk the organization is willing to take when making investment decisions. For example, if the organization is willing to take bigger risks and will make a decision if the probability of a decent return is at least 0.3, then we can read that value from the graph in Figure 9.12. Under this higher risk strategy, the organization has a 0.3 probability of making at least a $70,000 (or more) return on the investment.

The risk-based approach allows one to be precise about the accuracy of the input values and allows the tolerance of the organization to take risks to be accounted for in the decision making. We will look at some examples in Chapter 10.

9.7 Interpreting the ROI Values

This section explains how to interpret and use the calculated ROI values.

It must be recognized that the ROI calculations, cost savings, and project costs as presented in our models are estimates. Inevitably, there is some uncertainty in these estimates. The uncertainty stems from the variables that are not accounted for in the models (there are many other factors that influence project costs, but it is not possible to account for all of these because the model would then be unusable). Another source of uncertainty are the input values themselves. These values are typically averages calculated from historical data; to the extent that the future differs from the past, these values will have some error. However, by performing a sensitivity and risk analysis on the model and the input values, one incorporates the uncertainty about the values used in the results.

The calculated ROI is not an annual saving, but rather a saving in pre-release and post-release budgets. The development phase might span multiple years. Maintenance might also span multiple years. To annualize the savings, they must be allocated across multiple years. This is achieved by tabulating the cash flow over the lifetime of the product. We will illustrate this in the examples later in the book.

The calculated ROI values are for a single project. A software organization will have multiple ongoing and new projects. The total benefit of implementing software quality practices to the organization can be calculated by generalizing the results to the organization. For example, let the ROI for a single project be a 15 percent savings. Assuming that the input values are the same for other projects in the organization, then we can generalize to the whole organization and estimate that if software quality practices are implemented on all projects in the organization, the overall savings would be 15 percent. If the software budget for all the projects is, for example, $20 million, then that would translate into an estimated savings of $3 million.

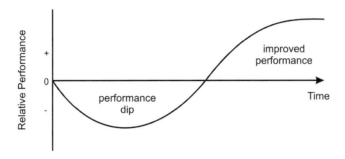

FIGURE 9.13   An illustration of how performance is expected to dip whenever a new practice is introduced.

If you are implementing quality improvement on a single project, then the costs of requiring any tools or the costs of training and consulting must be deducted from the single project savings. If you are implementing quality practices in the whole organization, then these costs will be spread across multiple projects. In such a case, these costs would be deducted from the organizational savings (the calculation of which is described above).

Whenever a new technology is introduced into a project, the performance of that project is expected to decrease temporarily as staff members master the technology.[8] This will likely be reflected by the depressed ROI results calculated after the introduction of a quality practice. The performance dip is illustrated in Figure 9.13. The first project that adopts a quality practice, which would typically be a pilot project, will probably not achieve the projected ROI. This should not be interpreted as an inaccuracy in the ROI calculations. Usually, the second and third projects, after wider deployment of the quality practice, will achieve higher ROI. Therefore, one should expect to see a gradual increase in savings over time as the staff master the quality practices and develop expertise in applying them.

9.8 Payback Period

When calculating ROI, it is important to understand how long the payback period will be. This section explains the relationship between payback period and the ROI models we have presented.

Conceptually, the relationships among payback, time, and a project's lifetime are shown in Figure 9.14. Payback is defined in terms of realizing the savings that are calculated according to our ROI models. Some of

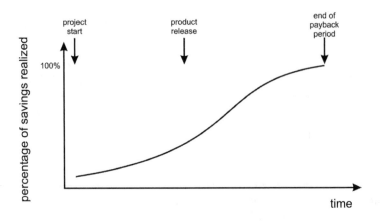

FIGURE 9.14 The relationship between payback in terms of savings and the passing of time as this relates to the lifetime of a software project.

these savings would be realized before a product is released, and some would be realized only post-release. All of the savings will be realized at the end of the payback period, which can be at product release or any period thereafter.

The exact shape of the curve will depend on how the funds are spent throughout the project. It is generally best to assume that expenses are incurred at the beginning of the year and savings are accrued at the end of the year. For pre-release savings, most of our examples assume that they will occur during testing. Therefore, pre-release savings materialize during the last year of the development portion of a project. The post-release savings are allocated equally to each of the maintenance years. This provides a reasonable basis for calculating the Present Value of the costs and the savings.

By presenting a cash flow analysis, as our examples do, we can determine the savings year by year and estimate when the breakeven point would be reached.

References

1. Kusumoto, S. Quantitative Evaluation of Software Reviews and Testing Processes, Ph.D. thesis, Osaka University, 1993.
2. Briand, L. et al. Using simulation to build inspection efficiency benchmarks for development projects, in *Twentieth International Conference on Software Engineering*, pp. 340–349, 1998.
3. Briand, L., Freimut, B., and Vollei, F. Assessing the Cost-Effectiveness of Inspections by Combining Project Data and Expert Opinion, Technical Report, International Software Engineering Research Network (ISERN), 99–14, 1999.

4. El Emam, K. and Goldenson, D. An empirical review of software process assessments, *Advances in Computers,* 53:319–423, 2000.

5. Boehm, B., Abts, C., Winsor Brown, A., Chulani, S., Clark, B., Horowitz, E., Madachy, R., Reifer, D., and Steece, B. *Software Cost Estimation with COCOMO II*, Prentice Hall, 2000.

6. Evans, M., Hastings, N., and Peacock, B. *Statistical Distributions*, John Wiley & Sons, 1993.

7. Vose, D. *Quantitative Risk Analysis: A Guide to Monte Carlo Simulation Modeling,* John Wiley & Sons, 1996.

8. Kemerer, C. How the learning curve affects CASE tool adoption, *IEEE Software*, pp. 23–28, May 1992.

Chapter 10

Example ROI
Calculations

This chapter presents a number of examples of calculating ROI based on the ROI models articulated in the previous chapter and explained in detail in Appendix E. For each ROI example, one must make some assumptions about the defect detection life cycle. These assumptions will be stated for each of the examples below. The ROI results show the savings in development and maintenance costs, the reduction in delivery schedule, and the decrease in customer costs for a number of different software quality practices.

10.1 Context

All examples pertain to a single hypothetical project in an IT department of a large company in the financial business. Let us call this project PIONEER. This project was typical for the IT department in terms of its scope, size, duration, and user base.

The PIONEER project itself was estimated to have a two-year development phase and a three-year maintenance phase. After three years, it is expected that the product will be retired (the plan was to spin off the product to a separate company that can continue supporting it and offer it for sale to other companies).

A total of ten software developers have been assigned to this project during its development phase and six during its maintenance phase. The expected size is 300 KLOC written in the C programming language. Using the backfiring table in Appendix D, the size of this system can be estimated at 2344 Function Points.

It was expected that the productivity of this team would be around 0.07 Function Points per person-hour, which is the average for this type of system. The total development budget is $3 million and the total maintenance budget is $3 million. The development costs are divided equally among the two years, and the maintenance budget is divided equally among three years.

The user organization for the product is another branch of the same firm, and provides financial services to the ultimate customers of the financial institution. This user organization has 2000 end users who will be working with the system.

The discount rate assumed in all of the calculations is 5 percent.

The typical project in this organization does not have any software inspections. There are three types of testing being performed: (1) unit testing, (2) integration testing, and (3) acceptance testing. Unit testing is rather ad hoc but integration and acceptance testing are a bit more structured. Further defects are detected after release to the user organization (i.e., during deployment).

The first thing we do is establish a baseline for the PIONEER project so that we can perform the ROI calculations. For the baseline, a similar project that has already been delivered is used. This previous project was roughly the same size and complexity as PIONEER. We use the previous project's data to calculate some parameters that we will need for our calculations.

As an aside, if such a project did not exist, that would not be a problem. In such a case, we can just use benchmark data as an approximation.

The type of data we need from the previous project is shown in Figure 10.1. The project team documented each defect that was discovered, from unit testing onward. This team also documented the phase in which it was discovered. A causal analysis on the defects discovered identified the most likely phase where the defects were inserted.

The data in Figure 10.1 is very valuable for establishing a solid baseline. We can see that a total of 913 defects were discovered. Of these, the team was able to determine the source of 558 of these defects. It is assumed that the remaining defects (913 − 558 = 355) were originally inserted during the requirements and design phases of the project.

The data in Figure 10.1 can be used to construct the life-cycle model shown in Figure 10.2. We can see that 355 defects came in *before* coding. The coding phase itself added 467 new defects, making the total number of new defects in the code before it goes into unit testing 822. During unit testing, 394 defects were discovered and fixed. We can assume that 10 percent of the fixes introduce a new defect (see Appendix E); therefore, approximately 40 new defects were introduced during unit testing due to bad fixes. And furthermore, the total number of defects inserted during coding is 507 defects (467 + 40).

The effectiveness of unit testing can be calculated as 48 percent (394/822). Effectiveness is the proportion (or percentage) of defects in the code that are detected and fixed during the defect detection activity. It reflects the ability of unit testing to find the defects that are already in the code (before the code goes through unit testing).

After unit testing, 468 defects (822 + 40 −394) escaped into integration testing. Integration testing discovered 395 defects. Approximately 39 new defects were inserted due to bad fixes. The effectiveness of integration testing is calculated as 85 percent (395/468).

Only 112 defects (468 + 39 − 395) escaped from integration testing into acceptance testing. Acceptance testing found 77 defects but inserted eight new defects due to bad fixes. The effectiveness of acceptance testing can now be calculated as 69 percent (77/112).

After acceptance, 43 defects (112 + 8 − 77) escaped into the field. These are defects that are found by the customer. If we assume that all defects that can be found have been found when this data was collected, then the effectiveness of post-release is 100 percent.

These numbers assume that the defects discovered represent all the defects in the system. This will not be true; but for our purposes, we only care about the defects that will be detected by testers and customers. Other latent defects that are never discovered during the lifetime of a product are not of concern.

The costs to find and fix defects for the previous phases were calculated for the previous project and are summarized in Table 10.1. These were obtained by looking at time sheets and defect databases to calculate the average cost per defect. The defect detection life cycle for the project before introducing any quality practices is shown in Figure 10.3.

Now that we have established the baseline for the project, we can calculate the ROI for various quality practices. The ROI can be calculated in advance (i.e., before any practices are implemented, which can help management choose among them) or after the fact. We initially assume for now that the ROI is being calculated in advance and then we consider an example of after-the-fact ROI to evaluate whether or not the benefits of the quality practices actually materialized.

The quality practices that will be evaluated include:

- Code inspections
- An automatic defect detection tool
- Risk assessment to focus code inspections
- Test-driven development

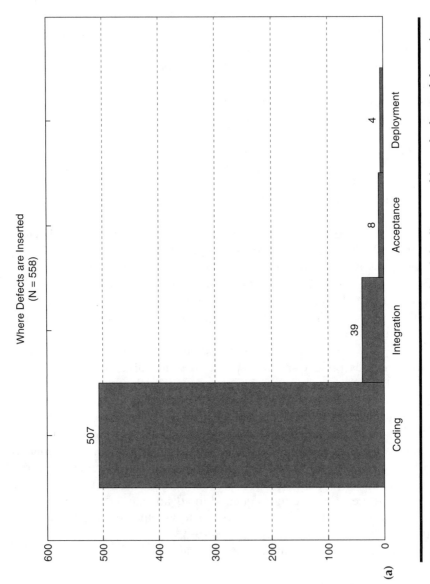

FIGURE 10.1 The number of defects (a) inserted and (b) discovered in each phase of the project.

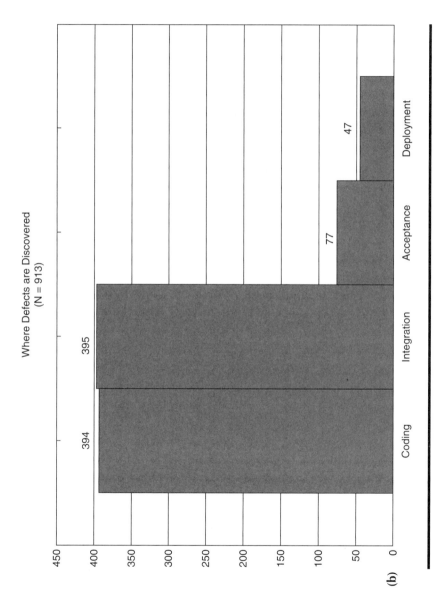

Figure 10.1 (continued)

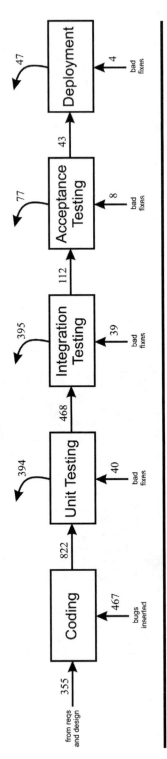

FIGURE 10.2   The number of defects inserted in each phase.

TABLE 10.1 Baseline Values for the Example (PIONEER) Project

Description	Value
Effectiveness of unit testing	48%
Effectiveness of integration testing	85%
Effectiveness of acceptance testing	69%
Cost to isolate and fix a defect during unit testing	$200
Cost to isolate and fix a defect during integration testing	$950
Cost to isolate and fix a defect during acceptance testing	$1700

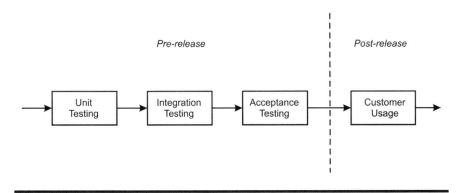

FIGURE 10.3   Schematic showing the defect detection activities *before* introducing code inspections.

10.2 Introducing Code Inspections

Software inspections have been around for more than 20 years. Despite the relatively long history, this is not a practice that is universally deployed in the North American software industry. Chapter 3 provided a brief description of the inspection process.

The focus here is on code inspections. After introducing inspections, the defect detection life cycle looks like Figure 10.4. We ignore unit testing for now because code inspections will be introduced after unit testing. Recall that, for our calculations of the ROI of a quality practice, we do not care about the activities that occur *before* it.

The two most important measures for evaluating software inspections are *effectiveness* and *efficiency*. Both of these are required to calculate the ROI. Effectiveness was defined previously as the proportion (or percentage) of defects in the code that is detected and fixed during the inspection.

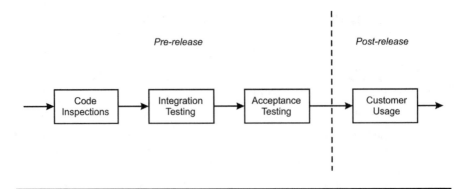

FIGURE 10.4 Schematic showing the defect detection activities *after* introducing code inspections.

TABLE 10.2 Results of the ROI Analysis for Deploying Code Inspections

Customer savings	38.5%
Pre-release ROI expressed as project savings	23.7%
Post-release ROI expressed as project savings	25.7%
Delivery schedule savings	8.2%

Efficiency is the average cost of finding and fixing a single defect. The benchmark values that we use for measuring the effectiveness and efficiency of inspections are given and justified in the appendix. We will convert the effort values for the efficiency of inspections to a dollar value of $75.

For the remaining values used in our calculations, we will use the defaults presented in Appendix E. We also assume that all the Scale Factors for calculating schedule reduction are Nominal.

The basic percentage savings results are shown in Table 10.2. We can see that customers will save just over a third of their cost of ownership caused by bug fixes. The pre-release and post-release cost savings run around a quarter of total budget, respectively. The projected reduction in delivery schedule is 8.2 percent, which translates to delivering about eight and a half weeks early.

The out-of-pocket expenses relate to training the developers to perform code inspections. This will cost $20,000. To coincide with when coding is expected to start, we assume that these costs will be incurred at the end of the first year. During the second year, some coaching and external consulting is needed to help the development team with its inspections

TABLE 10.3   Cash Flow and Total Savings from the Implementation of Code Inspections for our Example Project

Year	Costs	Dev. Savings	User Savings	Discounted Costs	Discounted Dev. Savings	Discounted User Savings
1	$20,000	0	0	$19,040	0	0
2	$10,000	$710,298	0	$9,520	$644,240	0
3	0	$256,500	$278,559	0	$221,360	$240,396
4	0	$256,500	$278,559	0	$211,100	$229,254
5	0	$256,500	$278,559	0	$200,840	$218,111
Total				$28,560	$1,277,540	$687,761

implementation. This is estimated to cost $10,000 at the beginning of the second year. These are all of the expected additional expenses that the project must cover.

The costs and benefits are summarized in Table 10.3. This table provides the actual and discounted costs and savings for each of the five years of the project lifetime. The savings by the development organization are separated out from the savings by the user organization. Years 3 to 5 are the maintenance period for the product.

There is expected to be $710,298 in savings pre-release. This is because the integration effort will be reduced dramatically due to fewer defects. Isolating and fixing defects takes the most time during testing. The project manager can reduce the staff load by around four people once integration starts. It is also expected that the project will finish early.

The break-even point for this investment is reached at the end of year 2, whereby the savings overtake all expenditures thus far.

The post-release savings accumulate over three years. The reduction in defects detected by the customer means that less effort would be spent fixing them. The total discounted savings for the development organization over the lifetime of the project is expected to be approximately $1.3 million.

For the user organization in the services industry, a recent NIST[1] study estimated that the cost per defect in applications per employee per annum is $362 on average. If we multiply that by the 2000 users of the user organization, then we can get a sense of the total cost of buggy software to the users. With the deployment of code inspections, the user organization will save $687,762 over the three years. This is a saving simply because the software that they will be using is expected to be of higher quality.

Because, under the current scenario, the development and the user organization belong to the same enterprise, the total cost savings to the enterprise from code inspections is estimated at around $2 million. This is for implementing code inspections on a single project.

The total benefit-cost ratio over the lifetime of this product is almost 71 times (this includes the developer and user organization savings). Therefore, the case is very compelling for deploying inspections on this project.

To gain a better understanding of which factors have the largest influence on the savings, we performed a sensitivity analysis. The variable with the most influence is the effectiveness of code inspections. We had used the benchmark average of 57 percent (see Appendix C for justifications and literature review). The maximum value for inspection effectiveness reported in the literature is 70 percent. At 70 percent, the development savings would be around $1.6 million and the user savings would be around $850k. Therefore, improving the effectiveness of inspections as much as possible by adopting best-in-class practices and continuously improving them can maximize the savings.

The effort per defect for inspections was ranked tenth in the sensitivity analysis. This indicates that getting that value to be extremely accurate in the ROI calculation would probably not add much precision to the ROI results. The $75 we used is realistic, and making it much more accurate will not significantly improve the ROI estimates.

The other important variables that emerged in the sensitivity analysis were the proportion of pre-release and post-release effort that was rework. We assumed that this would be 50 percent in both cases. The graph in Figure 10.5 shows that the development savings can approach $1.6 million if the proportion of rework approaches 75 percent, and can go down to around $1 million if the proportion of rework is only 25 percent. This indicates that having a good sense of how much rework there is on a project can help make the ROI calculations more accurate.

There was uncertainty in some of the variables used in the calculations. It would be more appropriate to capture that uncertainty and incorporate it in the results. Here we focus on the variables that had the highest influence on ROI as discovered through our sensitivity analysis. The variables that were uncertain included:

- *The effectiveness of inspections.* As noted in the appendix, the minimum reported effectiveness is 0.19 and the maximum is 0.7. Therefore there is wide variation in how well inspections work.
- *The proportion of rework during development.* The analyst performing the ROI calculations was not able to get very precise numbers on pre-release rework but the data available indicated it could be as low as 40 percent and as high as 80 percent.

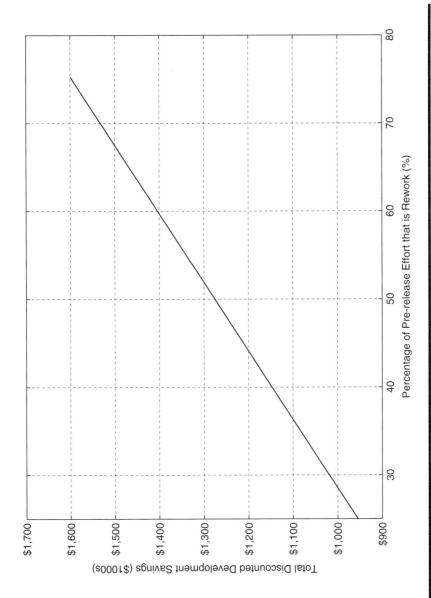

FIGURE 10.5   Sensitivity analysis for the proportion of pre-release rework versus the development savings.

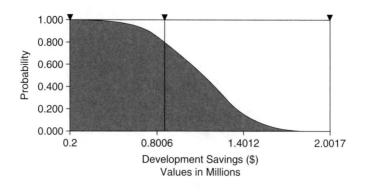

FIGURE 10.6   Graph showing the probability of achieving a given development saving. This organization was rather risk averse, so its threshold was a 0.8 probability of achieving that benefit.

- *The proportion of rework during maintenance.* The analyst performing the ROI calculations was not able to get very precise numbers on post-release rework but the data available indicated it could be as low as 25 percent and as high as 60 percent.
- *The cost per defect for integration testing.* This was found to be as low as $700 in some projects and as high as $1200 in others.
- *The cost per defect for acceptance testing.* This cost was found to be as low as $1500 and as high as $2200.

By incorporating all of these variables as triangular distributions in our ROI model and performing a Monte Carlo simulation, we obtained the graph in Figure 10.6. As is evident, at a threshold probability of 0.8, the expected savings are approximately $855,051 or more. This means that the probability of saving at least $855,051 during development is 0.8.

Figure 10.7 shows the same graph for the savings in the user organization. At the 0.8 threshold probability, the user organization can save at least $463,752 over the three years.

Both of these numbers (i.e., $855,051 and $463,752) were sufficiently compelling for the organization that it decided to go ahead and implement software inspections. In addition, the risk the organization would be taking to realize substantial benefits was sufficiently low and within the its risk tolerance such that management was comfortable with the investment.

10.3   Evaluating Code Inspections *after* Deployment

We now revisit the decision that was made in the previous section to invest in implementing code inspections. Let us say that the development

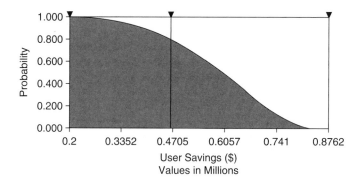

FIGURE 10.7 Graph showing the probability of achieving a given customer saving. This organization was rather risk averse, so its threshold was a 0.8 probability of achieving that benefit.

TABLE 10.4   Results of the ROI Analysis for Deploying Code Inspections Calculated *after* the Development Period Was Over

Customer savings	32%
Pre-release ROI expressed as project savings	19%
Post-release ROI expressed as project savings	21%
Delivery schedule savings	6.5%

period is over and now the product is in maintenance. Code inspections were implemented and used during development as planned. Did the returns that were anticipated actually materialize?

An initial examination indicated that the effectiveness of inspections on this project was 47 percent rather than 57 percent. Also, it was found that the cost per defect for code inspections was $100 instead of the anticipated $75. This is not surprising, as this project was the first one that implemented code inspections in this organization. Therefore, not achieving the industry average effectiveness is somewhat expected. The increase in cost is not going to have a dramatic effect on the ROI because the sensitivity analysis revealed that cost per defect ranked quite low in terms of influential variables.

When we recalculated the ROI, we obtained the percentages in Table 10.4 and the cash flow calculations in Table 10.5. There has been a reduction in the benefits, but this is expected given the considerable reduction in effectiveness.

TABLE 10.5   Cash Flow and Total Savings from the Implementation of Code Inspections for our Example Project Calculated *after* the Development Period Was Over

Year	Costs	Dev. Savings	User Savings	Discounted Costs	Discounted Dev. Savings	Discounted User Savings
1	$20,000	0	0	$19,040	0	0
2	$10,000	$569,412	0	$9,520	$516,457	0
3	0	$211,500	$229,689	0	$182,525	$198,222
4	0	$211,500	$229,689	0	$174,065	$189,034
5	0	$211,500	$229,689	0	$165,605	$179,846
Total				$28,560	$1,038,652	$567,102

The cost savings for the development organization are estimated at $1,038,652. This number is consistent with the results of the risk analysis performed *before* implementing code inspections. Recall that we estimated a 0.8 probability of achieving at least an $855,051 savings pre-release. The project managed to actually achieve a savings slightly larger than that. The schedule reduction was also only 6.5 weeks, instead of 8.5 weeks.

The savings on the customer side were also within the range expected. The projection was a 0.8 probability of at least a $463,752 savings. The project was able to achieve savings of $567,102 for the user organization.

This example highlights the value of performing a sensitivity analysis and a risk analysis. These two activities set expectations appropriately in advance of implementing quality practices so that there are few surprises. In many cases, if the sensitivity and risk analyses are done well, the ultimate results are within expectations.

Based on the ROI analysis performed after the development phase of the project, the management of the organization decided to deploy code inspections across all new projects. The post-hoc analysis like the one presented here was key in making that decision.

Note that for subsequent examples that build on the code inspections results, we do use the ROI results calculated after deployment (i.e., Table 10.5) as the basis.

10.4   Automatic Defect Detection Tools

Now that the decision has been made to deploy code inspections on all projects, the improvement team is looking for additional quality practices that can further improve quality and reduce rework.

This section looks at automatic defect detection tools as a possible technology to deploy on software projects to improve quality. This would be deployed in addition to inspections. Management was considering purchasing a tool for use in future projects. This example considers two different licensing models for automatic defect detection tools to see which one results in the higher ROI for the project.

Automatic defect detection tools parse the source code and look for constructs or patterns that are indicative of potential software defects. These tools tend to have a high false positive rate, but they can find very subtle defects and can analyze a large amount of code very quickly.

In our calculations we make the assumption that an automatic defect detection tool accurately finds 5 percent of the defects in a piece of code. We also assume that it costs, on average, $25 to fix this defect. Finding a defect involves running a tool, and such a tool identifies the exact location of the defect. The cost of finding defects is that of running the tool, which is negligible. Also, isolation cost is negligible because these tools typically do identify the exact location of the defect.

While the tool will be deployed on projects that start after PIONEER, the project parameters are assumed to be similar to PIONEER in terms of planned budgets, duration, and life cycle. The reason is that PIONEER was a typical project.

There are two vendors of such tools. We will assume that, in terms of effectiveness and cost per defect, they are equal (other potential vendors were eliminated from the running because their tools were not as effective or did not pinpoint defects accurately). The difference between the two remaining vendors lies with their licensing arrangements.

Vendor A charges based on the size of the system and follows a pay-per-use model. The fee is $0.18 per line of code. The source code is shipped to the vendor, who then performs the analysis. This can only be realistically done just before integration testing. Therefore, to analyze the whole system once (at 300 KLOC), the total cost is $54,000. If we say that automatic defect detection will be run at least twice for the whole system, then the total cost is $108,000.

The defect detection life cycle for the pay-per-use model is shown in Figure 10.8. Here we ignore code inspections because they occur *before* the intervention. The code is analyzed twice: the first time to find problems and the second time to make sure that these problems have been fixed and that no new problems have been introduced.

The second license model from vendor B is an outright purchase. Because the tool can be used repeatedly at no incremental licensing costs, it is made available to all developers as a remote service to analyze their code when it is checked in. The defect detection life cycle after introducing the tool is shown in Figure 10.9. We will compare these life cycles with

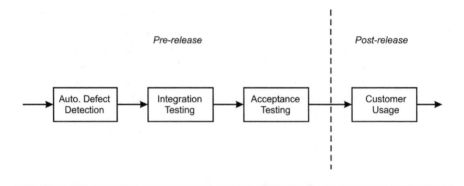

FIGURE 10.8 **The defect detection cycle for introducing an automatic defect detection tool where the licensing model is pay-per-use.**

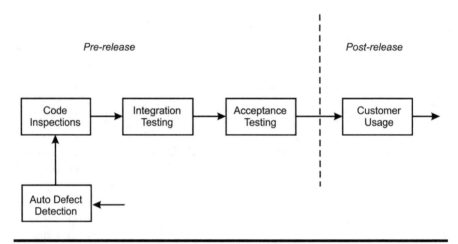

FIGURE 10.9 **The defect detection cycle for introducing an automatic defect detection tool where the licensing model is an outright purchase.**

the one in Figure 10.4, which includes the code inspections. Therefore, some defects are detected during inspections and testing and customers find the remaining defects.

The automatic defect detection tool is executed prior to inspections because we want to eliminate automatically as many defects beforehand as possible. It costs much less to find a defect using an automated tool than it is to find the defect using a manual process such as code inspections.

The license cost for the tool is $20,000 plus $4000 maintenance every year. An additional $20,000 will be used to train two developers to intelligently apply the tool and identify the false positives.

TABLE 10.6   Results of the ROI Analysis for Deploying an Automatic Defect Detection Tool with a Pay-per-Use Licensing Model

Customer savings	2.3%
Pre-release ROI expressed as project savings	1.7%
Post-release ROI expressed as project savings	1.7%
Delivery schedule savings	0.5%

TABLE 10.7   Cash Flow and Total Savings from Deploying an Automatic Defect Detection Tool with a Pay-per-Use Licensing Model (Vendor A)

Year	Costs	Dev. Savings	User Savings	Discounted Costs	Discounted Dev. Savings	Discounted User Savings
1	0	0	0	0	0	0
2	$108,000	$49,984	0	$102,816	$45,336	0
3	0	$16,650	$16,616	0	$14,369	$14,339
4	0	$16,650	$16,616	0	$13,703	$13,675
5	0	$16,650	$16,616	0	$13,037	$13,010
Total				$102,816	$86,445	$41,024

The two differing life cycles highlight the fact that the licensing model forces the tool to be used quite differently on both projects. We now look at the ROI from both of these approaches to see which one provides the better ROI results.

Table 10.6 and Table 10.7 show the ROI calculations for the pay-per-use approach. As we can see, the high costs make the returns rather small. The break-even point is reached at the end of year 4 for the whole enterprise. For the development group alone, the cost of the licenses is never recovered. The benefit-cost ratio is only greater than 1 when we include the user savings after the product goes into production. The total benefit over the lifetime of the project is $127,469, with a total benefit-to-cost ratio of around 1.2.

The results for the outright purchase licensing model shown in Tables 10.8 and 10.9 appear slightly worse than the pay-per-use model. The total savings are $126,739. However, the benefit-cost ratio is 2.7, which is higher than under the pay-per-use model. The break-even point is reached after

TABLE 10.8   Results of the ROI Analysis for Deploying an Automatic Defect Detection Tool *before* Inspections with an Outright Purchase Licensing Model

Customer savings	2.3%
Pre-release ROI expressed as project savings	1.6%
Post-release ROI expressed as project savings	1.7%
Delivery schedule savings	0.5%

TABLE 10.9   Cash Flow and Total Savings from Deploying an Automatic Defect Detection Tool *before* Inspections with an Outright Purchase Licensing Model (Vendor B)

Year	Costs	Dev. Savings	User Savings	Discounted Costs	Discounted Dev. Savings	Discounted User Savings
1	$44,000	0	0	$44,000	0	0
2	$4,000	$49,179	0	$3,808	$44,606	0
3	0	$16,650	$16,616	0	$14,369	$14,339
4	0	$16,650	$16,616	0	$13,703	$13,675
5	0	$16,650	$16,616	0	$13,037	$13,010
Total				$47,808	$85,715	$41,024

only three years. The reason is that the initial investment is lower with an outright purchase.

The above example provided management with the information to make the tool purchase decision and to reason about differing licensing models. In general, it would seem that, for this project, an outright purchase has a higher overall return. A sensitivity analysis indicates that the effectiveness of the tool has a substantial impact on the ROI. Therefore, if one of the competing tools does demonstrably have a higher effectiveness, then the ROI would tilt favorably toward that product.

10.5   Risk Assessment

One way to optimize software inspections is to only inspect the high-risk parts of the system (see Table 10.10 and Table 10.11). There is considerable evidence showing that a large percentage of defects reside in a small

TABLE 10.10   Results of the ROI Analysis for Deploying Risk Assessment to Focus Inspections

Customer savings	19%
Pre-release ROI expressed as project savings	12%
Post-release ROI expressed as project savings	13%
Delivery schedule savings	4%

TABLE 10.11   Cash Flow and Total Savings from Deploying Risk Assessment to Focus Inspections

Year	Costs	Dev. Savings	User Savings	Discounted Costs	Discounted Dev. Savings	Discounted User Savings
1	$10,000	0	0	$10,000	0	0
2	$10,000	$361,174	0	$9,520	$327,585	0
3	0	$126,900	$137,813	0	$109,515	$118,933
4	0	$126,900	$137,813	0	$104,439	$113,420
5	0	$126,900	$137,813	0	$99,363	$107,908
Total				$19,520	$640,900	$340,261

portion of the modules across a wide variety of systems [2-5]; however, the exact percentages do vary. In the telecommunications sector, for example, it has been noted that only 10 percent of modules changed from one release to another contributed to post-release defects on one system; that 80 percent of the defects came from 20 percent of the modules based on data from Nortel switches and that 20 percent of the modules contain about 40 to 80 percent of the defects at Alcatel.[6] During the development of the Rational Rose tool, it was found that 77 percent of source code defects were in subsystems that account for only 21 percent of the code.[7] During the development of the DOS operating system at IBM, it was found that 21 percent of the modules that had more than one defect accounted for 78 percent of the total defects.[8] In another IBM operating system, it was noted that 47 percent of post-release defects were associated with only 4 percent of the modules.[9]

The adoption of risk management practices allows the project to focus their scarce resources on the units of the system that are most likely to have a defect (i.e., the high risk ones). In this scenario, we look at the application of metrics-based risk management techniques to focus code inspections. As opposed to the example we saw earlier on whereby the project inspects everything (100 percent coverage), in this scenario we will assume that only the high-risk areas of the system are targeted for inspections. Chapter 3 provides a brief description of the general risk management approach.

One reason why project managers might wish to focus only on the high-risk parts of the system is that they would not need to train all of their developers on code inspections. Therefore, the initial investment may be smaller. For many organizations that have underfunding constraints, this is one way to get started with quality practices. Furthermore, if there is no organizational funding for process improvement, these funds may have to come out of the project budgets. In addition, because the effort is focused on modules with the largest density of errors, the effort to find a defect would be expected to decrease.

For this ROI calculation we will assume that risk assessment identifies the modules that have 60 percent of the defects. Given that resources are used more efficiently with risk assessment, the cost per defect is lower, at $50 instead of the initially calculated $100 (with 100 percent inspection coverage). We also assume that the effectiveness of inspections is at 47 percent, which is the value calculated after inspections were deployed on PIONEER.

The results are shown in Tables 10.10 and 10.11. The pre-release and post-release benefits are smaller than for having 100 percent inspection coverage (see Figures 10.4 and 10.5). However, this is expected because with a risk-based approach, not all of the defects are being targeted for detection. The total savings are $981,161 for the organization over the five years, compared to $1,605,752 for the 100 percent inspection coverage approach.

The initial costs for the risk assessment-based practice is only $19,520, compared to the $28,560 for 100 percent inspection coverage. This is probably the main reason why a project would follow a risk-based approach: the start-up costs are lower. From a benefits-to-cost ratio, the risk-based approach is about 50:1, whereas the 100 percent inspection is 56:1.

10.6 Test-Driven Development

This section looks at adding test-driven development (TDD) to future projects that have already deployed inspections. The pilot project that would evaluate TDD has the same parameters as the PIONEER project.

A recent study at IBM reported a 50 percent improvement in quality from using TDD compared to the incumbent unit testing method.[10] We

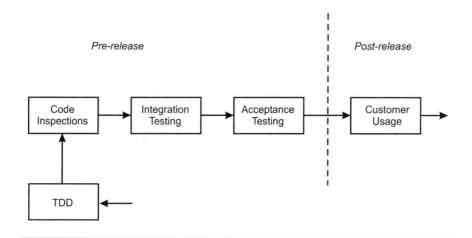

FIGURE 10.10 **The defect detection cycle for introducing TDD to replace the existing unit testing approach.**

therefore assume conservatively a 50 percent effectiveness for TDD when calculating its ROI. We also assume that each defect costs $25 to find and fix using TDD. This is reasonable because with TDD, development and testing are incremental, making it easy to spot program changes that made a test to fail.

For the following calculations we assume the life-cycle model shown in Figure 10.10. Here, TDD replaces the existing unit testing approach. Unit testing is performed before inspections. The benefits that are calculated are those accrued after the introduction of inspections (i.e., we are comparing the life cycle in Figure 10.10 with the life cycle in Figure 10.4).

For the ten developers, we assume that a commercial integrated development environment incorporating unit testing would be purchased at a cost of $10,000 a seat plus a 20 percent annual maintenance fee. Because unit testing must be performed throughout the maintenance period, maintenance fees are a cost that is incurred throughout the lifetime of the project. We also assume a $20,000 TDD training cost for the development team.

The results of the ROI analysis are shown in Tables 10.12 and 10.13. We can see that the breakeven point is reached at the end of the second year. The total development and user organization savings for the project are $1,267,391 from an investment of $210,900. This gives a benefits-to cost-ratio of about 6:1. The development schedule savings would be around six weeks.

It is clear that TDD is a very worthwhile investment, even after code inspections have already been introduced to a project.

TABLE 10.12   Results of the ROI Analysis for Deploying TDD

Customer savings	23%
Pre-release ROI expressed as project savings	16.4%
Post-release ROI expressed as project savings	16.6%
Delivery schedule savings	5.5%

TABLE 10.13   Cash Flow and Total Savings from Deploying TDD

Year	Costs	Dev. Savings	User Savings	Discounted Costs	Discounted Dev. Savings	Discounted User Savings
1	$140,000	0	0	$140,000	0	0
2	$20,000	$491,794	0	$19,040	$446,057	0
3	$20,000	$166,500	$166,158	$18,140	$143,690	$143,394
4	$20,000	$166,500	$166,158	$17,260	$137,030	$136,748
5	$20,000	$166,500	$166,158	$16,460	$130,370	$130,102
Total				$210,900	$857,147	$410,244

10.7 Multiple Practices

In some cases, an organization may wish to deploy multiple practices at the same time, rather than one by one. Under these conditions, we would want to calculate the ROI from multiple simultaneous deployments.

The approach to follow is to calculate ROI for each practice in order. For example, if we look at the case of deploying code inspections and TDD simultaneously, we would calculate the ROI for code inspections first and then add the ROI from TDD on top of that. This is exactly the order that we followed here. The combined inspections and TDD savings would be $857,147 + $1,038,652 = $1,895,799 for the development organization and $410,244 + $567,102 = $977,346 for the user organization. The combined costs would be $239,460. The total benefit to cost ratio is around 12:1.

When calculating the ROI from multiple quality practices, it is important to have the defect detection life cycle defined and the order of introducing the practices understood. For example, if we introduce TDD before code inspections, the ROI for TDD would be very different from that presented above. Let us consider that for a moment to illustrate the point.

TABLE 10.14   Results of the ROI Analysis for Deploying TDD *without* Code Inspections

Customer savings	33.75%
Pre-release ROI expressed as project savings	22%
Post-release ROI expressed as project savings	22%
Delivery schedule savings	7.6%

TABLE 10.15   Cash Flow and Total Savings from Deploying TDD *without* Code Inspections

Year	Costs	Dev. Savings	User Savings	Discounted Costs	Discounted Dev. Savings	Discounted User Savings
1	$140,000	0	0	$140,000	0	0
2	$20,000	$657,689	0	$19,040	$596,524	0
3	$20,000	$225,000	$244,350	$18,140	$194,175	$210,874
4	$20,000	$225,000	$244,350	$17,260	$185,175	$201,100
5	$20,000	$225,000	$244,350	$16,460	$176,175	$191,326
Total				$210,900	$1,152,049	$603,300

Table 10.14 and Table 10.15 show the ROI calculations for the case when TDD is introduced without inspections. The percentages in Table 10.14 pertain to the costs and schedule gains of TDD if it is introduced *before* inspections are introduced, whereas the percentages in Table 10.12 pertain to cost and schedule gains of TDD if it is introduced *after* code inspections are introduced.

The development cost savings are almost a quarter of a million dollars higher if TDD is introduced *before* (i.e., without) inspections. The user organization savings are around $200K higher. Therefore, before inspections, the benefits of TDD look much more impressive than if they are introduced after inspections have been deployed. However, the impact of having both practices in place is the same, irrespective of the order in which they were introduced.

The reason for this occurrence depends on a number of factors. One of them is that rework is reduced when inspections are introduced. Therefore, there are fewer opportunities for reducing rework. For example, let us say we have two practices X and Y. Each practice reduces rework by 50 percent. We also have 100 units of rework. If practice X is introduced first, it will bring rework down to 50 units. When practice Y is introduced, it will bring down rework to 25 units. In that order, practice X looks more impressive than practice Y, when in fact they have the same effect but X was introduced first. The opposite results would be obtained by reversing the order of introducing the practices. Therefore, the benefits of a single practice depend on the defect detection life cycle. The combined benefits are not affected by the order.

Each time a new practice is introduced, rework is reduced by a certain amount. The rework remaining after a quality practice is introduced is given by:

$$\frac{\text{Previous Rework} - \text{Savings}}{1 - \text{Savings}} \qquad (10.1)$$

If we take the results in Figure 10.4 for code inspections as an example, the savings were 19 percent. We assumed that the previous rework was 50 percent of the development (pre-release) effort. Therefore, using Equation (10.1), the remaining rework for any subsequent quality practices is 38 percent, which is down from the initial 50 percent. This is the equation that we used in our calculations in this chapter.

The second reason is that defects that are caught through TDD are saved from being caught through inspections. This is much cheaper than being saved from being caught by integration testing. Therefore, the savings from TDD catching defects when there are inspections are smaller than without inspections.

This example should illustrate that calculating the ROI for a quality practice independent of the defect detection life cycle can be quite inaccurate. Following the methodology described in this book should ensure that the calculations are correct.

References

1. NIST. The Economic Impacts of Inadequate Infrastructure for Software Testing, National Institute of Standards and Technology, U.S. Department of Commerce, 2002.
2. Moller, K.H. and Paulish, D. An empirical investigation of software fault distribution, *First International Software Metrics Symposium*, pp. 82–90, 1993.
3. Kaaniche, M. and Kanoun, K. Reliability of a commercial telecommunications system, *International Symposium on Software Reliability Engineering*, pp. 207–212, 1996.
4. Ohlsson, N. and Alberg, H. Predicting fault-prone software modules in telephone switches, *IEEE Transactions on Software Engineering*, 22(12): 886–894, 1996.

5. Fenton, N. and Ohlsson, N. Quantitative analysis of faults and failures in a complex software system, *IEEE Transactions on Software Engineering*, 26(8):797–814, 2000.
6. Shull, F. et al. What we have learned about fighting defects, *Eighth IEEE Symposium on Software Metrics*, pp. 249–258, 2002.
7. Walsh, J. Preliminary defect data from the iterative development of a large C++ program, *OOPSLA*, pp. 178–183, 1992.
8. Humphrey, W. *Managing the Software Process*, Addison-Wesley, 1989.
9. Myers, G. *The Art of Software Testing*, John Wiley & Sons, 1979.
10. Maximilien, E. and Williams, L. Assessing test-driven development at IBM, *International Conference on Software Engineering*, pp. 564–569, 2003.

Chapter 11

The Quality of Open Source Software

Thus far, we have examined in great detail how to calculate ROI with examples of some high-impact quality practices. But one additional question that I commonly receive is: What is the ROI from adopting open source software? There is an important quality dimension to this question because one of the main reasons why enterprises adopt open source software (OSS) is its perceived superiority compared to closed source software (CSS) or proprietary software. It is said that open source is cheaper, more reliable, and has less security vulnerabilities. The argument is that "open sourceness" is a characteristic that endows a software product with superior quality. Each OSS system is said to be worked on by a community of thousands or even millions of developers, debuggers, and reviewers around the world. If that is true, then we should be able to make a business case for migration to OSS rather easily because OSS would have a low cost of ownership. Coupled with the perceived low cost of adoption of OSS, the ROI from adopting OSS looks like it should be respectably high.

In an effort to answer the above question, this chapter presents a comprehensive review of the evidence on the quality of OSS and the cost to enterprises of adopting OSS. In terms of calculating ROI, the data presented here can be used with the methodology presented in this book to evaluate the ROI from adopting specific open source systems.

The purpose of this chapter is to analyze carefully the claims of higher-quality OSS and draw some conclusions about whether or not we can make a broad business case for software purchasers/users to adopt OSS.

11.1 Adoption of OSS

The adoption of OSS is increasing. Some open source systems, such as the Apache Web server, the Linux operating system, and the MySQL database, are becoming highly respected and emerging as real alternatives to incumbent CSS.

Some of the popular OSS applications are large, and their development is in the same league as large commercial projects. For example, Debian Linux has been estimated to be larger than 50 million lines of code.[1] Red Hat Linux (version 7.1) was counted to have more than 30 million lines of code, with the kernel at more than 2.4 million lines of code.[2] Windows 3.1 was 3 million SLOC, Windows 95 was 15 million LOC, and Windows 2000 is 29 million SLOC.[3,4]

We begin by presenting some data on the extent of adoption of OSS and the reasons behind it.

11.1.1 Definition Open Source Software

OSS software comes in many guises. The most common definition of an OSS product is:

- The source code is made available.
- The user can sell, give away, or redistribute the source code.
- The source code can be modified and extended, and must be distributed under the same licensing terms as the original license.

There are additional requirements for an application to qualify as OSS (these are defined at the Open Source Initiative Web site <www.opensource.org>), but the ones above are the most critical. There are many licensing schemes for OSS that are discussed elsewhere;[5] however, the GNU General Public License is by far the most commonly used.

11.1.2 Reasons for Adoption

Surveys show that enterprises adopt OSS primarily because they believe it is cheaper to acquire than alternative CSS solutions and that they have a lower total cost of ownership.[6,7] Many IT managers believe that OSS is free.[8] Close behind is the belief that OSS is more reliable and more secure than CSS.[6]

11.1.3 Adoption of OSS

When evaluating the adoption of OSS, we can look at specific examples of adoption to illustrate potential.

Sendmail, which is an open source e-mail server, was found to power 42 percent of all e-mail servers and Microsoft Exchange was found to have 18 percent of the market.[9] Almost 95 percent of the domain name servers use the open source program BIND.[10] PHP, a popular scripting language, is powering about a quarter of the Web sites.[10]

Netcraft (www.netcraft.com) statistics on Web servers have shown over the years that Apache has dominated the public Internet Web server market since 1996. When counting active Web sites, Apache has 66 percent of the market and Microsoft's IIS (the main contender) has around 24 percent (in September 2002). When counting IP addresses instead of sites (because many sites can be hosted on the same server), 54 percent are using Apache while 35 percent are using IIS. A May 2003 update reported that Apache was used in 66.52 percent of active Web sites. Therefore, it would seem that Apache rates are at a plateau, but a high one.

A large-scale survey performed by the Yankee Group found that 33 percent of IT administrators had no plans to change Windows servers to Linux, 25 percent were planning to migrate a portion of their Windows servers to Linux, and 11 percent were planning to migrate all of their Windows servers to Linux.[8] The same survey found that Microsoft commands 94 percent of the desktop market and 66 percent of the server operating system market, while Linux holds 20 percent of the server operating system market.

While the growth of some OSS applications has been substantial over the past few years, Lewis[11] notes that in a friction-free economy, market share growth becomes more difficult as the percentage increases. One can double one's market share easily when it is at 2 percent; but when it reaches 20 or 30 percent, increasing market share becomes much more difficult and the increase slows down. Therefore, it may not be possible to sustain such rapid growth rates for OSS for much longer (i.e., the previous growth rate is not necessarily a predictor of future adoption rates).

11.1.4 Number of Developers of OSS

One survey[12] found that 49 percent of OSS projects have only one developer, and only 15 percent have two or three developers. A majority,

73 percent, have only one stable developer (who regularly contributes). A subsequent study of only the OSS projects that seem to be currently active found that a vast majority of them have less than five developers.[13] An examination of 27,918 SourceForge (an incubator of OSS projects) projects found that 67 percent of them have a single developer.[14] The average project size was two developers.

An examination of the GNOME project, a desktop environment for users and an application framework for developers,[15] found that the top 15 programmers contributed 48 percent of the code and the top 52 programmers contributed 80 percent of the code over its lifetime. A clustering of the developers did find that there was a core group of 11 developers who were most active. The peak staffing for this project was around 130 developers working on it at the same time.

An analysis of 3149 OSS projects found that more than 70 percent of the contributed code was authored by 10 percent of the authors.[16] An analysis of 100 of the mature projects on SourceForge found that the median number of developers involved in an OSS project is four and the mode is one.[17] Only 29 percent of all projects had more than five developers.

Another examination of more than 46,000 OS projects found that the median number of developers on these projects was one, and 95 percent of them had five or fewer developers working on them.[18]

This has caused some authors to state that the "findings raise questions about the scope and accuracy of existing theories of OSS development [... the open source image] does not capture the fact that the typical project has one developer, no discussion or bug reports, and is not downloaded by anyone".[18] In addition, it has been asserted that the model of open source production with thousands of developers does not match reality.[9]

In fact, when a project grows in popularity, it becomes more and more attractive so that developers are likely to join it. Given the predominant motivations of individuals to participate in OSS projects, they are most likely to increase their reputation if more people are looking at their code. The opposite happens with unpopular projects that do not succeed in attracting a large base of programmers.[9] Therefore, it does not make sense to talk about open source projects in general because most open source projects do not fit the common description of the OSS model. Rather, we need to focus only on the very small minority of popular OSS projects.

11.1.5 The OSS Process

The development process for OSS projects has been characterized by Mockus et al.[19] and Sharma et al.[20]

- There is a development team that is geographically distributed.
- Work is not assigned; people undertake the work they choose to undertake.
- There is no explicit system-level design, nor even detailed design.
- There is no project plan, schedule, or list of deliverables.
- There is the use of coordination mechanisms that emphasize asynchronous communication.
- There is no formal organizational structure for the team.

The activities that go into a release include problem discovery, finding volunteers to work on the problem, solution identification, code change and testing, code change review, code commit into the version control system, and release management.[20]

11.2 The OSS Advantage

A number of reasons have been put forth to explain why OSS projects will, inherently, result in higher-quality software. Here we examine some of these claims and the evidence that supports them.

11.2.1 Incremental Software Process

Raymond[21] argues that the success of OSS development is due to not using traditional and rigid software development practices. Rather, more flexible development practices with frequent small releases are encouraged. However, these types of practices are not unique to open source[22] — for example, rapid prototyping, incremental and evolutionary development, the spiral life cycle, and rapid application development. In fact, these practices are at the core of many agile methods. These practices have been used at Microsoft for some time in its daily build process.[23] Therefore, the uniqueness of the OSS process is an argument that does not hold water under minimal scrutiny and will not be discussed further.

11.2.2 Users Fix Bugs

It is argued that many users of OSS software do not just report bugs, but actually track them down to their root causes and fix them. To the extent that an application is popular, the user community represents a large pool of debuggers, thus relieving the core development teams from the arduous task of replicating, isolating, and fixing defects.

If there is a large pool of debuggers, much larger than one would see for a CSS application, then that would be a good reason why OSS would be of higher quality. Unfortunately, that is usually not the case.

A study by the SEI[24] of the Apache project found that the majority (93 percent) of changes (implementations, patches, and enhancements) were made by the core group of developers. The total number of people reporting bugs was 5116, but only 200 individuals actually contributed patches. The difficult and critical architectural changes were made by an even smaller subset of the core group.[24]

Another investigation of Apache[25] found that more than 83 percent of the modification requests, 88 percent of added lines of code, and 91 percent of deleted lines of code came from the top 15 developers. About 66 percent of bug fixes were produced by the top 15 developers, but 182 individuals submitted bug fixes out of 3060 who submitted bug reports.[19] The top 15 problem reporters submitted only 5 percent of the problem reports. These numbers indicate that a small core team develops new functionality but that there is slightly wider participation in bug fixes.

An interesting informal survey performed at a computer science department among UNIX users (comprising researchers, staff, and students) asked if they had encountered bugs and if they had reported them.[26] All of the respondents who had encountered bugs, some serious, did not bother to report them. To the extent that this behavior is common among technical users (UNIX users tend to be rather technically savvy), many users will not bother to report bugs even if they do discover them. In the case of Apache, it was estimated that less than 1 percent of all Apache users submit problem reports.[19]

Therefore, with the above numbers, it is very difficult to make a general claim that OSS applications have a large pool of debuggers (developer-users). To have thousands of debuggers who actually contribute fixes, as some OSS advocates claim, requires an OSS application to have millions of users. Very few match that description.

The most successful OSS applications that we commonly hear about (e.g., Apache) do have a relatively large core team of developers and contributors. However, these are the exception rather than the norm. In fact, these successful examples are far from being the average OSS project. Examples from flagship projects such as Linux and Apache should not be taken as the rule for all OSS projects.[13] Even for some of the more popular projects, most of the people who report bugs do not actually submit any fixes. A small proportion of those who report problems are really debuggers.

Contrast these numbers with the development team for Windows 2000. It was reported that the development team consisted of 1400 developers and 1700 testers.[3] These are full-time staff. If we wish to convert those numbers to OSS developer equivalents, then we can conservatively double these numbers (most OSS developers contribute to OSS projects on a part-time basis).

11.2.3 Large-Scale Peer Reviews Improve Quality

One of the fundamental assumptions for the success of OSS software is that there will be many developers looking over the source code. The popularized statement "given enough eyeballs, all bugs are shallow" captures that assumption[21] Because so many developers and users would be looking at the source code of an OSS application, this amounts to a very large-scale peer review process. Some authors are talking about millions of programmers out there performing peer reviews on OSS code.[27]

It is well established in software engineering that peer reviews are one of the best methods for defect detection.[28] In addition, the prospect of having their code available for scrutiny by their peers motivates most programmers to be more careful.[29,30]

Peer reviews are relatively common practice in OSS projects. For example, on the FreeBSD project, 57 percent of respondents working on the project had distributed code for review in the month prior to the survey,[30] and 86 percent of those who distribute code for review do get feedback from their peers.

Unfortunately, a vast majority of OSS projects do not have a large number of developers or users. Therefore, the large-scale peer review simply does not occur, except with the very few projects that do have a large contributor and user base.

Even if there are many developers, a critical point to note is that the benefits of peer reviews do plateau after a certain number of reviewers. For example, if we make the reasonable assumption that peer reviewers are (statistically) independent in an OSS project, then a simple simulation will illustrate the point. Let us say that a peer reviewer has a probability of 0.25 of finding a defect (i.e., a reviewer will only find, on average, a quarter of all the defects in the code through a review). This is the minimum reported value in the literature for the effectiveness of code reviews.[28]

If we have ten peer reviewers, then the overall probability of finding a defect is 0.95. This means that it is almost certain that all defects that can be found by peer review will be found. If we have 20 peer reviewers, then the probability of finding a defect is around 0.995 — which is higher, but the increment is rather small. Therefore, adding more peer reviewers reaches a point of diminishing returns very rapidly. This is illustrated in Figure 11.1.

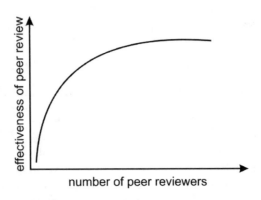

FIGURE 11.1 **Addition of peer reviewers reaches a point of diminishing returns rather rapidly.**

In reality, peer reviewers are likely to have a probability of finding a defect that is larger than 0.25. Therefore, the plateau of effectiveness will be reached earlier than ten reviewers.

The implication is that, even if there are hundreds of peer reviewers looking over the code, that does not add tremendous value as along as at least five or six developers review the code. Beyond that number of reviewers, the incremental defect detection benefit decreases substantially.

How does this compare to CSS projects? As summarized previously, one survey found that 52 percent of companies perform code reviews;[31] while another survey found that 71 percent of respondents in the United States use code reviews, around 82 percent in Europe, and 74 percent in Japan.[32] Therefore, there is evidence that a majority of CSS projects do use some form of peer review. In practice, the recommended team size ranges from 2 to 12.[33-45] Given that the benefits of adding reviewers reach a plateau with relatively few reviewers, one can make the argument that CSS peer reviews are comparable to OSS peer reviews in terms of their ability to find defects.

This raises the question of how big the peer review advantage really is in OSS software compared to CSS software. Based on the above data, one can conclude that the performance of peer reviews for OSS software would, at best, be as good as for CSS software.

Another important issue to note is that the hardest defects to find and fix, such as those creating dangerous security vulnerabilities, are design flaws rather than coding errors.[46] Without the availability of good design documentation, it would be very difficult to find these defects through a code review. Most OSS projects do not have good design documentation.

Peer reviews are the main mechanisms for defect detection in OSS projects. The other defect detection practice, testing, is not practiced systematically on OSS projects. One study based on an investigation of 80 OSS projects and interviews with OSS developers found that in OSS projects, formal testing is not very common.[47] An examination of quality practices in various well-known OSS projects demonstrated that formal testing is not prevalent.[48] A survey of open source developers found that their testing practices were not thorough.[49] It has been argued that OSS contributors tend to be more interested in coding than in documenting and testing.[47] There is evidence that the test coverage for the Linux kernel test suite is very low.[50]

In CSS projects, some form of testing is almost always performed before a product is released.[31,32] There is evidence that peer reviews and testing find different types of defects and, in fact, they are complementary rather than alternatives.

Therefore, the strong focus on reviews to the detriment of testing would have a negative impact on quality because defects that are most likely to be detected by testing will escape into production code.

Finally, developers making changes to an OSS program will typically focus on the parts that are relevant to that change, rather than focus on the whole system. Therefore, the parts of the system that tend to be changed frequently are reviewed more often, and the parts that are not changed get examined less frequently. Therefore, to the extent that peer reviews are performed, they tend to be uneven across the system.

11.2.4 Large-Scale Beta Testing

One of the arguments made in support of superior OSS quality is that it tends to have a large number of end users who effectively beta test the software every time it is released. This large and free beta testing ensures that any bugs that escape development will be discovered relatively quickly.

This argument has merit. It is known that defect discovery is affected by usage. Therefore, the more users a product has, the more defects will be discovered.

Most (80 percent) OSS projects have less than 11 users (where subscribers is used as a surrogate for users).[12] Only 1 percent have more than 100 users.[12] A Pareto analysis of active projects on SourceForge found that half the active projects had between 0 and 70 downloads per month,[52] and that a very small number of projects are popular, with the vast majority not experiencing many downloads. Following a Pareto distribution means that the number of projects with more than a given number of downloads tails off exponentially.

As shown above, most OSS projects do not have a large number of users. Therefore, this argument can only apply to the very few OSS products that are very popular.

11.2.5 OSS Projects Have Good Programmers

The developers working on OSS projects are experienced programmers who get involved in OSS projects on a part-time basis. Many improve their skills rapidly because of all the peer reviews they do and the feedback they get.

There has been accumulating evidence that individual skills and capability have a significant impact on productivity and quality. Therefore, if the team is good, the chances of a good product increase.

The open source development model appears to encourage meritocracy, in which programmers organize themselves based on their contributions. The most effective programmers write the most crucial code, review the contributions of others, and decide which of the contributions make it into the next release.

Having good programmers, however, is not an exclusive advantage of OSS projects. Many a CSS project will have good programmers; and the better they are, the greater the probability that they will be responsible for critical code.

11.2.6 Fewer Schedule Pressures

OSS projects do not face the same type of resource and time pressures that commercial projects do. OSS software is rarely developed against a fixed deadline. Development continues until the code is ready.

The lack of schedule and budget pressures affords more opportunity to peer review and beta test as needed before release. This is a considerable advantage. Projects with tight deadlines frequently have to make difficult choices about which defects to fix, and many are released with known bugs.

Contemporary CSS software is updated and patched on a regular basis. This is performed physically with update disks or over the Internet. In either case, the CSS vendor has the opportunity to fix bugs in these patches and updates. Even if the software is shipped with defects and this is caused by schedule pressures, the patches will fix these problems rapidly. However, many users do not install these patches. Installing patches can be expensive and disruptive.

Is it enough to make the case for superior quality software? Most OSS developers work part-time (they have day jobs) and therefore the ability to take longer arguably compensates for their inability to devote their time exclusively to the OS projects.

11.2.7 Requirements Uncertainty

One study of a relatively large sample of OSS products found that the most common application domains were "Internet," "System," "Software Development," "Communications," and "Multimedia."[12] This means that a large majority of OSS applications (66 percent) are intended to serve the software development community rather than some other community (e.g., health care or insurance).

The developers must be users because there is generally no formal requirements elicitation process in OSS projects[47, 53–55] and the developers themselves are assumed to be the domain experts. Only what this group of user-developers thinks are important features will get developed. Systems with highly uncertain requirements, where access to users who are not part of the development team is required, will have a more difficult time under the OSS development model.

Requirements uncertainty is a major cause of software project failure. Therefore, the fact that OSS projects focus mostly on low uncertainty projects is an important advantage that reduces the development risks.

11.2.8 Summary

The above discussion went through the inherent reasons why OSS projects may have higher quality. Some of the mechanisms concern the OSS methodology, while other factors such as people skills have been claimed to also play a role.

The case for OSS has centered on the thousands or millions of debuggers and reviewers who would find all of the defects. The data presented above indicates that this rarely, if ever, actually happens. In theory, it is a good idea and would work, but practice has not yet followed this theory.

What is evident is that for a large majority of OSS projects, the conditions that are necessary to make them superior do not exist. Therefore, the broad statements that OSS projects are somehow inherently better can neither be supported nor justified.

In reality, the only advantages that OSS projects have that do not exist for CSS projects is that there is no deadline — and hence no schedule pressure. Also, the types of projects that are pursued tend to have low functional uncertainty.

There are a small minority of very successful OSS projects, such as Linux, Apache, MySQL, etc. Keeping in mind that these are not representative of OSS projects but rather the exceptions, we examine below in further detail how these example OSS applications compare to CSS applications.

11.3 The Cost of Adopting OSS

The perception that OSS is free is one of the main reasons that attract individuals and organizations to look at adopting it. This means that the software can be downloaded at no cost from the Internet. Users can download ready-to-execute binaries on the specific platform(s) that they choose or download the source code and compile it for a specific platform.

The cost of ownership is one of the critical dimensions of ROI. Therefore, we examine the extent to which OSS changes our understanding of cost of ownership.

In reality, OSS is far from free. There are many hidden costs and risks involved in the use of OSS. To repeat from a previous chapter, we can categorize the costs as:

- *Purchase costs.* These include the cost of looking for the software and evaluating it, as well as the licensing costs.
- *Installation costs.* These are the costs incurred during installation, which include integration with existing systems and any necessary data migration.
- *Operational costs.* These are the technical service and support costs, as well as upgrade and maintenance costs.

Given that code is contributed by many people from around the world, there is the risk of proprietary code or copyrighted materials inadvertently making its way into an OSS application. Successful OSS products are being commercialized very rapidly. This commercialization is necessary to migrate OSS to the enterprise. Therefore, the notion that OSS is free is best suited for fairy tales. The adoption costs are discussed below.

11.3.1 Purchase Costs

As an enterprise, it would not be prudent to just download and install OSS. This approach is suitable for individuals and maybe even small companies; but for medium-sized or large organizations, this is not a realistic option. Availability of support is one of the main problems encountered by adopters of OSS and one of the main fears of those who do not adopt OSS.[6]

The typical process for getting support with OSS is to post a query on a forum that is frequented by experts. Anecdotally, many people have had a good experience with this process. However, this will not work for a typical enterprise for three reasons:

1. End users who are not technical but who are using an open source application are not likely to frequent a forum to post questions. And the responses to these questions are typically from the developers. Therefore, the end users are not likely to be able to parse the responses because they would be too programmer oriented. There would have to be different levels of support geared toward different user types.

2. Good responsiveness would be a challenge if there were 500 end users from each enterprise posting queries every day. The volume of queries would be substantial. This would not be a problem if every single user is prepared to respond to queries as well as post them. However, an enterprise would not want its staff providing application support to other companies that may be competitors.
3. Enterprises will want written guarantees that support will be available and can handle the load. Good intentions of a group of volunteers will just not be convincing enough.

An internal support group within an enterprise is the most appropriate way to deal with OSS support if a vendor does not provide such support. Therefore, there would be a cost for OSS support either way.

The better option is to purchase a license from one of the companies that supports OSS software (e.g., Red Hat, Novell, HP, or IBM, to name a few). With such a license, you will get a distribution that has a legal entity standing behind it and will provide some warranties on the product. Furthermore, the licensed products will have the proprietary system and network management tools that are necessary to run large installations. They may also have performance-enhancing add-ons that are required for high loads.

Some insurance companies are offering copyright insurance for OSS software. The premiums are high but that is another avenue that can be pursued. Insurance does provide some protection and should be looked at on a case-by-case basis. However, insurance does increase the purchase cost for OSS.

11.3.2 Installation Costs

OSS has a reputation of not being user friendly, and typically it lives up to its reputation. For example, real converts describe their first Linux installation as "an exhilarating succession of problem-solving challenges."[56] Although things are getting better, it will take some years for OSS to reach the usability levels of common CSS applications.

If your site has many UNIX administrators, then that is a good start. UNIX administrators are accustomed to command line interfaces and writing a lot of scripts to get things to work. If you are a Windows shop, then a bigger shift in expertise is required.

There will be some costs incurred in training the IT staff to install and manage an open source system or to hire new staff or consultants. If we take Linux as an example, in North America today, there is a premium for individuals who have that expertise, especially as demand picks up. This means that if you hire people with that expertise, you will be paying them more than your other staff with expertise in UNIX and Windows. This is likely to change in the next few years as the talent pool increases.

There is a lack of good documentation and training materials on many OSS applications, except perhaps the most popular ones (e.g., there are a number of very good books on Linux and Apache). The lack of documentation means that the installation and setup period may be longer if you do not hire external experts.

Integration with legacy applications can become expensive. OSS tends to follow standards but legacy applications do not necessarily follow standards. Therefore, data exchange between them may be problematic. Many OSS products were not built to integrate with CSS systems. The cost of integration may involve changing the OSS code, which can add substantially to the overall cost.

11.3.3 Post-purchase Costs

Once the OSS is in place, there are ongoing operational costs. These include the annual license costs to the vendor that is providing the OSS support and upgrades.

Some argue that fewer administrators are required to manage an OSS installation than to manage a CSS installation. While this may be true to some extent, the comparative numbers used without substantiating evidence are very large — making that argument very difficult to believe. For example, one study argued that a Linux administrator can manage 50 percent more servers than a Windows administrator.[57]

Costs due to quality and security problems will be comparable to CSS systems. As will be argued further below, the reliability and security differential between OSS and CSS software, at least for the more popular OSS applications, is absent. Therefore, costs due to service interruptions from patches and updates will be similar.

If operating in a regulated industry, then each time the OSS system is upgraded or modified, it may have to be recertified. Certification costs can be substantial. These costs are comparable to recertifying custom applications.

An additional cost is that of making changes to OSS software.

Depending on the license that the OSS falls under, you may be obliged to make your changes to the OSS available to anyone who asks if you distribute the software. The GNU General Public License makes such a stipulation. For example, if you give the modified OSS system to your customers, suppliers, or business partners, then this may be construed as distribution. You may then be obliged to make your source code, including your changes, available under the same license to outsiders who ask for it. This is risky if the changes you made include competitive business logic.

The risks are higher if some of the code that your staff includes in the OSS system distributed finds its way back to your other CSS systems. Then these other systems must be open sourced if you distribute them. What this means is that if you decide to make changes to an OSS product, a very effective audit function must be in place to ensure that OSS code does not "infect" your other CSS systems, and to ensure that any changes do not expose competitive information.

Furthermore, if you modify an OSS application, then future updates to that application, security patches, and or drivers for new hardware may no longer work on your customized version of the OSS. Therefore, your staff would have to scrutinize each patch and each update to see if it warrants integration with your specific version of the OSS application. In practice then, this amounts to your organization inheriting a large legacy application that was developed by an external team with little or no supporting documentation. The consequence is that they will not be able to maintain your custom version of the OSS application for very long before problems (mainly quality problems and an inability to integrate functionality fast enough) start to occur without making additional investments in developer strategy.

Most companies that modify OSS code do not share it back with the community. Although this goes against the spirit of OSS, not contributing back to the community is the current reality. But, if you have to modify code, then the better long-term solution is to share it with the OSS community. This will ensure that the version that the rest of the OSS community is working on matches the version that you are running in your enterprise.

Procedures must be in place for sharing software with the open source community. These should be coordinated with the lawyers. In addition, a budget must be put aside for this, as some effort will have to be expended.

However, a risk with contributing source code to an OSS project is that the contribution may not be accepted. The core development team for the OSS project may not perceive the additions or changes as relevant to the whole community or may reject it for some other reason. This is something that cannot be controlled by the contributing enterprise. Therefore, your internal customized versions of the OSS system may permanently diverge from the standard OSS version. One option you may have is to create a new fork of the OSS system and manage it yourself. But then your company would end up coordinating an OSS project. This will require substantially more investment on your side to allocate your staff to that.

Many OSS vendor licenses do not provide any protection if you change the code. This means that if your staff changes OSS code and these modified OSS systems are distributed to clients, suppliers, or business partners, you will be liable for any damages that may occur due to the software. Although the changes you made to the software may be minor, you will likely be unable to pass the risk onto someone else if any of the software that is distributed causes damages.

As a general rule, it is best not to modify any OSS that you use.

11.3.4 Summary

Most organizations do not perform a serious total cost of ownership analysis before adopting OSS applications. Disliking a certain CSS vendor or a certain CSS vendor's practices is not a sound basis for making a large IT investment. It is strongly recommended that a cost analysis go beyond the cost of purchase and consider the total cost of operating a system that is based on OSS, and then make a decision.

Being able to change the code for OSS systems is little more than a red herring. In practice, the costs for enterprises to do so and the risks involved are substantial. This is more so if your IT department does not wish to get into the OSS business.

The lowest risk scenario for adopting OSS is when you get support licenses for OSS from a commercial vendor and do not need to make any changes to the code to implement customizations that your business needs; or if the OSS software is at the middleware or operating system level, in which case you can add your customizations on top of it. For example, if you adopt Linux, then you can develop your own applications on top of it without having to modify the operating system itself.

11.4 Comparing OSS and CSS Software Reliability

We now examine the data from head-to-head reliability comparisons of OSS and CSS. Notwithstanding the questions raised above about the mechanisms that would allow OSS to be superior, one can say that, ultimately, the reliability comparisons provide the proof.

11.4.1 Complexity of OSS

One of the arguments made in favor of OSS is that it fosters less complex code.[58] This means that OSS will be more modular and have less coupling than CSS.

An empirical study comparing three successful OSS products with three commercial CSS products found that the OSS products tended to be more

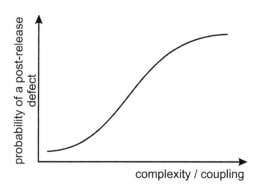

FIGURE 11.2 Relationship between complexity and post-release defects.

complex.[59] The same result was found for whole systems and for individual functions. This is contradictory to the claims made by OSS advocates. Furthermore, the results of that study found that coupling tended to be much higher for OSS systems than for the CSS systems examined. As a general software engineering principle, higher coupling indicates bad design for two reasons: systems with high coupling (1) are more difficult to understand and (2) suffer from more ripple effects due to changes. The latter means that whenever a change is made in a module, other modules are affected. Such side effects increase the probability of inadvertently introducing defects while making changes.

A second study that looked specifically at coupling among modules within the Linux kernel found exponential growth over time.[60] Such a growth trajectory suggests deterioration in modularity over time. Another study found that just under a half of unchanged Linux kernel modules suffered from increasing levels of clandestine common coupling. This means that these modules are affected by changes in other parts of the kernel, potentially resulting in higher risks of inadvertent side effects during changes.[60]

The implication of the results is that OSS projects are likely to have *more* defects than CSS products. The reason is that the relationship between complexity/coupling and defects is well established in software engineering. The functional form of this relationship is shown in Figure 11.2. This does not necessarily mean that all OSS is less modular and more complex than CSS. However, it does mean that some of the better-known OSS applications have similar structural problems as they grow, as we have witnessed in CSS applications in the past.

Another study analyzed 100 OSS projects using software metrics.[61] The basic idea is to collect common metrics that are leading indicators of

TABLE 11.1   Recommendations after Static Analysis of 100 Open Source Components in Linux using Complexity Metrics

Recommendation Using Calculated Metrics	Mean (%)
ACCEPT (acceptable quality)	50.18
COMMENT (requires further commenting)	30.95
INSPECT (needs to be inspected)	8.55
TEST (requires additional testing)	4.31
REWRITE (the component must be rewritten)	5.57
UNDEFINED	0.42

Note: The mean number of components for each of the 100 Linux applications that fell in the recommendation categories.

quality based on previous research work. Then these metrics are compared to established thresholds obtained from CSS. The thresholds indicate whether or not the quality is acceptable. Four dimensions of quality were evaluated: (1) testability, (2) readability, (3) simplicity, and (4) self-descriptiveness. The results are summarized in Table 11.1. About half of the OSS applications were acceptable by CSS software quality standards, and around 10 percent of the applications require further testing or need to be rewritten because their quality levels were deemed too low.

Having good self-documentation within the code is critical for the success of these efforts because of the distributed nature of the projects.[63] According to the authors, it was found that the level of code comments in OSS was rather low compared to general CSS standards (one comment per ten lines of code).[61] This is of concern because OSS uses code comments as the main documentation mechanism.

The traditional OSS process has difficulty supporting complex code because it is more difficult to have a distributed team design complex functionality. The developers of FreeBSD, an OSS operating system, could not use their typical continuous release process to develop a complex feature (SMP).[30] This feature had to be taken outside and managed as a separate project with design, documentation, and a more formal project plan.

Therefore, OSS is clearly not less complex than comparable CSS applications. And for the large OSS systems, they are suffering substantial increases in code complexity.

11.4.2 *Evaluation of Software Failures*

There have been a number of studies that evaluated the quality of OSS and CSS directly by comparing failure rates. Note that a failure is not the same as a defect. For example, if there are 100 inputs to a program that causes it to fail, there may be a single underlying defect causing all of these failures. However, failures are what the end user will experience. These studies are summarized below.

A series of tests, commonly known as the Fuzz tests, were performed over a ten-year period from 1990 to 2000. The basic idea behind the Fuzz tests was to generate random black-box test cases and inject them into OSS and CSS programs. If the programs crashed or hung (i.e., did not respond), then that is considered a failure.

The intention of these studies was not to compare CSS with OSS. However, given the nature of the systems they tested, the results can be used to compare the two development paradigms.

The first Fuzz tests were performed on 90 UNIX utilities on seven different versions of UNIX.[26] The authors were able to crash 24 to 33 percent of the programs on each of the UNIX systems. Some of the UNIX versions were commercial and some were OSS.

The second Fuzz tests[64] tested over 80 utility programs on nine different UNIX platforms, seven of which were commercial versions. The authors also tested network services and the X-Windows servers and applications. The failure rate of the utilities on commercial versions of UNIX (including Sun, IBM, SGI. DEC, and NEXT) ranged from 15 to 43 percent. The failure rate on Linux was only 9 percent, and the failure rate on the GNU utilities was a low 6 percent. The authors could not crash any of the network services that were tested, nor the X-Windows servers. However, more than half of the time, the X-Window applications crashed with random input, and more than 25 percent of the time the input stream was valid.

Although the tests they ran on these applications were random and not all of them represented valid inputs, the failure rates reported here sound astounding, especially when the space of inputs that are valid that have not yet been covered by these tests is very large. However, with random testing, one is not using the system with the same usage profile as a regular user (i.e., random testing does not follow the operational profile for the system). Therefore, the reported failure rates will not necessarily match the failure rates that a user will encounter in practice.

The most recent series of tests performed focused on Windows NT.[64] Two types of tests were performed. First, Windows applications were subjected to keyboard and mouse events, and random (often invalid) input messages. The input messages were injected through the Win32 message interface. Overall, 21 percent of the NT applications crashed when presented with random valid keyboard and mouse events. An additional 24 percent of the NT applications hung when presented with random valid keyboard and mouse events. Up to 100 percent of the applications crashed or hung when presented with random input streams through the messaging interface. This latter result is a consequence of the way that the messaging interface is designed in Windows, thus making it rather easy to crash it.

The above studies counted the number of programs that failed at least once during the testing. The rates do not reflect the probability that a particular application will fail. For example, if I tested ten utilities and, after running all of the tests that I have, five of the utilities failed once, then the reported "Fuzz" rate is 50 percent. This does not mean that if I use any of the five utilities, they will fail 50 percent of the time.

Another study examined Windows reliability in a different way. Here, the authors generated anomalous input rather than completely random input.[66] Instead of generating random input that does not meet the syntax of the program's input, they generated input using the input grammar of the Windows programs. Failure in this study was defined as an incorrect exit code, unhandled exceptions, hung processes, insecure behavior, or a system crash.

The authors tested the Windows NT command-line utilities. Only 0.338 percent of the test cases resulted in failure. The same study evaluated the open source GNU utilities that have been ported to Windows.[65] These failed 10.64 percent of the time. For all of these tests, the distribution of failures was heavily skewed toward memory access violations. This points to potential vulnerabilities in the GNU utilities to buffer overrun attacks (a common form of security vulnerability).

The large discrepancy in the GNU and Windows numbers compared to the Fuzz tests is due to the way the failure rates were counted. The way the Fuzz rates are calculated is more conducive to dramatic numbers.

Another study focused on operating systems.[66] Here, the authors injected invalid inputs into operating system calls (which are the basis for most applications written on top of these operating systems). A failure was defined as an incorrect error/success return code from the call, abnormal termination, or hanging the system. None of the operating systems had catastrophic failures. However, HP-UX (a version of UNIX) had 30 restarts out of 2059 tests (1.4 percent) and QNX (a commercial real-time operating system) had 35 restarts out of 1564 tests (2.2 percent).

11.4.3 Evaluation of Defect Levels

A company called Reasoning did a series of interesting evaluations of defects in OSS and compared them to a database that it had of defects from CSS. The basic approach they used was static analysis.

TABLE 11.2 Types of Defects that Discovered through Static Analysis

Defect Type	Description
Null pointer dereference	When the code dereferences a NULL pointer. This would terminate execution of the program (or current thread).
Out-of-bounds array access	When an array index is outside the lower or upper bounds of the array. This will typically result in termination of the program or the thread.
Resource leak	When a resource is allocated but never released, such as memory, file descriptors, and socket handles.
String comparison	When two strings are incorrectly compared.
Bad deallocation	When inappropriate memory is released or memory that was never explicitly allocated is deallocated.
Uninitialized variable	When local and dynamic variables are not explicitly initialized prior to use. This can cause unpredictable program behavior.

With static analysis, a tool is used to parse the source code of the program and look for problematic patterns. These patterns have a high probability of being a defect. The types of defects that can be detected through this kind of analysis are summarized in Table 11.2 for C, C++, and Java programs.

The Reasoning studies (which at the time of writing could be downloaded from <http://www.reasoning.com/>) are interesting for two reasons. First, they are the first to do a serious static analysis of OSS and compare the results to CSS results. Second, they are being frequently quoted and cited in the quality of OSS debate.

Not all of the detected defects are true defects. There are two classes of untrue defects:

1. The first class of untrue defects is *false positives*. These are cases where it looks like the problematic pattern exists but after further manual examination, it is discovered that the problem does not exist.
2. The second class is true patterns but that will not cause a problem in practice because the combination of prerequisites for the defect to manifest itself is impossible. This is determined by a manual examination.

The results of their analysis are shown in Table 11.3. Note that the above defect levels are only for the defect types in Table 11.2. They are

TABLE 11.3 Summary of the Defects Discovered through the Reasoning Static Analysis

Program	No. Defects Discovered	Total SLOC	Defect Density (defects/KSLOC)
MySQL	21	235,667	0.09
Apache	31	76,208	0.53
Linux TCP/IP	8	125,502	0.097
Tomcat	26	127,553	0.2

Note: The defect density is calculated by dividing the number of defects by size in SLOC. The SLOC shown in the table includes all header files (for C and C++ programs). The defect density calculation does not include the header files.

TABLE 11.4 Commercial Software Benchmark Used for Interpreting the OSS Numbers

Defect Density Range	Percentage
Less than 0.36 defects/KSLOC	33
Between 0.36 defects/KSLOC and 0.71 defects/KSLOC	33
Greater than 0.71 defects/KSLOC	33

Note: The benchmark consists of three groups. One third of the commercial products had more than 0.71 defects/KSLOC; one third had less than 0.36 defects/KSLOC; and one third had defect densities in between.

not total defect densities for these applications and they represent only a subset of all of the defects in an application.

To interpret these numbers, Reasoning has provided a benchmark from CSS. Reasoning makes its living by analyzing commercial products in the same manner and therefore has a large database of results from CSS. The benchmark presented in Table 11.4 is based on data from 200 projects totaling 35 million SLOC.

The results of the OSS analysis can now be interpreted. We can see that MySQL and Linux are in the top third and very comparable to the best CSS products. Apache is in the middle in terms of quality. Tomcat is also in the top third of applications. None of the OSS applications were in the bottom third.

The basic interpretation from these numbers is that there is variation in the quality of OSS as there is variation in the quality of CSS. Furthermore, not all OSS is comparable to the best CSS in terms of this limited measure of quality. Also note here that we are comparing CSS against the most

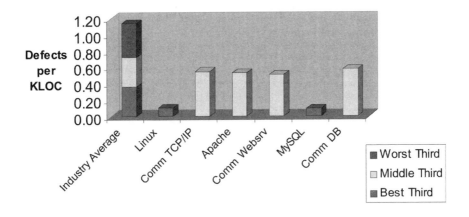

FIGURE 11.3 Comparison of defect density among OSS and CSS software. These numbers already remove the false positives. (*Source:* From Kamperman, J. Is Open Source Software Better than Commercial Software? Ottawa Software Quality Association (www.osqa.org), 2004.

successful and popular OSS applications (i.e., the ones where many of the ideal OSS conditions are met).

Another comparison is revealing.[68] Here, each of the OSS applications was matched with a CSS application in the same domain. The results are shown in Figure 11.3. In all cases, the CSS applications fare worse in terms of defects discovered through static analysis, although the difference between Apache and the commercial Web server is rather small.

I discuss the MySQL comparison in detail because I have more information about that.

The version of MySQL that was analyzed consists of a quarter of a million lines of code. The commercial database that it was compared against has tens of millions of lines of code and has been around for a couple of decades. The substantial size difference between the two products makes such a comparison questionable. Recall from a previous discussion in this book that there is a size effect and that the relationship between size and defects is not linear. Therefore, comparing two products with such a discrepancy in size is problematic.

The second issue to raise is that 8 of the 21 MySQL defects, as determined by the MySQL team, would not manifest themselves in the field. I spoke with one of the project managers of the commercial database product that was being compared to MySQL. His comments on the defects discovered through this static analysis indicated that many of the reported defects would not manifest themselves in the field. Therefore, the MySQL numbers and the commercial database numbers that are being compared are questionable to say the least. This basically means that if we make

TABLE 11.5 Comparison of Post-release Defect Levels in Apache with Four Commercial Products

	Apache	Commercial A	Commercial B	Commercial C	Commercial D
Defects per KLOC added	2.64	0.11	0.1	0.7	0.1
Defects per thousand deltas	40.8	4.3	14	28	10

approximate adjustments for all of these error sources, there is really no difference between MySQL and the commercial database in terms of quality.

Another evaluation of post-release defect levels in Apache found that the defect density was higher than in a number of commercial products in the telecommunications field.[19,25] These numbers are summarized in Table 11.5. A source code review by the Software Engineering Institute (SEI) of an OSS product, Enhydra, revealed that there were 87 easy-to-find defects in the C code and substantive errors in the Java code.[24] This was despite the claims made that thousands of programmers were working on the OSS system. The authors concluded that it was "no better than commercial source code we have reviewed in the past."

The above results on defect levels are not very surprising. An analysis of the code coverage during testing (the percentage of statements actually executed during a run of a test suite) for the Linux kernel test suite produced the results summarized in Table 11.6.[50] Two notes of caution should be mentioned here. First, statement coverage is not the best measure of test coverage. Second, some of those subsystems were quite large. However, we can see that the test coverage is very low and the test suite does not cover a number of important subsystems in the Linux kernel.

11.4.4 Summary

The review of data on the quality of OSS software does not reveal a substantive and general discrepancy between OSS and CSS. There have been many attempts to find a consistent gap in quality using varied techniques, but no compelling difference has been discovered. Therefore, making an OSS adoption based on a general quality differential between OSS and CSS cannot be supported empirically.

TABLE 11.6   Test Coverage Results after Running on the Test Suite on the Linux Kernel

Linux Kernel Subsystem	Test Coverage (%)
/usr/src/linux/arch/i386/kernel	9
/usr/src/linux/arch/i386/mm	11.65
/usr/src/linux/fs	29.51
/usr/src/linux/fs/autofs4	0
/usr/src/linux/fs/devpts	3.31
/usr/src/linux/fs/ext2	28.24
/usr/src/linux/fs/isofs	9
/usr/src/linux/fs/lockd	0.13
/usr/src/linux/fs/nfs	0
/usr/src/linux/fs/nfsd	0
/usr/src/linux/fs/partitions	0
/usr/src/linux/fs/proc	25.44
/usr/src/linux/ipc	46.02
/usr/src/linux/kernel	25.63
/usr/src/linux/mm	24.5
/usr/src/linux/net	48.4
/usr/src/linux/net/802	0
/usr/src/linux/net/core	12.87
/usr/src/linux/net/ethernet	28.21
/usr/src/linux/net/ipv4	18.37
/usr/src/linux/net/netlink	0
/usr/src/linux/net/packet	0
/usr/src/linux/net/sched	3.36
/usr/src/linux/net/sunrpc	0
/usr/src/linux/net/unix	47.8

Note: According to the author of the study that generated these data, all tests in the test suites except networking tests were executed to gather this data.

Source: From Iyer, M. *Analysis of Linux Test Project's Kernel Code Coverage,* IBM, 2002.

This is further reinforced in a study where the percentages of changes that are corrective maintenance are compared among two OSS systems and a CSS system.[69] Overall, it was found that the two types of software have the same percentage of corrective maintenance changes.

Concluding that there is no quality difference is based on evaluating the most popular OSS applications. I would conjecture that for the vast majority of OSS applications, that are not popular, there would be a significant quality difference when compared against commercial versions.

11.5 Comparing OSS and CSS on Security

Software defects can lead to security vulnerabilities. Therefore, the following security discussion is an extension of the quality discussion presented above except that different data was used to make the various points.

11.5.1 The Open Source Advantage?

The claim of OSS advocates is that the extensive peer review process (the "many eyeballs" argument) ensures that any security vulnerabilities will be promptly discovered, and either fixed by the reviewers (who would have to be pretty good programmers themselves if they have the skill to discover security defects) and send in the patch or at least report it. Therefore, the consequence would be that OSS is very secure and certainly more secure than CSS.

A common example to demonstrate the OSS advantage is that of "back door" code. This type of code is malicious and is inserted in legitimate programs to allow the bad guys access to the program (and data, the system, and possibly the network) by bypassing any existing security mechanisms that are in place. OSS proponents would say that because so many people read the code, such a situation would be discovered very fast. One example is the TCP Wrapper software that was hacked, into which back door code fragment was added. The malicious code was discovered and corrected — within a day.[69]

On the other hand, Borland/Inprise Interbase database software had a back door inserted by Borland's programmers (probably for debugging purposes) that allows access to the data in the database and the settings (CERT Advisory CA-2001-01). Stored procedures can be added and executed by anyone who knows about this back door account. This vulnerability took nine years to discover — and only after the vendor open sourced the database application.

The risk of using software with malicious code increases with network installs and automatic network updates. With many OSS users, they simply download binaries over the network (rather than source code that they would then compile themselves). This is potentially dangerous. In 2003, the GNU FTP server, which is the download mothership for GNU, was compromised and the compromise was detected after a month (or more).[70] CERT characterized this as a "serious threat" (CERT Advisory CA-2003-21). Similarly, four servers belonging to the Debian project were broken into in 2003, although this was detected within 24 hours.[71,72]

The point is that back door vulnerabilities are not exclusive to OSS or to CSS — both are vulnerable.

The proponents of CSS argue that because of source code availability, the peer review process gives bad guys the opportunity to identify vulnerabilities themselves and write exploits.[73] Therefore, it is more secure not to have the source code available.

Furthermore, with CSS, the bad guys will not discover security defects by reading code and therefore it will be much more difficult for them to write exploits (not impossible, just more difficult than if the source code was there). Any undiscovered security defects will therefore have no impact on the security of the systems.

Both the OSS and CSS arguments concede that having access to the source code makes finding security defects easier. They only differ in the motives behind that. One side views that as a good thing because the good guys will find the security defects first. The other side views it as a risk because the bad guys will find the security defects first.

There are counter examples on both fronts.

There was a leak of code from Microsoft a short while ago (or at least it was publicized a short while ago). One thing did not happen — there is no evidence that the existence of the source code on the Internet resulted in new vulnerabilities being discovered and new exploits derived from the source code.[74] This indicates two things: (1) having open source does not necessarily mean that the bad guys will be able to find security vulnerabilities and, (2) therefore, open sourcing code is not necessarily a high-risk activity as the defenders of CSS would argue.

Serious security defects existed in the GNU Mailman program, which is OSS, for three years without anyone noticing, despite considerable interest and usage of the application itself.[75] Furthermore, there were buffer overflows in MIT's Kerberos distribution for more than ten years that no one discovered.[69,75]

So why did the programmers working on these projects not find them? There are a number of reasons.

First, recall that for OSS projects, there is not a large pool of developers working on them. The developer population for any application tends to be very small for most applications. Therefore, the "many eyeball" argument fails.

Second, finding security defects requires special skills. These defects can be very complex and subtle. Most programmers do not receive any training on security. Furthermore, to be able to do it effectively requires a deep understanding of the application domain. For example, if one is writing an e-mail server, then a detailed knowledge of e-mail protocols is needed to detect situations or inputs that are risky. Very few programmers will have that kind of domain experience.

Finally, OSS code tends to be complex and lacks documentation. As seen in the data presented earlier, code complexity for some popular OSS applications is high and increasing over time. In addition, documentation is not the top priority of programmers. This makes it more difficult to find security defects, especially those caused by subtle design assumptions.

11.5.2 Security Evaluation

Payne[76] performed a study to compare the security of OSS and CSS software. He examined Debian, OpenBSD, and Solaris. The evaluation involved examining each operating system's security-related features and known vulnerabilities. Features were rated based upon their effectiveness and importance, while vulnerabilities were scored according to the extent of their impact, the ease of exploiting the flaw, and the difficulty of solving the problem. Each item was then classified into one or more of the four security dimensions: confidentiality, integrity, availability, and audit. A quantitative scoring was derived to present and aggregate the results of the individual item scoring.

Confidentiality included, for example, cryptographic file systems and other mechanisms for encrypting data. Integrity included preventing processes from modifying files in certain ways. Availability included the ability to control the amount of resource usage to prevent a malicious user from over-utilizing a shared resource. Audit included the ability to log network packets and calls to the kernel.

The results of this analysis are quite revealing, and are summarized in Table 11.7. We see that the two OSS operating systems — OpenBSD and Debian — are indeed more secure than the CSS operating system, Solaris. For example, OpenBSD had only five security vulnerabilities, whereas Solaris has more than four times that number.

However, if the OSS "improves peer review security" argument is true, then one would expect both OpenBSD and Debian to have equal scores. This is not the case. OpenBSD is significantly more secure than Debian. They are both OSS products. If security were an inherent open source advantage, then surely Debian would score very high as well.

TABLE 11.7 Security Evaluation Results of Three Operating Systems, Two of which Are Open Source

	Debian	Solaris	OpenBSD
Features			
Confidentiality	5.9	6.08	7.5
Integrity	5.88	6.17	7.38
Availability	7.00	5.75	6.00
Audit	6.9	5.67	7.25
Number	15	11	18
Average	6.42	5.92	7.03
Vulnerabilities			
Confidentiality	6.75	8.13	4.5
Integrity	7.7	7.4	4.25
Availability	8.1	7.00	8.0
Audit	8.33	8.42	0
Number	12	21	5
Average	7.72	7.74	4.19
Final Score	**–1.0**	**–3.5**	**10.2**

Note: The individual scores are based on a scheme devised by the researcher who did the study, but it is monotonic (i.e., larger values are better). The final score uses a special scaling to balance features with vulnerabilities.

In fact, making a program open source does not, by itself, ensure security. The OpenBSD project explicitly and purposefully aims to be secure and specifically targets and pours substantial resources into security reviews of all of the source code looking for security defects. It is this deliberate action that accounts for the high rating of OpenBSD. Also note that the OpenBSD team is not actually very large — it is a small dedicated team with a strong focus.

There is no reason why a deliberate action on security should not be taken by CSS vendors, and a number of high-profile vendors have started to do so. In the past there was no motivation for software vendors to pay attention to security. However, things have changed. With the bad publicity that ensues from security vulnerability and the increasing liability risks, vendors are starting to pay attention.

The security of the product does not depend on whether it is CSS or OSS. It depends on whether the development team focuses on security. Some OSS projects focus on security and some do not. Some CSS products focus on security and some do not. It is really that simple!

11.5.3 Comparing Vulnerabilities and Exploits

Another way to evaluate whether or not OSS is better than CSS is to compare the number of reported vulnerabilities over time.

Before interpreting the actual data, it is important to consider the following issues:

- Vulnerabilities have different severities. Some can be very mild with little impact or are difficult to take advantage of. Others may be serious and easy to exploit. Not all the vulnerability data considered severity.

- When comparing OSS and CSS operating systems, it should be noted that what is included within the scope of the operating system may be very different. For example, many Linux distributions will include a Web server or two, a database or two, and an office suite. The standard distribution of Windows will not include all of these applications. It is not clear in the numbers that are published what the scope of each platform is. This will also influence the size of the platforms. According to the discussion earlier about size and defects, it is not appropriate to compare, for example, a 30 million LOC distribution with a 2 million LOC distribution because the former will very likely have more vulnerabilities reported simply due to its size. Matters are actually worse because in many instances the vulnerability counts are not even adjusted by size.

- Platforms that are more widely deployed are more likely to have a larger number of vulnerabilities. Recall the usage argument that was made earlier in this book: the more usage, the greater the probability that latent defects will be discovered. For example, Windows desktop platforms tend to be much more widely deployed than Linux desktops. Therefore, desktop defects are more likely to be discovered on Windows than on Linux.

- Some reports of vulnerabilities sum across Linux distributions or Linux versions. This does not make sense. Many of the Linux distributions have common code; therefore, summing across the distributions effectively counts the same vulnerabilities more than

TABLE 11.8 Tally of Vulnerabilities Reported in 2001 by Obasonjo based on Data from the Security Focus Vulnerability Archive

Platform	Number of Recorded Vulnerabilities
AIX	10
Debian	13 + 1 Linux kernel
FreeBSD	24
HP-UX	25
Mandrake	17 + 12 Linux kernel
OpenBSD	13
Red Hat	28 + 12 Linux kernel
Solaris	38

Source: From Obasango, D. The Myth of Open Source Security Revisited v2.0. Available at: http://www.developer.com/open/article.php/990711.

once. In the numbers presented below, the data is presented per platform.

■ It has been argued that for CSS, not all vulnerabilities are publicized; while in the OSS community, vulnerabilities are openly discussed and therefore cannot be hidden. To the extent that this is the case, then the CSS vulnerabilities are underestimated.

■ The distribution of vulnerabilities throughout the year is not uniform. There may be more during a certain period and fewer during another period. The arbitrary choice of dates in many of the reports makes it difficult to determine whether a different "date window" would change the conclusions about which platform has the most vulnerabilities.

Below are some of the security vulnerability data that have been published in the recent past comparing different distributions.

The data in Table 11.8 shows that the largest number of vulnerabilities is in an OSS distribution (Red Hat), followed closely by a CSS operating system (Solaris). The lowest number of vulnerabilities is in AIX, which is a CSS version of UNIX, closely followed by OpenBSD, an OSS operating system.

The data in Table 11.9 shows that Debian had the largest number of security vulnerabilities, including the highest number of high-severity ones.

TABLE 11.9 Security Vulnerabilities Reported between June 1, 2002, and May 31, 2003, for Various OSS and CSS Platforms

Platform	Total Number of Vulnerabilities	Number of High Severity Vulnerabilities
Microsoft	128	86 (67%)
Red Hat	229	128 (56%)
Debian	286	162 (57%)
Mandrake	199	120 (60%)
SuSe	176	111 (63%)

Source: From Koetzle, L. *Is Linux More Secure Than Windows?* Forrester, 2004.

TABLE 11.10 Vulnerability Data Released by SecurityFocus for 2001 until August of That Year

Platform	Number of Vulnerabilities
Windows	24
Red Hat	28
Debian	26
Mandrake	33
Solaris	24

Source: From Middleton, J. Windows More Secure than Linux? Available at http://www.vnunet.com/.

Other OSS distributions do not fare much better. The Microsoft platform had the lowest number of vulnerabilities overall and the fewest high-severity ones. However, Microsoft had the largest proportion of its vulnerabilities classified as high severity.

The data in Table 11.10 shows that the two CSS platforms had the fewest vulnerabilities compared to the OSS platforms. This is consistent with the results in Table 11.9. The data in Table 11.11 focuses on the OSS platforms only and shows vulnerabilities throughout 2001. The numbers here appear to be much higher than those in Table 11.8 although they are supposed to be for the same time period.

The numbers in Table 11.12 show that the two CSS platforms have higher security vulnerabilities than Linux.

TABLE 11.11 Number of Security Updates to Linux Distributions in 2001

Platform	Number of Security Updates
Debian	81
Mandrake	81
Red Hat	56
SuSe	44

Source: From Middleton, J. Fans Should 'Weep' over Linux Bugs. Available at http://www.vnunet.com/.

TABLE 11.12 Security Tracker Statistics for Operating System Vulnerabilities Reported between April 2001 and March 2002

Platform	Number of Vulnerabilities
UNIX	51
Microsoft	36
Linux	19

Source: From SecurityTracker. SecurityTracker Statistics. Available at http://www.securitytracker.com/.

As one can see, the data that has been reported, and this is only a subset, is all over the place. What this means is that we cannot really draw any compelling conclusions from vulnerability data. By selecting any one of the above tables it is easy to say that OSS is better than CSS in terms of security vulnerabilities, or vice versa. But in fact, depending on which dates you look at, whether severity is considered and how vulnerabilities are counted, one can draw very different conclusions.

The bottom line is that vulnerability and security update numbers that are typically published do not inform us much about the relative security merits of OSS versus CSS. One can conclude, based on the existing evidence, that there is not much of a difference. OSS platforms do have security vulnerabilities reported against them. These do not get as much airplay in the trade and regular press. Also, reporting vulnerabilities in OSS does not make as good a story as reporting vulnerabilities in CSS applications. Because they do not get much airplay does not mean that they do not exist.

11.5.4 Days of Risk

That software will have security vulnerabilities is a given. The important question is: how long does it take to fix these vulnerabilities and distribute the fixes? If it takes a long time, then the user community is at risk of an exploit for a longer period of time.

We can use Figure 11.4 to illustrate some concepts related to the evaluation of the security exposure risk. When a software application is released, it is likely to have some security vulnerabilities. At release, it is likely that no one will know of these vulnerabilities (unless they were deliberately inserted by the developers or through a back door — which we will not consider for now). While the risk to an end user of that vulnerability being exploited is not zero, it is quite small because few, if any, people will know about it.

At some point in time later on, someone will discover that vulnerability. This can occur either through reading the source code or by black-box testing of the application if the source code is not available. The discovery can be disclosed right away or at a later point in time.

There is a debate in the community about how fast to disclose a vulnerability. One approach to disclosure requires informing the software developer of the vulnerability and not informing anyone else. This will give the developer some time to produce a fix. So when someone else discovers the vulnerability at a later point, a fix will already exist. Another approach, called responsible disclosure, is for the discoverer of the vulnerability and the developer of the software to coordinate and work together, and announce the vulnerability and the fix at the same time.

When the vulnerability is discovered, the risk to the end user increases slightly. After the vulnerability is disclosed, the risk starts to increase more rapidly. At that point, the bad guys will start looking at ways to exploit the vulnerability. At some point, one of the bad guys will develop an automated script for the exploit(s). This is when the risk starts to increase rapidly. Now, relatively inexperienced attackers can use the script to launch their own attacks.

At the same time, the vendors and developers are trying to produce a fix. There is always a delay between disclosure and a fix being released. Vendors and developers have finite resources and must prioritize the vulnerabilities that must be addressed and regression tested, and a new patch prepared. In the timeline shown here, we assume that automation of the exploit will precede the fix being available.

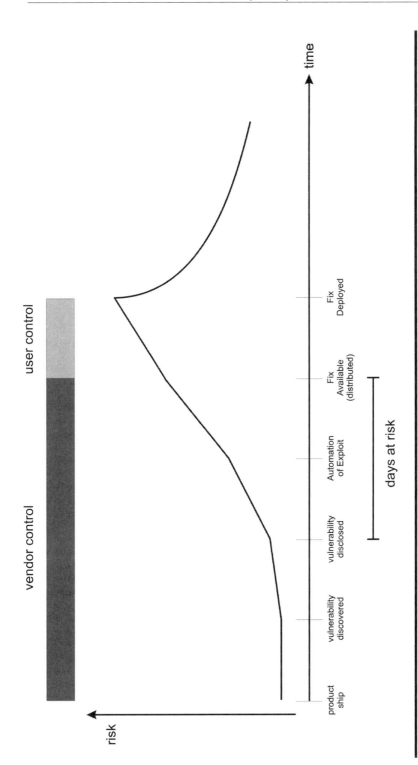

FIGURE 11.4 The milestones in the lifetime of a vulnerability. (*Source:* From Koetzle, L. *Is Linux More Secure Than Windows?* Forrester, 2004; Schneier, B. Full Disclosure and the Window of Exposure. Available at: http://www.schneier.com/crypto-gram-0009.html; Schneier, B. Closing the Window of Exposure. Available at: http://www.legamedia.net/dy/articles/article_15801.php.

Once the fix is available, then end users can start to install it. However, many end users will not install fixes right away. In fact, many will not even know that the fixes exist. For example, imagine your typical home computer user. They are very unlikely to keep their home desktop updated on a regular basis. Even enterprise customers will not be able to install fixes immediately. Typically, enterprises will want to perform acceptance tests on new patches before they deploy them. Acceptance testing is expensive. For example, some updates change application settings back to the default. Imagine an enterprise with a few thousand users having all of their office suite settings defaulted overnight. This would not be acceptable and therefore it is prudent to perform this acceptance testing. Some types of acceptance tests require specialized equipment. The consequence is that fixes are accumulated and installed at once in a batch or never installed unless there is a known attack going on.

From a risk perspective, the risk will continue to increase over time until the user installs the fix. However, after the fix is distributed, the rate of increase of the risk is not as high. The reason is that some vulnerabilities require other users to have the security defect (i.e., they rely on a network effect). That network effect is diluted overtime because other users install the fix.

Once the fix is installed, the risk goes down rapidly. It does not go all the way down to zero right away because there is a non-zero probability that the fix introduced another vulnerability inadvertently. However, the risk trend is downward as there is a natural tendency to upgrade systems anyway over time.

From the time of the release until the fix is distributed, the risk is under the vendor's control. After the fix is distributed, then the risk is under the user's control. The days of risk, or the amount of time when a user is at risk due to the vendor, is shown in Figure 11.4. It spans the time from when the vulnerability is disclosed until the time the vulnerability is fixed and the fix distributed.

The results of some analyses that were performed to evaluate the average days of risk for different vendors and platforms are shown in Table 11.13 and Table 11.14. The former is for 1999 while the latter is more recent.

For the two vendors that are on both lists, one OSS and one CSS, it is clear that the days at risk has increased (more than doubled) since 1999. In terms of recent rankings, Microsoft is seen as having the shortest delay and Mandrake is seen as having the longest delay.

Some of the reasons why Microsoft vulnerabilities seem to affect many more people is a function of the large installed base and because users do not install fixes that are available. However, there seems to be a good responsiveness in terms of getting fixes out by industry standards.

TABLE 11.13   Average Days of Risk Based on an Analysis of 1999 Advisories

Vendor	Average Days of Risk
Red Hat	11.23
Microsoft	16.1
Sun	89.5

Source: From Reavis, J. Linux vs. Microsoft: Who Solves Security Problems Faster. Available at http://csoinformer.com/research/solve.shtml.

TABLE 11.14   Average Days of Risk Based on Analysis of Vulnerabilities between June 1, 2002, and May 31, 2003

Vendor/Platform	Average Days of Risk
Microsoft	25
Red Hat	57
Debian	57
Mandrake	82
SuSe	74

Source: From Koetzle, L. *Is Linux More Secure than Windows?* Forrester, 2004.

The implication from these numbers is that OSS does not necessarily have an advantage or a monopoly in terms of making and distributing fixes quickly. The CSS vendor on that list demonstrates a reasonably fast turnaround time (in fact, the shortest) as well.

11.5.5 Summary

To summarize the results by looking at the security of OSS compared to CSS, it is not evident that either is really consistently superior to the other. The claims made about large-scale peer reviews in the OSS world do not really hold up under scrutiny, and therefore there does not seem to be a supportable inherent reason within the OS paradigm for it to work better than the CS paradigm. While the "many eyeballs" argument is theoretically very appealing, in practice that is not what happens. In addition, having many eyeballs ceases to add substantial value after a few eyeballs.

The bottom line is that if a project has competent people dedicated to security and to identifying security vulnerabilities, there will be fewer security defects in that system. This should be considered on a case-by-case basis and on a platform-by-platform basis rather than by whether it is an OSS or a CSS project.

11.6 Conclusions

As becomes evident after reading this chapter, the real advantages of OSS development are difficult to see in existing OSS projects. Putting the rhetoric away for a moment, it is difficult to make justifiably broad statements about the superiority of OSS or CSS development.

Making a decision to adopt OSS or not because of some generalities about the OSS approach to software development being better/worse than the CSS approach is indefensible and negligent. There is no compelling evidence that the OSS approach works consistently much better or much worse, in terms of reliability and security, than the CSS approach. And this only applies to the popular OSS applications. For the large number of less popular OSS applications, their risk profile is likely much higher and should not realistically be considered for enterprise adoption.

References

1. Gonzelez-Barahona, M., Perez, M., Quiros, P., Gonzalez, J., and Olivera, V. Counting Potatoes: The Size of Debian 2.2., 2001.
2. Wheeler, D. More Than a Gigabuck: Estimating GNU/Linux's Size. Available at http://www.dwheeler.com/.
3. Lucovsky, M. From NT OS/2 to Windows 2000 and beyond — A software-engineering odyssey. Paper presented at *4th USENIX Windows Systems Symposium,* 2000.
4. Schneier, B. Software Complexity and Security. Available at http://www.schneier.com/crypto-gram-0003.html.
5. Dooley, B. *Open Source and the Cathedral.* Cutter Consortium, 6(2):2003.
6. Giera, J. *The Costs And Risks of Open Source.* Forrester, 2004.
7. Hunt, F., Probert, D., and Barratt, S. Adopting new technology: the case of open source software at Marconi. Paper presented at *The 12th International Conference on Management of Technology (IAMOT 2003),* 2003.
8. Didio, L. *Linux, Unix and Windows TCO Comparison, Part 1.* The Yankee Group, 2004.
9. Bonaccorsi, A. and Rossi, C. *Contributing to the Common Pool Resources in Open Source Software: A Comparison between Individuals and firms.* Institute for Informatics and Telematics (IIT-CNR), Pisa, Italy, 2003.

10. Wheeler, D. Why Open Source Software/Free Software (OSS/FS)? Look at the Numbers. Available at www.dwheeler.com.

11. Lewis, T. The open source acid test. *IEEE Computer,* 128:125–127, 1999.

12. Capiluppi, A., Lago, P., and Morisio, M. Characteristics of open source projects. *Seventh European Conference on Software Maintenance and Engineering,* 2003.

13. Capiluppi, A. Models for the evolution of OS projects. *International Conference on Software Maintenance,* 2003.

14. Kienzle, R. Sourceforge Preliminary Project Analysis. Available at http://www.osstrategy.com/sfreport.

15. Koch, S. and Schneider, G. Effort, co-operation and co-ordination in an open source software project: GNOME. *Information Systems Journal,* 2002:12:27–42.

16. Ghosh, R. and Prakash, V. The Orbiten Free Software Survey. Available at http://www.orbiten.org/ofss/01.html.

17. Krishnamurthy, S. *Cave or Community? An Empirical Examination of 100 Mature Open Source Projects.* University of Washington, May 2002.

18. Healy, K. and Schussman, A. *The Ecology of Open-Source Software Development*: Department of Sociology. University of Arizona, 2003.

19. Mockus, A., Fielding, R., and Herbsleb, J. Two case studies of open source software development: Apache and Mozilla. *ACM Transactions on Software Engineering and Methodology,* 11(3):309–346, 2002.

20. Sharma, S., Sugumaran, V., and Rajagoplan, B. A framework for creating hybrid-open source software communities. *Information Systems Journal,* 12:7–25, 2002.

21. Raymond, E. The cathedral and the bazaar. Available at http://www.first-monday.dk/issues/issue3_3/raymond/.

22. Fuggetta, A. Open source software — An evaluation. *Journal of System and Software,* 66:77–90, 2003.

23. Cusumano, M. and Selby, R. *Microsoft Secrets.* The Free Press, 1995.

24. Hissam, S., Weinstock, C., Plakosh, D., and Asundi, J. *Perspectives on Open Source Software.* Software Engineering Institute, CMU/SEI-2001-TR-019, 2001.

25. Mockus, A., Fielding, R., and Herbsleb, J. A case study of open source software development: the Apache server. *International Conference on Software Engineering,* 2000.

26. Miller, B., Fredriksen, L., and So, B. An empirical study of the reliability of Unix utilities. *Communications of the ACM,* 33(12):32–44, 1990.

27. Greiner, S., Boskovic, B., Brest, J., and Zumer, V. Security issues in information systems based on open source technologies. *EUROCON 2003,* 2003.

28. El Emam, K. *Software Inspection Best Practices.* Cutter Consortium (E-Project Management Advisory Service), 2(9):2002.

29. Bagchi, S. and Madeira, H. Panel: Open source software — A recipe for vulnerable software, or the only way to keep the bugs and the bad guys out? *Fourteenth International Symposium on Software Reliability Engineering,* 2003.

30. Jorgensen, N. Putting it all in the trunk: Incremental software development in the FreeBSD open source project. *Information Systems Journal,* 11:321–336, 2001.

31. MacCormack, A., Kemerer, C., Cusumano, M., and Crandall, B. Trade-offs between productivity and quality in selecting software development practices. *IEEE Software,* September/October, 78–84 2003.

32. Cusumano, M., MacCormack, A., Kemerer, C., and Randall, B. Software development worldwide: the state of the practice. *IEEE Software,* November/December, 28–34, 2003.

33. Bisant, D. and Lyle, J.R. A two-person inspection method to improve programming productivity. *IEEE Transactions on Software Engineering,* 15:1294–1304, 1989.

34. Bottger, P.C. and Yetton, P.W. An intregration of process and decision scheme explanations of group problem solving performance. *Organizational Behavior and Human Decision Processes,* 42:234–249, 1998.

35. Buck, F.O. Indicators of Quality Inspections. Technical Report 21.802, IBM, Kingston, NY; September 1981.

36. Eick, S., Loader, C., Long, M., Votta, L., and Weil, S.V. Estimating software fault content before coding. *Fourteenth International Conference on Software Engineering,* 1992.

37. Fagan, M. Design and code inspections to reduce errors in program development. *IBM Systems,* 15(3):182–211, 1976.

38. Gilb, T. and Graham, D. *Software Inspection.* Addison-Wesley Publishing, 1993.

39. Grady, R.B. *Practical Software Metrics for Project Management and Process Improvement.* Prentice Hall, 1992.

40. Lau, L., Jeffery, R., and Sauer, C. Some Empirical Support for Software Development Technical Reviews. Unpublished manuscript, 1996.

41. Madachy, R., Little, L., and Fan, S. Analysis of a successful inspection program. *18th Annual NASA Software Engineering Laboratory Workshop,* 1993.

42. Porter, A., Siy, H., and Votta, L. A Review of Software Inspections. Technical report. 1996.

43. Porter, A., Votta, L., and Basili, V. Comparing detection methods for software requirements inspections: a replicated experiment. *IEEE Transactions on Software Engineering,* 21(6):563–575, 1997.

44. Strauss, S. and Ebenau, R. *Software Inspection Process.* McGraw-Hill, 1994.

45. Weller, E.F. Lessons from three years of inspection data. *IEEE Software,* 10(5):38–45, 1993.

46. Schneider, F. Open source security: visiting the bazaar. *IEEE Symposium on Security and Privacy,* 2000.

47. Gacek, C. and Arief, B. The many meanings of open source. *IEEE Software,* January/February, 34–40, 2004.

48. Halloran, T. and Scherlis, W. High quality and open source software practices. Paper presented at *Second Workshop on Open Source Software Engineering,* 2002.

49. Zhao, l. and Elbaum, S. Quality assurance under the open source development model. *Journal of System and Software,* 66:65–75, 2003.

50. Iyer, M. *Analysis of Linux Test Project's Kernel Code Coverage.* IBM, 2002.

51. Hunt, F. and Johnson, P. *On the Pareto Distribution of Sourceforge Projects.* Engineering Department, Cambridge University, 2003.

52. Mockus, A. and Herbsleb, J. Why not improve coordination in distributed software development by stealing good ideas from open source? Paper presented at *Second Workshop on Open Source Software Engineering,* 2002.

53. Scacchi, W. Understanding the requirements for developing open source software systems. *IEE Proceedings — Software,* 149(1):24–39, 2002.

54. Scacchi, W. Free and open source development practices in the game community. *IEEE Software,* January/February, 59–66, 2004.

55. Sanders, J. Linux, open source, and software's future. *IEEE Software,* September/October, 88-91, 1998.

56. Staff. *Total Cost of Ownership for Enterprise Applictation Workloads.* Robert Francis Group, 2004.

57. O'Reilly, T. Lessons from open-source software development. *Communications of the ACM,* 42(4):33–37, 1999.

58. Paulson, J., Succi, G., and Eberlein, A. An empirical study of open-source and closed-source software products. *IEEE Transactions on Software Engineering,* 30(4):246–256, 2004.

59. Schach, S., Jin, B., Wright, D., Heller, G., and Offutt, A. Maintainability of the Linux kernel. *IEE Proceedings — Software,* 149(1):18–23, 2002.

60. Schach, S., Jin, B., Wright, D., and Offutt, J. Quality impacts of clandestine common coupling. *Software Quality Journal,* 11:211–218, 2003.

61. Stamelos, I., Angelis, L., Oikomomou, A., and Bleris, G. Code quality analysis in open source software development. *Information Systems Journal,* 12:43–60, 2002.

62. Bollinger, T., Nelson, R., Self, K., and Turnbull, S. Open source methods: peering through the clutter. *IEEE Software,* 16(4):8–11, 1999.

63. Miller, B., Koski, D., Lee, C., et al. *Fuzz Revisited: A Re-examination of the Reliability of Unix Utilities and Services*: Computing Sciences Department, University of Wisconsin, 1995.

64. Forrester, J. and Miller, B. An empirical study of the robustness of Windows NT applications using random testing. *4th USENIX Windows System Symposium,* 2000.

65. Ghosh, A., Schmid, M., and Shah, V. Testing the robustness of Windows NT software. *International Symposium on Software Reliability Engineering,* 1998.

66. Koopman, P., Sung, J., Dingman, C., Siewiorek, D., and Marz, T. Comparing operating systems using robustness benchmarks. *IEEE Symposium on Reliable Distributed Systems,* 1997.

67. Kamperman, J. Is open source software better than commercial software? Ottawa Software Quality Association (www.osqa.org), 2004.

68. Schach, S., Jin, B., Yu, L., Heller, G., and Offutt, J. Determining the distribution of maintenance categories: survey versus measurement. *Empirical Software Engineering,* 8:351–366, 2003.

69. Gerfinkel, S. Open Source: How Secure? Available at http://www.simson.net/clips/99.WideOpen.Security1.htm.
70. Naraine, R. GNU Project Hacked by Intruder. Available at http://www.esecurityplanet.com/trends/article.php/2248811.
71. Vaughan-Nichols, S. Debian: Attack Didn't Harm Source Code. Available at http://www.eweek.com.
72. Fisher, D. Debian Linux under Attack by Hackers. Available at http://www.eweek.com/.
73. Hissam, S., Plakosh, D., and Weinstock, C. Trust and vulnerability in open source software. *IEE Proceedings — Software,* 149(1):47–51 2002.
74. Seltzer, L. Was the Windows Source Leak a Bust? Available at http://www.eweek.com/.
75. Viega, J. The Myth of Open Source Security. Available at http://itmanagement.earthweb.com/secu/article.php/621851.
76. Payne, C. On the security of open source software. *Information Systems Journal,* 12:61–78, 2002.
77. Obasango, D. The Myth of Open Source Security Revisited v2.0. Available at http://www.developer.com/open/article.php/990711.
78. Koetzle, L. *Is Linux More Secure Than Windows?* Forrester, 2004.
79. Middleton, J. Windows More Secure than Linux? Available at http://www.vnunet.com/.
80. Middleton, J. Fans Should 'Weep' over Linux Bugs. Available at http://www.vnunet.com/.
81. SecurityTracker. SecurityTracker Statistics. Available at http://www.securitytracker.com/.
82. Schneier, B. Full Disclosure and the Window of Exposure. Available at http://www.schneier.com/crypto-gram-0009.html.
83. Schneier, B. Closing the Window of Exposure. Available at http://www.legamedia.net/dy/articles/article_15801.php.
84. Reavis, J. Linux vs. Microsoft: Who Solves Security Problems Faster. Available at http://csoinformer.com/research/solve.shtml.

Chapter 12

Making the Business Case

There are two approaches you can follow to evaluate the ROI from improved software quality. First, use an ROI analysis performed by another company and assume that the numbers used and the benefits extrapolate to your company. Second, use your own numbers and assumptions, and develop an ROI model specific to your business.

Sheard[1] makes a convincing case that no one would believe an ROI analysis for improving software development that came from somewhere else. However, it is important that these external ROI results do exist. The existence of other company ROI evidence demonstrates that benefits are possible with a particular practice or tool. Because companies will only publicize success stories, if there are no other ROI analyses available, then one should question whether a practice has benefited anyone at all.

The type of ROI evidence, as well as evidence on intangible benefits, for any software engineering practice follow an evolutionary path that matches the practice's maturity. For example, when software inspections were first introduced, there were only a handful of case reports at IBM and other companies demonstrating their benefit. Now, more than 20 years later, the ROI analyses done on software inspections are very sophisticated and the evidence includes many controlled experiments. Appendix G on "Expecting and Interpreting Evidence" discusses how evidence evolves with a software engineering technology.

Of course, it is best to develop your own ROI analysis. This provides a much more compelling basis for action than an external ROI. The contents of this book should go a long way toward helping you achieve that.

The advantage of having your own ROI analysis is illustrated through an example. Let us say that a published ROI case demonstrates that improving a firm's process maturity on the SW-CMM has a cost/benefit ratio of 1:7. This is quite an impressive number. However, to get that return, an investment in process improvement of $1 million was required. Small companies, while convinced that the return is seven times the investment, simply cannot invest that kind of money. They have, say, $10,000 to invest in quality improvement. Then the seven times benefit does not seem real to their particular context anymore. Small companies need to develop their own ROI for an investment of $10,000.

To result in actual investments in software quality, a convincing ROI analysis must be embedded within a larger business case. There are common obstacles faced when presenting such a business case to decision makers. This chapter reviews these common obstacles and discusses some remedies. It is important to be cognizant of the issues presented here as they can hamper the successful introduction of quality practices if not addressed.

12.1 Wariness about Initial Investments

Quality does not come freely, at least not at the outset. Management must make an initial investment to reap the benefits. The investment would cover the costs of tool acquisitions, piloting, training, and the temporary productivity dip that occurs when software practices are changed. After those investments are made, the returns start to accrue.

However, for some organizations, making an investment in software quality is difficult. There is evidence that many software organizations do not even have a Quality Assurance (QA) function. One survey found that a sizeable portion of organizations developing software have neither an explicit QA function nor a metrics program to collect data about their performance (see Table 12.1).[2] For those organizations, investments in improving software quality are more difficult because they have neither a culture supportive of QA nor do they have experiences with QA practices. They also have no data showing the extent to which bugs are eating up resources and capacity.

Furthermore, many organizations, including those with QA functions, are cutting costs aggressively. In such an environment, the general belief tends to be that we do not have funds to make investments in quality. Or, some make half-hearted investments that do not cover the total cost of a quality initiative (e.g., buy the tools but do not bother with the training), which increases the risk of the returns from that investment not materializing.

TABLE 12.1 Percentage of Organizations that Have QA and Metrics Efforts in Place Based on a Worldwide Survey

	Existence of a QA Function (%)	Existence of a Metrics Program (%)
Aerospace	52	39
Computer manufacturing	70	42
Distribution	16	—
Finance	57	25
Government	30	5
Health	51	8
Manufacturing	52	25
Oil and gas	40	20
Software	60	36
Telecommunications	54	44
Transportation	33	33
Utility	40	10

Source: From Rubin, H. and Yourdon, E. Industry Canada Worldwide Benchmark Project, Industry Canada, 1995.

Some decision makers perceive that they simply do not have the funds to make these initial investments, even if they are convinced that the returns will materialize in the short term. To the extent that this is the case, then there is not much to go on — making the business case for quality will be extremely difficult.

On a positive note, however, in practice, funds are typically available. As Reifer points out, there are always funds available in most organizations — you just have to find them.[3] For example, many divisions and groups do not spend all the money allocated to them in their budgets. It may be possible to tap some of that unused money.

12.2 Length of Payback Period

In some cases, an appropriate investment is made in improving quality. However, executives then have an expectation of immediate returns. For this reason, it is critical that initial quality investments should focus on bringing benefits to the ongoing projects. Quality practices that benefit the organization as a whole or span multiple projects should be implemented afterward. It is important to speed tangible returns to ongoing projects.

Most quality improvement practices demonstrate their benefits unequivocally over the duration of the whole project. It is therefore also important to start with projects that are small and that last only a few months. This will give executives rapid feedback as to the benefits of practices that improve software quality. Ideally, a pilot project should be performed. Guidelines on selecting pilot projects are provided in Sidebar 12.1.

Failure to adopt these two strategies can result in the decision makers cutting the funding to the quality initiatives before tangible evidence of their benefits has emerged. It is usually very difficult to restart an aborted quality improvement initiative for quite some time afterward.

12.3 Hardware Culture

Companies that develop embedded systems tend to have many decision makers more accustomed to hardware development than to software development. This results in substantial investments going into the improvement of hardware quality, with little attention paid to the software. In some cases, firmware problems are classified as hardware issues to justify diverting funds to the hardware divisions to fix the problems.

In one organization I work with, the software problem reports are at least three times more frequent than the hardware problem reports from the field. However, fixing software problems is seen as trivial compared to the difficult hardware issues. This has resulted in a dearth of investment in improving software quality and eventually, at the time of writing, the real possibility of the company's biggest customer switching to a competitor because of software failures.

A recent field report noted "practitioners were more positive and knowledgeable about quality if they were trained software engineers. Practitioners with a science rather than a computing background, and a hardware rather than a software background were generally more negative about quality."[4] In the same study, the authors noted that there was a correlation between knowledge about quality systems and positive attitudes toward quality. A lack of knowledge about software quality makes practitioners anxious and anticipate the worst. Therefore, having a predominantly non-software engineering culture amplifies this problem.

To alleviate the negative attitudes toward software quality, it is necessary to educate the development staff. This may entail sending them to conferences, organizing invited presentations in-house, courses, providing

▼

SIDEBAR 12.1   Selecting and Staffing Pilot Projects

Pilot projects are typically aimed at evaluating a new technique or tool, and also serve to collect feedback for tailoring or customizing a new technique or tool. The manner in which these projects are run can have a substantial impact on the successful adoption of the technique or tool in an organization.

The selection of projects or personnel for pilot projects must balance three concerns[1,2]: (1) the risk of failure, (2) achieving the benefits that are expected (and having the evidence to demonstrate the benefits), and (3) their representativeness and credibility to the rest of the organization.

If, for example, a low-risk project is selected for the quality initiative to survive politically, it may not provide benefits or be representative. If the personnel selected were the most capable in the organization, then it would not be clear from the pilot outcomes whether the benefits were due to the people or the new tools and techniques. The same applies if the worst capable personnel were selected. The motivation of participants or project managers taking part in the pilot should also be examined. If such personnel are not too eager, then the pilot project may fail. Conversely, if such personnel exhibit too much enthusiasm, this may be indicative of another agenda that might place the pilot at risk. Some general recommendations on selection of personnel are[3]:

- Do not allow technology champions to run pilot projects.
- Use normal procedures to staff pilot projects; do not select people who are particularly enthusiastic nor particularly cynical about the practices and tools.

The pilot project should be sufficiently small and simple that its outcomes are clear quickly. It must also be large and complex enough to be credible to the remainder of the organization and to provide realistic feedback for tailoring the tools and techniques to the organization's specific processes and culture.

It is critical that the participants in the pilot project receive adequate training in any new practices and tools. Training is neither an overview nor a briefing session. A training course will properly prepare the participants to use the new quality practices and tools to solve realistic problems.

References

1. Leonard-Barton, D. and Kraus, W. Implementing new technology. *Harvard Business Review,* pp. 102–110, 1985.
2. Veryard R. Implementing a methodology. *Information and Software Technology,* 29(9):46–74, 1987.
3. Kitchenham, B., Linkman, S., and Law, D. Critical review of quantitative assessment. *Software Engineering Journal,* 9(2):43–53, 1994.

▲

online education, and making books on quality available. It would also be advantageous to hire developers from companies with good quality practices. They tend to be advocates for good software engineering practices, and having at least one quality champion would help reverse the negative attitudes.

Another approach that frequently works under these conditions is to present executives with data. In the above example, when data on defect levels, the problems customers complained about the most, and the cost of software defects was presented to management, a change in attitude soon followed.

12.4 Software Culture

Software engineers, especially those who have never worked on large projects, tend to have an inherent resistance to quality practices. For starters, most university graduates are not well educated in software quality because curricula do not have extensive coverage of this topic.[8,9] Therefore, many development staff were not taught quality practices in the past and perceive such practices as unnecessary.

As noted above, the lack of knowledge about quality is associated with negative attitudes toward quality. These negative attitudes create resistance to change. They also feed rumors about what quality practices are like. One study reported the "apocryphal horror stories about quality" being circulated among developers in a company that can only be described as decidedly anti-quality.[4]

In many small and medium-sized companies, there is also an acceptance of 80-hour weeks, sacrificed personal lives, and late nights as hallmarks of the road to success. In fact, it is almost a badge of honor and a point of personal pride to operate in that way. More recently, rather than being optional, the threat of layoffs has pushed more employees to put forth additional effort to prove themselves.[10] There is an expectation that those with a job will have to work harder and longer to keep the job.[11]

This inevitably leads to burnout. The cost of burnout to software companies can be substantial.[11] Staff experiencing extreme burnout may leave or have serious health problems. There is a cost of replacement for experienced employees. In addition, staff experiencing burnout tend to make more errors and are less accurate in their work. There is evidence demonstrating that software engineers experiencing high levels of mental and physical stress tend to produce more defects.[12,13] This results in lower software quality.[10,11,14] In addition, burnout results in the absence of motivation and excessive criticism of new initiatives in the organization.[10]

This further impedes the organization's ability to introduce practices to improve software quality. Therefore, it is really a double hit: (1) more defects and (2) a stronger reluctance to change practices.

The implementation of practices to improve quality, as demonstrated in this book, would give the organization additional capacity so that the working conditions can be improved. Quality improvement is one way out of the vicious cycle, but it is not at all easy to introduce new practices in these companies.

I have also been to organizations where the developers see quality practices as academic and something that does not actually work in the real world. With such beliefs it is no surprise that they would not want to adopt them and change their current practices. Even when presented with evidence that other organizations are employing quality practices and their benefits are demonstrated, a common comeback is "we are different — this will not work here."

Some organizations perceive that quality practices "depress and demotivate highly creative people. ... Practitioners in this company thought that quality systems did not improve quality, but instead created work in quality departments for less able developers and 'empire building' managers."[4]

Companies with a culture that is very adverse to quality practices will not embark on a change unless there is extreme pain; this means, for example, a key customer deserting, constant resourcing problems, near misses (averting a disaster through a coincidence), or the failure to get a big contract. If the company is small and does not have deep pockets, it may be too late to help them. Large organizations with cash reserves are, at that point of extreme pain, ready to receive a business case.

12.5 Time-to-Market Is King

Contemporary small and medium-sized companies rush products to market to build market share using any approach that works. The argument then goes that they can work on quality later on if the market accepts the product.[15] These companies find it more difficult to justify explicit investments in quality and may also perceive quality practices as slowing them down and adding more "bureaucracy." There are also instances when a company believes that it can achieve quality results without quality practices, for example, by hiring good people instead.[4]

Time-to-market is the primary driver for many projects, especially in small companies. Sutton notes that "Although other factors contribute to the success of a new software product or producer, for a start-up company that aims for 'better, faster, cheaper,' 'faster' usually takes precedence."[16] For start-ups, quality is usually not even on the radar screen: "The first resources invested in a company typically focus on outward-looking activities: getting the product out, promoting the product, and building strategic alliances."[16] Reifer amplifies this for Internet development projects by stating that "many time-tested software engineering practices were jettisoned based on the faulty belief that teams do not have time to put these practices to work."[17] One report from U.K. companies noted that "quality went out of the window when deadlines loomed."[4]

Further anecdotes specific to quality are provided by Hieatt and Mee. "Often, valuable software engineering principles are discarded, simply because they are perceived as being too time-consuming and lacking significant payoff, and testing is a common casualty".[18] Baker states that "In many cases, due to poor project planning or project management, little time is available to test adequately."[19] Lest you think that these are isolated examples, a recent survey found more than 40 percent of respondents admitting that the development team is often pressured to release software prematurely due to business schedule considerations.[20]

Some organizations make an implicit threat to their developers that if they do not meet the deadlines, by whatever means, then they would be replaced by developers who could meet them.[4] Such job threats often motivate taking quality shortcuts.

The logical flaw here is that with good quality practices, these companies would make it to market faster (as you saw in the schedule reduction numbers in Chapter 10). Improved software quality means less rework effort throughout the project and hence a shorter project interval.

The only time when the above time-to-market argument actually makes sense is if the products are not adequately tested. If minimal or no proper testing is performed on products before they ship or go live, then adding quality practices will indeed take longer. There are companies that follow this approach[20,21] and survive through luck and users with low expectations about quality. The latter is more common with very innovative products, where the low quality is perceived as the cost of innovation. However, for more mature product segments, this is less the case.

An additional risk that companies focusing on rushing products to market are taking is that if a product is successful, there will be considerable demand on customer support and for new features. A buggy product is a much larger liability if it succeeds because the costs of support and fixes can eat away at revenues. Furthermore, demand for many new features from a larger customer base requires larger development teams. Ad hoc quality practices that may have worked in small teams do not scale up. I have seen this attempted and the consequence is typically a serious case of an inability to deliver and regular product release delays.

Therefore, the time-to-market argument against software quality does not hold much water when examined in depth. And, the conditions under

TABLE 12.2 Brief Summary of Approaches to Overcome the Obstacles Discussed in This Chapter

Obstacle	Approach to Deal with It
Wariness about initial investment	Find unused funds rather than allocate "new money" and focus on quick gains
Length of payback period	Small pilot to demonstrate ROI
Hardware culture	Increase software engineering and quality education to reduce anxiety and uncertainty about what quality practices mean Compare the costs of hardware versus software problems and the impact on customers using company data
Software culture	In extreme cases, just wait for the pain of not changing (i.e., implementing quality practices) to become unsustainable
Time-to-market	Convincing ROI case demonstrating schedule reduction benefits and reduce project scope

which it is logical (i.e., no or little testing) are desperate indeed. If time-to-market is important, and the schedule reductions from implementing quality practices are too small, then the other reasonable option is to reduce the scope of the project.

12.6 Summary

The above sections highlighted typical obstacles. A business case using a believable ROI analysis can go a long way to overcome these obstacles. A few additional things to note are:

- *Anecdotes and experience reports of successful software quality improvements are frequently quite convincing.* These can come from conference presentations, magazines, and consultants. A good story always makes the numbers seem more real.
- *Peer and competitive pressure helps.* If there is information (e.g., press releases or articles) that competitors are embarking on a quality improvement initiative, this motivates management to pay attention. If there is a chance that the competition is "going to eat your lunch" through quality improvements, it is time to start catching up.

A summary of the approaches discussed is provided in Table 12.2.

References

1. Sheard, S. and Miller, C. The Shangri-La of ROI, Software Productivity Consortium (Technical Report), 2000.
2. Rubin, H. and Yourdon, E. Industry Canada Worldwide Benchmark Project, Industry Canada, 1995.
3. Reifer, D. *Making the Software Business Case: Improvement by the Numbers*. Addison-Wesley, 2002a.
4. Hall, T. and Wilson, D. View of software quality: A field report in *IEE Proceedings on Software Engineering*, 144(2):111–118, 1997.
5. Leonard-Barton, D. and Kraus, W. Implementing new technology. *Harvard Business Review*, pp. 102–110, 1985.
6. Veryard, R. Implementing a methodology, *Information and Software Technology*, 29(9):46–74, 1987.
7. Kitchenham, B., Linkman, S., and Law, D. Critical review of quantitative assessment, *Software Engineering Journal*, 9(2):43–53, 1994.
8. Lethbridge, T. A survey of the relevance of computer science and software engineering education. *Eleventh Conference on Software Engineering Education and Training*, pp. 56–66, 1998.
9. Lethbridge, T. What knowledge is important to a software professional? *IEEE Computer*, 33(5): 44-50, May 2000.
10. Ramanathan, N. Be aware and be prepared: dealing with burnout in the IT profession. *Cutter IT Journal*, 15(12):20–26, 2002.
11. Thomsett, R. Hitting the buttons: effective and low-cost techniques for preventing burnout. *Cutter IT Journal*, 15(12):5–11, 2002.
12. Furuyama, T., Arai, Y., and Lio, K. Fault generation model and mental stress effect analysis. *Journal of Systems and Software*, 26:31–42, 1994.
13. Furuyama, T., Arai, Y., and Lio, K. Analysis of fault generation caused by stress during software development. *Journal of Systems and Software*, 38:13–25, 1997.
14. Russell, L., Leading out of IT burnout, *Cutter IT Journal*, 15(12):12–19, 2002.
15. Baskerville, R. et al. How Internet software companies negotiate quality. *IEEE Computer*, pp. 51–57, 2001.
16. Sutton, S. The role of process in a software startup, *IEEE Software*, July-August, 33–39, 2000).
17. Reifer, D. Ten deadly risks in Internet and Intranet software development. *IEEE Software*, pp. 12–14, 2002b.
18. Hieatt, E. and Mee, R. Going faster: testing the Web application. *IEEE Software*, 19(2):60–65, March/April 2002.
19. Baker, E. Which way, SQA?. *IEEE Software*, pp. 16–18, 2001.
20. Bennatan, E. Software testing — Paying Now or Paying Later. I. Paying Now, Agile Project Management Advisory Service — Executive Update, *Cutter Consortium*, 4(8), 2003a.
21. Rokosz, V. Long-term testing in a short-term world. *IEEE Software*, 20(3): 64–67, May/June 2003.

Appendix A

Definition of Application Domains

This appendix provides a brief summary of four broad application domains that are referred to repeatedly throughout the book. These definitions come from Jones[1] and are included here for completeness.

Military Software

These types of applications are built according to military or U.S. Department of Defense standards and procedures. While these contain largely weapons systems, the category also covers support and logistics software applications, as well as payroll and accounting systems, which all have to follow military standards.

Systems Software

These types of applications are typically embedded and control hardware and other physical devices, such as software in aircraft, in automobiles, and telephone switches.

Commercial Software

Commercial applications are developed for lease or sale to external customers. Shrink-wrap applications such as PC-based word processors and e-mail client programs fall into this category. Large mainframe applications such as enterprise planning systems are also considered commercial applications if they are sold externally.

MIS (Management Information Systems)

These are applications developed by an internal IT department for use within the organization itself. Most large companies and government agencies will have their own dedicated IT group that develops custom applications to run their business. These range from traditional accounting and payroll systems running on mainframes to more modern web-based systems running on distributed architectures.

References

1. Jones, C. Variations in software development practices. *IEEE Software*, November-December, 22–27, 2003.

Appendix B

Overview of the Data Sets

This appendix provides a descriptive summary of two of the data sets that were used for quality benchmarking purposes.

B.1 The ISBSG Data Set

The 2003 quality benchmark had data from 315 projects. Table B.1 shows the distribution of projects by business domain. Financial projects are the most prevalent business domain in this data set. This is followed by insurance.

The distributions by country for the data set are shown in Table B.2. The largest contributors of defect density data are Australia, the Netherlands, India, and Japan. However, there remains good representation from North America and other countries in Europe.

Another view of the projects is by deployment platform, as shown in Table B.3. The largest subset consists of mainframe projects. PC projects make up a small minority of the projects.

The distribution of projects by development type is shown in Table B.4. The data is almost evenly distributed among development and maintenance projects.

One of the questions in the benchmark is whether a methodology was used. Table B.5 reveals the distribution of methodology use. Most projects have used a methodology (approximately 71 percent of those who responded). However, it will be noticed that a large minority of respondents did not answer this question, and another healthy minority indicated that they do not know if they used a methodology or not.

TABLE B.1 Distribution by Business Domain of ISBSG Projects that Provided Defect Data

Business Domain	Count (Percentage)
Sales	15 (5%)
Financial (excluding banking)	43 (14%)
Insurance	35 (11%)
Accounting	19 (6%)
Inventory	8 (2.5%)
Banking	22 (7%)
Manufacturing	18 (6%)
Telecommunications	12 (4%)
Marketing	8 (2.5%)
Legal	8 (2.5%)
Engineering	10 (3.2%)
Personnel	5 (1.6%)
Logistics	4 (1.3%)
Fine enforcement	4 (1.3%)
R & D	3 (1%)
Network management	3 (1%)

Note: The totals do not add up to 100 percent because there was missing data on this variable, and business domains with only one or two projects are not shown.

Further examination of the methodology question is shown in Table B.6. Here we see that a large majority of projects use a methodology that was developed in-house. Few projects purchase external methodologies.

B.2 The MIT Data Set

The MIT-led study collected data from 104 projects worldwide.[1] A questionnaire was administered over the Web and respondents around the world were invited to participate. The basic descriptive summary of all the responses is included in Table B.7.

TABLE B.2   Distribution by Country of Origin of ISBSG Projects that Provided Defect Data

Country of Origin	Count (Percentage)
Australia	86 (27%)
Brazil	1 (0.3%)
Canada	11 (3.5%)
Germany	4 (1.3%)
India	49 (15.5%)
Japan	52 (16.5%)
Malaysia	3 (0.95%)
Netherlands	51 (16%)
New Zealand	1 (0.3%)
Republic of South Africa	1 (0.3%)
United Kingdom	33 (10.5%)
United States	17 (5.4%)

TABLE B.3   Distribution by Deployment Platform of Projects that Provided Defect Data

Platform	Count (Percentage)
Mainframe	153 (49%)
Midrange	48 (15%)
PC	59 (19%)

Note: The percentages do not add up to 100 because some projects did not provide this data.

TABLE B.4   Distribution by Development Type of Projects that Provided Defect Data

Development Type	Count (Percentage)
New development	165 (52%)
Enhancement	142 (45%)
Re-development	8 (3%)

TABLE B.5 Distribution by Use of a Formal Methodology of Projects that Provided Defect Data

Methodology Use	Count (Percentage)
Yes	160 (51%)
No	64 (20%)

Note: The percentages do not add up to 100 because some projects did not provide this data.

TABLE B.6 Distribution by How Methodology Was Acquired of Projects that Provided Defect Data

How Methodology Acquired	Count (Percentage)
Developed in-house	122 (76%)
Purchased	13 (8%)
Combined (in-house/purchased)	24 (15%)

TABLE B.7 Descriptive Statistics for the Data Collected through the MIT Study

	India	Japan	United States	Europe and Other	Total
No. projects	`24	27	31	22	104
Software Type					
System	7 (29.2)	5 (18.5)	4 (12.9)	4 (18.2)	20
Applications	4 (16.7)	4 (14.8)	7 (22.6)	5 (22.7)	20
Custom	11 (45.8)	16 (59.2)	19 (61.3)	10 (45.5)	56
Embedded	2 (8.3)	2 (7.4)	1 (3.2)	3 (13.6)	8
Level of Reliability					
High	8 (33.3)	12 (44.4)	8 (25.8)	4 (18.2)	22
Medium	14 (58.3)	14 (51.9)	20 (64.5)	18 (81.8)	66
Low	2 (8.3)	1 (3.7)	3 (9.7)	0 (0)	6
Hardware Platform					
Mainframe	2 (8.3)	6 (22.2)	3 (10)	1 (4.5)	12
Workstation	16 (66.7)	16 (59.2)	19 (63.3)	15 (68.2)	66
PC	3 (12.5)	4 (14.8)	7 (23.3)	1 (4.5)	15
Other	3 (12.5)	1 (3.7)	1 (3.3)	5 (22.7)	10
Customer Type					
Individual	0 (0)	1 (3.7)	2 (6.7)	2 (9.1)	5
Enterprise	23 (95.8)	23 (85.2)	21 (70)	17 (77.3)	84
In-house	1 (4.2)	3 (11.1)	7 (23.3)	3 (13.6)	14

Note: The numbers in parentheses are percentages.

Source: From Cusumano, M. et al. Software development worldwide: the state of the practice, *IEEE Software*, November/December, 28–34, 2003.

References

1. Cusumano, M. et al. Software development worldwide: the state of the practice, *IEEE Software*, November/December, 28–34, 2003.

Appendix C

The Effectiveness and Efficiency of Software Inspections

This chapter presents a literature review to calculate values for effectiveness and efficiency that we used in evaluating the ROI from software inspections. Effectiveness is the proportion of defects in the code (or design or any other artifact) that are found during an inspection. Thus, an effectiveness of, for example, 0.5 means that 50 percent of the defects in that code are found. Efficiency pertains to the cost of inspections. Cost is usually computed per defect. The values we derive are the average from published articles. This review is based on the one already published and is included here for completeness.[1]

The following criteria were used to deem an article appropriate for inclusion in this average:

- There should be a clear indication that the published data is based on actual projects rather than being mere opinions or a rehashing of someone else's numbers. There are many opinion articles that were excluded.
- It should be clear what is being measured. For example, if we are looking at inspections, then it should be clear that inspections actually took place and the data pertains to the inspections.

- The unit of observation should be clear. For example, for inspection data, it should be stated whether the data pertains to all inspections performed on a project or to a single inspection.

The exceptions to the above criteria were review articles that already summarized evidence. In such a case, quality judgment on the review methodology was performed to decide whether the data from the review should be included.

C.1 Effectiveness of Defect Detection Activities

The following presents the articles that give data on effectiveness.

Fagan[2] presented data from a development project at Aetna Life and Casualty. Two programmers wrote an application program of eight modules (4439 non-commentary source statements) in COBOL. Design and code inspections were introduced into the development process, and the number of inspection participants ranged between three and five. After six months of actual usage, 46 defects had been detected during development and usage of the program. Fagan reported that 38 defects were detected by design and code inspections together, yielding defect detection effectiveness for inspections of 82 percent. The remaining eight defects were found during unit test and preparation for acceptance testing.

In another article, Fagan[3] published data from a project at IBM. Seven programmers developed a program of 6271 LOC in PL/1. Over the life cycle of the product, 93 percent of all defects were detected by inspections. He also mentioned two projects of the Standard Bank of South Africa (143 KLOC) and American Express (13 KLOC of system code), each with a defect detection effectiveness for inspections of over 50 percent without using trained inspection moderators.

Weller[4] presented data from a project at Bull HN Information Systems, which replaced inefficient C, code for a control microprocessor, with Forth. After system testing was completed, code inspection effectiveness was around 70 percent.

Grady and van Slack[5] reported on experiences from achieving widespread inspection use at Hewlett-Packard. In one of the company's divisions, inspections (focusing on code) typically found 60 to 70 percent of the defects.

Shirey[6] stated that defect detection effectiveness of inspections is typically reported to range from 60 to 70 percent.

Barnard and Price[7] cited several references and reported a defect detection effectiveness for code inspections varying from 30 to 75 percent.

In their environment at AT&T Bell Laboratories, the authors achieved a defect detection effectiveness for code inspections of more than 70 percent.

McGibbon[8] presented data from Cardiac Pacemakers Inc., where inspections are used to improve the quality of life critical software. They observed that inspections removed 70 to 90 percent of all faults detected during development.

Collofello and Woodfield[9] evaluated reliability-assurance techniques in a case study — a large real-time software project that consisted of about 700,000 lines of code developed by more than 400 developers. The project was performed over several years, recording quality-assurance data for design, coding, and testing. The respective defect detection effectiveness was reported to be 54 percent for design inspections, 64 percent for code inspections, and 38 percent for testing.

Kitchenham et al.[10] reported on experiences at ICL, where approximately 58 percent of defects were found by software inspections. The total proportion of development effort devoted to inspections was only 6 percent.

Gilb and Graham[11] included experience data from various sources in their discussion of the costs and benefits of inspections. IBM Rochester Labs published values of 60 percent for source code inspections, 80 percent for inspections of pseudo-code, and 88 percent for inspections of module and interface specifications.

Grady[12] performed a cost-benefit analysis for different techniques, among them design and code inspections. He stated that the average percentage of defects found for design inspections was 55 percent, and 60 percent for code inspections.

Jones[13] discussed defect-removal effectiveness in the context of evaluating current practices in U.S. industry. He gave approximate ranges and averages of defect detection effectiveness for various activities.

Franz and Shih[14] presented data from code inspection of a sales and inventory tracking systems project at HP. This was a batch system written in COBOL. Their data indicated that inspections had 19 percent effectiveness for defects that could also be found during testing.

Meyer[15] performed an experiment to compare program testing to code walkthroughs and inspections. The subjects were 59 highly experienced data processing professionals testing and inspecting a PL/I program. Myers[16] reported an average effectiveness value of 0.38 for inspections.

To summarize this data, we assume that effectiveness follows a triangular distribution. A triangular distribution has a maximum value, a minimum value, and a most likely value (Evans et al.[17]). When little is known about the actual distribution of a variable, it is common to adopt a triangular distribution (Vose[18]).

The maximum value for the effectiveness of design inspections was reported by Gilb and Graham[19] from IBM Rochester Labs. This value was 0.84 (average for two types of design document). The minimal value was reported by Jones[13] as 0.25 for informal design reviews. The most likely value is the mid-point of the data from Collofello and Woodfield[9] and the industry mean reported in Jones[13], which is 0.57.

For the minimum value of code inspection effectiveness, only the data from Franz and Shih[14] is used (0.19). The maximum value of 0.7 was obtained by Weller[4]. For the most likely value, the data from Meyer,[15] Collofello and Woodfield,[9] Jones,[13] Gilb and Graham,[19] and Grady[12] was used to produce an average, which was 0.57.

C.2 Average Effort per Defect

This section summarizes the data on the average effort per defect for various defect detection techniques (design inspections, code inspections, and testing).

Ackerman et al.[20] presented data on different projects as a sample of values from the literature and from proprietary reports. These are described below.

The development group for a small warehouse-inventory system used inspections on detailed design and code. For detailed design, they reported 3.6 hours of individual preparation per thousand lines, 3.6 hours of meeting time per thousand lines, 1.0 hours per defect found, and 4.8 hours per major defect found (major defects are those that will affect execution). For code, the results were 7.9 hours of preparation per thousand lines, 4.4 hours of meetings per thousand lines, and 1.2 hours per defect found.

A major government-systems developer reported the following results from inspection of more than 562,000 lines of detailed design and 249,000 lines of code. For detailed design, 5.76 hours of individual preparation per thousand lines, 4.54 hours of meetings per thousand lines, and 0.58 hours per defect were found. For code, 4.91 hours of individual preparation per thousand lines, 3.32 hours of meetings per thousand lines, and 0.67 hours per defect were found.

Two quality engineers from a major government-systems contractor reported 3 to 5 staff-hours per major defect detected by inspections, showing a surprising consistency over different applications and programming languages.

A banking computer-services firm found that it took 4.5 hours to eliminate a defect by unit testing, compared to 2.2 hours by inspection (probably code inspections).

An operating-system development organization for a large mainframe manufacturer reported that the average effort involved in finding a design defect by inspections is 1.4 staff-hours, compared to 8.5 staff-hours of effort to find a defect by testing.

Weller[4] reported data from a project that performed a conversion of 1200 lines of C code to Forth for several timing-critical routines. While testing the rewritten code, it took 6 hours per failure. It was known from a pilot project in the organization that they had been finding defects in inspections at a cost of 1.43 hours per defect. Thus, the team stopped testing and inspected the rewritten code detecting defects at a cost of less than 1 hour per defect.

McGibbon[8] discussed software inspections and their return on investment as one of four categories of software process improvements. For modeling the effects of inspections, he uses a sample project of an estimated size of 39.967 LOC. It is assumed that if the cost to fix a defect during design is 1X, then fixing design defects during the test is 10X, and in post-release is 100X. The rework effort per defect for different phases is assumed to be 2.5 staff-hours per defect for design inspections, 2.5 staff-hours for code inspections, 25 staff-hours for testing, and 250 staff-hours for maintenance (customer-detected defects).

Collofello and Woodfield[9] discussed a model for evaluating the efficiency of defect detection. To conduct a quantitative analysis, they needed to estimate some factors for which they did not have enough data. They performed a survey among many of the 400 members of a large real-time software project who were asked to estimate the effort needed to detect and correct a defect for different techniques. The results were 7.5 hours for a design error, 6.3 hours for a code error, both detected by inspections, 11.6 hours for an error found during testing, and 13.5 hours for an error discovered in the field.

Kitchenham et al.[10] reported on experience at ICL, where the cost of finding a defect in design inspections was 1.58 hours.

Gilb and Graham[11] included experience data from various sources reporting the costs and benefits of inspections. A senior software engineer describes how software inspections started at Applicon. In the first year, 9 code inspections and 39 document inspections (other documents than code) were conducted and an average effort of 0.8 hours was spent to find and fix a major problem. After the second year, a total of 63 code inspections and 100 document inspections had been conducted and the average effort to find and fix a major problem was 0.9 hours.

Bourgeois[21] reported experience from a large maintenance program within Lockheed Martin Western Development Labs (LMWDL), where software inspections replaced structured walkthroughs in a number of projects. The analyzed program is staffed by more than 75 engineers who maintain and enhance over 2 million lines of code. The average effort for 23 software inspections (six participants) was 1.3 staff-hours per defect found and 2.7 staff-hours per defect found and fixed. Bourgeois also presented data from the Jet Propulsion Laboratory that is used as an industry standard. There, the average effort for 171 software inspections (five participants) was 1.1 staff-hours per defect found and 1.4 to 1.8 staff-hours per defect found and fixed.

Franz and Shih's data[14] indicated that the average effort per defect for code inspections was 1 hour and for testing was 6 hours.

In presenting the results of analyzing inspections data at JPL, Kelly et al.[22] reported that it takes up to 17 hours to fix defects during formal testing, based on a project at JPL. They also reported approximately 1.75 hours to find and fix defects during design inspections, and approximately 1.46 hours during code inspections.

Following the same logic as for effectiveness, we compute the average values of effort per defect for the various defect detection activities.

Considering the average effort per defect for design inspections, Ackerman et al.[20] provide the maximum value of 2.9 hours, on average, per defect for different design documents on a project. The same article also provides the minimum value obtained from another project, which was 0.58 person-hours. The most likely value was the average of another project in Ackerman et al.,[20] Kitchenham et al.,[10] and Kelly et al.[22] This was 1.58 hours.

Considering the average effort per defect for code inspections, Bourgeois[21] reported the maximum value for code inspections of 2.7 hours per defect. Ackerman et al.[20] reported the minimal value. The most likely value was the mean of values reported in Ackerman et al.,[20] Kelly et al.,[22] Weller,[4] and Franz,[14] which was 1.46 hours.

Finally, for the average effort per defect for testing, the maximum value of 17 was obtained from Kelly et al.[22] The minimum of 4.5 was obtained from Ackerman et al.[20] The most likely value was the mean for projects reported in Weller[4] and Franz and Shih,[14] and was computed in 6 hours.

References

1. Briand, L., El Emam, K., Laitenberger, O., and Fussbroich, T. Using simulation to build inspection efficiency benchmarks for developmental projects, *Twentieth International Conference on Software Engineering,* 340–349, 1998.
2. Fagan, M. Design and code inspections to reduce errors in program development. *IBM Systems Journal,* 15(3):182–211, 1976.
3. Fagan, M. Advances in software inspections. *IEEE Transactions on Software Engineering,* 12(7):744–751, 1986.

4. Weller, E. Lessons from three years of inspection data. *IEEE Software,* 10(5): 38–45, September 1993.

5. Grady, R. and Slack, T. Key lessons in achieving widespread inspection use. *IEEE Software,* 11(4):46–57, 1994.

6. Shirey, G. How inspections fail, in *Proceedings of the Ninth International Conference on Testing Computer Software,* pp. 151–159, 1992.

7. Barnard, J. and Price, A. Managing code inspection information. *IEEE Software,* 11:59–69, 1994.

8. McGibbon, T. Business Case for Software Process Improvement, A DACS State-of-the-Art Report. Available at www.dacs.com/techs/roi.soar/soar.html, 1996.

9. Collofello, J. and Woodfield, S. Evaluating the effectiveness of reliability-assurance techniques. *Journal of Systems and Software,* pp. 191–195, 1989.

10. Kitchenham, B., Kitchenham, A., and Fellows, J. The effects of inspections on software quality and productivity. *ICL Technical Journal,* 5(1):112–122, 1986.

11. Gilb, T. and Graham, D. *Software Inspection,* Addison-Wesley Publishing Company, 1993.

12. Grady, R. *Practical Software Metrics for Project Management and Process Improvement,* Prentice Hall, 1992.

13. Jones, C. Software defect removal efficiency. *IEEE Computer,* 29(4):94–95, 1991.

14. Franz, L. and Shih, J. Estimating the value of inspections and early testing for software projects. *Hewlett-Packard Journal,* pp. 60–67, 1994.

15. Meyer, G. A controlled experiment in program testing and code walk-throughs/inspections. *Communications of the ACM,* 21(9):760–768, 1978.

16. Myers, W. Can software for the SDI ever be error-free?. *IEEE Computer,* 19(10):61–67, 1986.

17. Evans, M., Hastings, N., and Peacock, B. *Statistical Distributions,* John Wiley & Sons, 1993.

18. Vose, D., *Quantitative Risk Analysis: A Guide to Monte Carlo Simulation Modeling,* John Wiley & Sons, 1996.

19. Gilb, T. and Graham, D. *Software Inspection,* Addison-Wesley Publishing Company, 1993.

20. Ackerman, A., Buchwald, L., and Lewski, F. Software inspections: an effective verification process. *IEEE Software,* 6 (3):31–36, 1989.

21. Bourgeois, K. Process insights from a large-scale software inspection data analysis. *Crosstalk: The Journal of Defense Software Engineering,* 9(10): 17–23, 1996.

22. Kelly, J., Sheriff, J., and Hops, J. An analysis of defect densities found during software inspections. *Journal of Systems Software,* 17:111–117, 1992.

Appendix D

Backfiring Table

Backfiring is the process of converting lines of code to Function Points and vice versa. The former is useful as a quick way to determine the functional size of a system from its Lines of Code (LOC) measure. While approximate, it does provide a serviceable estimate in some instances. The latter is useful when wishing to interpret Function Point numbers, for example, figuring the defects per thousand lines of code from the defects per function point.

The recent backfiring table for common programming languages is shown in Table D.1. As an example of how to use this, let us assume that we have a Visual Basic program that has a defect density of 0.1 defects per Function Point. This means a low of 2.7 defects per thousand lines of code and a high of 5 defects per thousand lines of code. The average defect density would be 3.1 defects per thousand lines of code.

TABLE D.1 Backfiring Table from Jones

Language	Source Statements per Function Point		
	Low	Average	High
Basic Assembly	200	320	450
Macro Assembly	130	213	300
C	60	128	170
FORTRAN	75	107	160
COBOL	65	107	150
Pascal	50	91	125
PL/I	65	80	95
Ada83	60	71	80
C++	30	53	125
Ada95	28	49	110
Visual Basic	20	32	37
Smalltalk	15	21	40
SQL	7	12	15

Note: This assumes IFPUG 4.1 Function Point counting rules.

Source: From Jones, C. *Software Assessments, Benchmarks, and Best Practices,* Addison-Wesley, 2000.

Appendix E

The ROI Model

This appendix presents the complete ROI model, explains its derivation, and justifies all of its components. The unit of analysis for this model is the software project.

E.1 Definitions

E.1.1 Total Project Cost

The elements of the total project cost can be broken down as shown in Table E.1. The assumption is made that the generic support costs are carried by the organization because the support function should be provided for all projects.

All costs, except the fixed and overhead costs, are really made up of effort (i.e., labor costs). In most software projects, effort is such a large part of the total budget that frequently effort and budget are used interchangeably. Furthermore, the fixed and overhead costs can be calculated per head; therefore, converting effort into total project dollars is straightforward.

E.1.2 Defect Detection Costs

To formulate ROI properly, it is also necessary that we break down the costs of defect detection activities. Table E.2 shows the notation that we will use to define the individual effort items for each instance of a defect detection activity. The instance is denoted by i. For example, if we are

TABLE E.1   Notation Used for the Cost Elements on a Software Project

Cost Element	Notation
Fixed and overhead costs	C_1
Construction costs	C_2
Defect detection costs (pre-release)	C_3
Pre-release rework costs	C_4
Post-release rework costs	C_5
Post-release new feature costs	C_6
Total pre-release costs	$C_A = C_1 + C_2 + C_3 + C_4$
Total post-release costs	$C_B = C_5 + C_6$

TABLE E.2   Notation Used for the Effort to Find and Fix a Defect

Effort Definition	Notation
Effort to create or recreate a failure or detect a defect in defect detection activity f	$E_{1, f, i}$
Effort to isolate a defect in defect detection activity f	$E_{2, f, i}$
Effort to fix a defect in defect detection activity f	$E_{3, f, i}$
Effort to finalize a defect (retesting, documentation, and packaging) in defect detection activity f	$E_{4, f, i}$
Total effort to find and fix a defect in defect detection activity f	$E_{f, i} = E_{1, f, i} + E_{2, f, i} + E_{3, f, i} + E_{4, f, i}$

talking about inspections, then this is the effort for a single instance of an inspection.

A project will have multiple instances of a defect detection activity. For example, a project will have many code inspections. We use f to denote a type of defect detection activity, such as the code inspection.

For specific defect detection activities, some of the effort values may be zero or very small. For example, during a code inspection, the isolation effort would be close to zero because the inspection itself identifies the exact location of the defect.

E.1.3 Defect Counts

An important definition when evaluating reduction in rework is the number of defects that exist in a document (e.g., a design or source code) prior to any defect detection activity:

$$\left|\alpha_{f,i}\right| = \left\{ x \left| \begin{array}{l} \text{x is a defect that exists in the} \\ \text{document prior to defect detection} \end{array} \right. \right\} \quad \text{(E.1)}$$

This applies to a specific instance of a defect detection activity: instance i. The total number of defects is therefore given by the size of this set.

The actual defect detection activity will also find a certain number of defects. This is defined as:

$$\left|\lambda_{f,i}\right| = \left\{ x \left| \begin{array}{l} \text{x is a defect that exists in the} \\ \text{document during defect detection} \end{array} \right. \right\} \quad \text{(E.2)}$$

This applies to a specific instance of a defect detection activity: instance i. The total number of defects found is therefore given by the size of this set.

Two important measures that characterize the defect detection activity should be defined. The first is the effectiveness of defect detection. For a single instance of a defect detection activity (instance i), this is given by:

$$p_{f,i} = \frac{\left|\lambda_{f,i}\right|}{\left|\alpha_{f,i}\right|} \quad \text{(E.3)}$$

This gives the effectiveness for a single instance. Effectiveness is really the fraction of defects in the document that were found. An effectiveness of 0.5 means that half of the defects in the document were found during defect detection.

For all of the defect detection activities on a project (across all instances), we take the average:

$$\hat{p}_f = \overline{\left(\frac{\left|\lambda_{f,i}\right|}{\left|\alpha_{f,i}\right|}\right)} \quad \text{(E.4)}$$

Therefore, where f = "code inspections," then $\hat{p}_{\text{code inspections}}$ is the average effectiveness of all code inspections on the project. In this formulation we make the assumption that the variation in the defect content of the document is small.

E.1.4 Defect Detection Effort

The second important measure is the effort it takes to find and fix a defect:

$$\varepsilon_{f,i} = \frac{E_{f,i}}{|\lambda_{f,i}|} \tag{E.5}$$

This gives the effort per defect for a single instance i of the defect detection activity. For example, if the value is 2 hours for a given code inspection, then this means that it took 2 hours, on average, to find and fix a single defect during the code inspection.

For all of the defect detection activities on a project, we take the average:

$$\hat{\varepsilon}_f = \overline{\left(\frac{E_{f,i}}{|\lambda_{f,i}|} \right)} \tag{E.6}$$

Therefore, where f = "code inspections," then $\hat{\varepsilon}_{\text{code inspections}}$ is the average (find and fix) effort per defect of all code inspections on the project. Here we make the assumption that variation in the number of defects discovered is small.

E.1.5 Bad Fixes

The above formulations do not take into account the possibility that some of the fixes are bad fixes. We therefore have to account for the bad fix ratio, β. Let us say that if β is 0.1, this means that one in ten fixes are bad. The proportion of correct fixes is given by $(1-\beta)$. Now we have the following for effectiveness:

$$\hat{p}'_f = \overline{\left(\frac{|\lambda_{f,i}|}{|\alpha_{f,i}|} \right)}(1-\beta) \tag{E.7}$$

This is true effectiveness, correcting for bad fixes. And for the cost per defect, we have:

$$\hat{\varepsilon}'_f = \overline{\left(\frac{|E_{f,i}|}{|\lambda_{f,i}|} \right)}\left(\frac{1}{1-\beta} \right) \tag{E.8}$$

This is effort per defect corrected for bad fixes. The more bad fixes, the higher the effort per defect, on average.

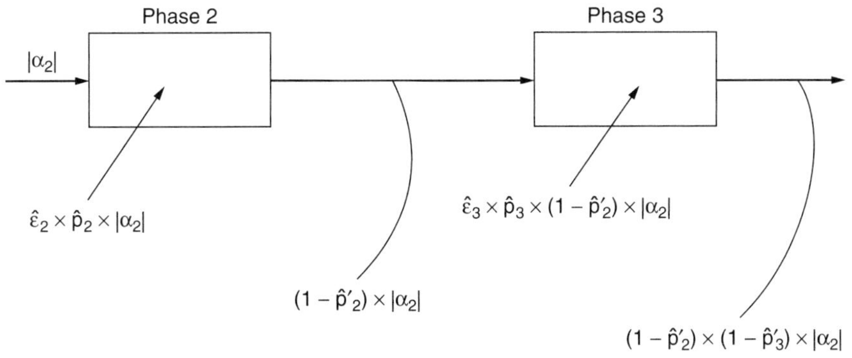

Phase 2

$|\alpha_2|$

$\hat{\epsilon}_2 \times \hat{p}_2 \times |\alpha_2|$

$(1 - \hat{p}'_2) \times |\alpha_2|$

Phase 3

$\hat{\epsilon}_3 \times \hat{p}_3 \times (1 - \hat{p}'_2) \times |\alpha_2|$

$(1 - \hat{p}'_2) \times (1 - \hat{p}'_3) \times |\alpha_2|$

FIGURE E.1 A two-stage defect detection process. The diagram shows the effort to perform each of the defect detection activities in each of the two phases (the arrows pointing to the boxes), as well as the defects that enter and escape each phase.

E.2 Defect Detection Stages

Before providing the ROI model in detail, it is instructive to derive a number of equations to illustrate how one can estimate the costs and effectiveness of defect detection activities. We use the modeling notation that is used in the body of the book to illustrate how these equations can be derived.

The main drivers of ROI in our models (except when we account for productivity gains due to reuse) are:

■ Reduced rework throughout the life cycle
■ Fewer delivered defects

Both are due to defect detection activities. These can be inspections and testing. We assume that there are n consecutive defect detection activities, for example, design inspections, code inspections, testing, and post-release. These will be numbered incrementally from 1 to n, where n is the last pre-release activity in the series of defect detection activities. In the example we will be using for illustration, n = 3.

For each of the defect detection activities (or phases), we will derive the equations characterizing the effectiveness and effort under different scenarios. Such examples make it easier to understand how the ROI models are constructed and applied.

Consider Figure E.1. Here we have two sequential defect detection phases. As per our notation, $|\alpha_2|$ is the number of defects, on average, that exist in the documents that enter Phase 2. The term $\hat{\varepsilon}_2 \times \hat{p}_2 \times |\alpha_2|$ gives the total effort expended on defect detection and fixing the defects in Phase 2. This captures the total effort for all of the defects that have been discovered during that defect detection phase.

The escapes from Phase 2 are given by $(1 - \hat{p}_2') \times |\alpha_2|$. This term captures escapes after accounting for the fact that some of the defects that were fixed during Phase 2 resulted in new defects being injected (i.e., the bad defect ratio is not zero).

We apply the same equations to Phase 3 as for Phase 2 except now instead of the defects coming into Phase 3 being $|\alpha_2|$, they are the escapes from Phase 2.

Based on the above example, we can generalize and compute the total defect detection effort expended as follows:

$$\text{Defect Detection Effort} = \sum_{t=2}^{n} \hat{\varepsilon}_t \times \hat{p}_t \times |\alpha_2| \times \chi_t \qquad (E.9)$$

where n is the maximum index value of our defect detection phases. In the example above, this was 3 (i.e., the highest index value was 3). We also have:

$$\chi_t = \begin{cases} 1 & , \quad t = 2 \\ \prod_{k=2}^{t-1}(1 - \hat{p}_k'), & t > 2 \end{cases} \qquad (E.10)$$

And the total number of defects that escape the series of defect detection phases is given by:

$$\text{Escapes} = |\alpha_2| \times \prod_{t=2}^{n}(1 - \hat{p}_t') \qquad (E.11)$$

Now consider Figure E.2. Here we have added a new phase, Phase 1, preceding the other two phases in the series. This new phase is intended to improve the software's quality. We wish to derive some equations showing the impact of this new phase by comparing the two figures.

First, we assert that by $|\alpha_1| = |\alpha_2| = |\alpha|$ because the total defects coming into the defect detection series will be the same. Then we can compare the defect detection effort for Phases 2 and 3 as depicted in Figure E.1 and Figure E.2 (we will not count Phase 1 for the moment). The comparison

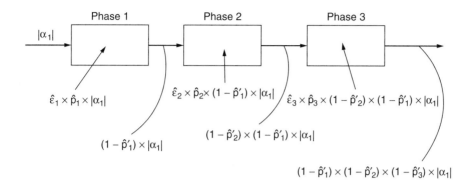

FIGURE E.2 **A three-stage defect detection process. The diagram shows the effort to perform each of the defect detection activities in each of the three phases, as well as the defects that enter and escape each phase.**

involves computing the cost difference between the two-phase and the three-phase series. It is given by:

$$\text{Effort Savings} = \left[\text{Two Phase Series Cost}\right] - \left[\text{Three Phase Series Cost}\right] \quad \text{(E.12)}$$

which translates to:

$$\text{Effort Savings} = |\alpha| \times \left(\left(\hat{\varepsilon}_2 \times \hat{p}_1' \times \hat{p}_2\right) + \left(\hat{\varepsilon}_3 \times \hat{p}_1' \times \hat{p}_3 \times \left(1 - \hat{p}_2'\right)\right)\right) \quad \text{(E.13)}$$

We also define:

$$\left|\lambda_1\right| = \hat{p}_1 \times |\alpha| \quad \text{(E.14)}$$

which is the number of defects found by Phase 1. Then we can re-express our savings in Phases 2 and 3 as:

$$\text{Effort Savings} = \left(\hat{\varepsilon}_2 \times \hat{p}_2 \times \left|\lambda_1\right| \times \left(1 - \beta\right)\right) + \left(\hat{\varepsilon}_3 \times \hat{p}_3 \times \left(1 - \hat{p}_2'\right) \times \left|\lambda_1\right| \times \left(1 - \beta\right)\right) \quad \text{(E.15)}$$

We can now generalize the savings as follows:

$$\text{Effort Savings} = \sum_{t=2}^{n} \hat{\varepsilon}_t \times \hat{p}_t \times \left|\lambda_1\right| \times \left(1 - \beta\right) \times \chi_t \quad \text{(E.16)}$$

where n is the maximum index value of our defect detection phases. In the example above, this was 3 (i.e., the highest index value was 3).

We can also compute the defect reduction between the two-phase process and the three-phase process shown in Figures E.1 and E.2. The defect reduction is given by:

$$\text{Defect Reduction} = \hat{p}_1' \times \left(1 - \hat{p}_2'\right) \times \left(1 - \hat{p}_3'\right) \times |\alpha| \qquad \text{(E.17)}$$

We can generalize this to any number of phases:

$$\text{Defect Reduction} = |\alpha| \times \hat{p}_1' \times \prod_{t=2}^{n} \left(1 - \hat{p}_t'\right) \qquad \text{(E.18)}$$

With the above equations, we are in a good position to derive all of the different ROI models that we require.

E.3 The Customer Cost Savings Model

Recall that the customer savings from better quality software is expressed in terms of defect density as follows (see Equation 6.8):

$$\text{Percentage Savings} = \frac{Q_B - Q_A}{Q_B} \times 75 \qquad \text{(E.19)}$$

If we assume that the size of the software is the same, then the above equation can be expressed in terms of actual defects found. The numerator is the defect reduction, which was derived as (see Equation E.18):

$$\text{Defect Reduction} = |\alpha| \times \hat{p}_1' \times \prod_{t=2}^{n} \left(1 - \hat{p}_t'\right) \qquad \text{(E.20)}$$

The denominator of the percentage savings equation is the total number of delivered defects before making any improvements to quality, which we showed above was:

$$\text{Escapes} = |\alpha| \times \prod_{t=2}^{n} \left(1 - \hat{p}_t'\right) \qquad \text{(E.21)}$$

Therefore, the percentage savings is given by:

$$\text{Percentage Savings} = \frac{|\alpha| \times \hat{p}'_1 \times \prod_{t=2}^{n}\left(1 - \hat{p}'_t\right)}{|\alpha| \times \prod_{t=2}^{n}\left(1 - \hat{p}'_t\right)} \times 75 = \hat{p}'_1 \times 75 \quad \text{(E.22)}$$

This means that the savings to the customer can be calculated as the effectiveness of the new defect detection technique that would be introduced by the development project multiplied by a constant.

E.4 The Financial ROI Model

The financial ROI model consists of three elements:

$$\text{Financial ROI} = \left[\text{PreRelease ROI}\right] + \left[\text{PostRelease ROI}\right] + \left[\text{ROI from reuse}\right] \quad \text{(E.23)}$$

Below we start putting the whole ROI model together with all the appropriate parameterizations to account for the benefits of quality practices.

The pre-release savings would be given by (based on Equation 9.3):

$$\text{PreRelease ROI} = \frac{\left(\sum_{t=2}^{n} \hat{\varepsilon}_t \times \hat{p}_t \times |\lambda_1| \times (1-\beta) \times \chi_t\right) - \left(\hat{\varepsilon}_1 \times |\lambda_1|\right)}{\sum_{t=2}^{n} \hat{\varepsilon}_t \times \hat{p}_t \times |\alpha_1| \times \chi_t} \times \frac{C_3 + C_4}{C_A} \quad \text{(E.24)}$$

which can be further simplified to:

$$\text{PreRelease ROI} = \hat{p}_1 \frac{\left(\sum_{t=2}^{n} \hat{\varepsilon}_t \times \hat{p}_t \times (1-\beta) \times \chi_t\right) - \hat{\varepsilon}_1}{\sum_{t=2}^{n} \hat{\varepsilon}_t \times \hat{p}_t \times \chi_t} \times \frac{C_3 + C_4}{C_A} \quad \text{(E.25)}$$

where:

$$\chi_t = \begin{cases} 1 & , \quad t = 2 \\ \prod_{k=2}^{t-1}\left(1 - \hat{p}'_k\right), & t > 2 \end{cases}$$ (E.26)

The $\left(\hat{\varepsilon}'_l \times |\lambda_1|\right)$ term reflects the effort spent on quality practices to reduce rework effort. For example, if the quality practice was the automated detection of defects, then this term is the effort to find and fix the defects that were found. In the simplified form (Equation E.25), this term becomes $\left(\hat{\varepsilon}_1\right)$.

For the post-release ROI model, we compute the total post-release effort as:

PostRelease Effort = effectiveness × effort per defect × delivered defects (E.27)

To compute the savings in post-release effort, we compute the post-release effort before quality improvement and subtract from that post-release effort after quality improvement. For example, in Figures E.1 and E.2, we get:

PostRelease effort savings = $\hat{\varepsilon}_{\text{post}} \times \hat{p}_{\text{post}} \times \left(1 - \hat{p}'_2\right) \times \left(1 - \hat{p}'_3\right) \times |\alpha| - \hat{\varepsilon}_{\text{post}}$

$$\times \hat{p}_{\text{post}} \times \left(1 - \hat{p}'_1\right) \times \left(1 - \hat{p}'_2\right) \times \left(1 - \hat{p}'_3\right) \times |\alpha|$$ (E.28)

which simplifies to:

PostRelease effort savings = $\hat{\varepsilon}_{\text{post}} \times \hat{p}_{\text{post}} \times \left(1 - \hat{p}'_2\right) \times \left(1 - \hat{p}'_3\right) \times \hat{p}'_1 |\alpha|$ (E.29)

The value of $(\hat{p}_{\text{post}})$ captures the proportion of all post-release defects that are actually fixed. However, some of those fixes introduce more defects (bad fixes). These bad fixes (or new defects) need to be fixed as well. These secondary fixes introduce more defects, and so on. The true effectiveness of post-release defect detection activities for a very long period of time is:

$$\hat{p}_{\text{post}} \times \left(1 + \prod_{i=1}^{\infty} \beta^i\right) = \hat{p}_{\text{post}}$$ (E.30)

Because the post-release effectiveness will converge as shown above, and for the sake of simplicity, we will leave the effectiveness as $(\hat{p}_{\text{post}})$.

Going back to our financial ROI model:

$$\text{ROI} = \frac{\text{Costs Saved} - \text{Investment}}{\text{Original Cost}} \qquad (E.31)$$

For the post-release phase, there are no additional costs consumed for quality improvement, as defined here, because all of these costs have been accounted for during the pre-release phase. We therefore have a simplified version:

$$\text{ROI} = \frac{\text{Costs Saved}}{\text{Original Cost}} \qquad (E.32)$$

which translates to:

$$\text{PostRelease ROI} = \frac{\left(\hat{\varepsilon}_{\text{post}} \times \hat{p}_{\text{post}} \times \left(1 - \hat{p}_2'\right) \times \left(1 - \hat{p}_3'\right) \times \hat{p}_1' \times |\alpha|\right)}{\hat{\varepsilon}_{\text{post}} \times \hat{p}_{\text{post}} \times \left(1 - \hat{p}_2'\right) \times \left(1 - \hat{p}_3'\right) \times |\alpha|} \times \frac{C_5}{C_B} \qquad (E.33)$$

And this simplifies to:

$$\text{PostRelease ROI} = \frac{\hat{p}_1' \times C_5}{C_B} \qquad (E.34)$$

Now we can compute the savings from reuse, which are given by:

$$\text{ROI from reuse} = \left(\frac{\text{RLOC}}{\text{TLOC}} \times \left(1 - \text{RCR}\right)\right) - \frac{\kappa}{C_A} \qquad (E.35)$$

where the definitions in Table E.3 apply.
In practice, all that is needed is the RLOC/TLOC ratio, which is the proportion of the total system that would be reused.

TABLE E.3 Notation Used to Calculate the Benefits of Reuse

Definition	Notation
Lines of code that will be reused	RLOC
Relative cost of reuse	RCR
Total size of the system	TLOC

The RCR value captures the notion that reuse is cheaper than development from scratch. It quantifies the relative cost of reuse compared to development. RCR is typically used when evaluating the benefits of software reuse.[1]

The κ value is the cost of reuse. It is expressed as κ/C_A. This means we can express it as a proportion of the total pre-release project budget.

If a particular investment does not result in reuse benefits, then the reuse ROI term would be zero because RLOC would be zero and κ would also be zero.

The three parts of this ROI model can be used individually or in unison to compute the savings from quality practices.

E.5 Schedule ROI

The schedule ROI applies only to the pre-release part of a software project. We can therefore combine the pre-release ROI model (in Equation E.25) with the SCEDRED model in Equation 9.12 to get the following development schedule ROI model:

$$\text{Schedule ROI} = 1 - \left(1 - \left(\hat{p}_1' \times \frac{\left(\sum_{t=2}^{n} \hat{\varepsilon}_t \times \hat{p}_t \times (1-\beta) \times \chi_t\right) - \hat{\varepsilon}_1}{\sum_{t=2}^{n} \hat{\varepsilon}_t \times \hat{p}_t \times \chi_t} \times \frac{C_3 + C_4}{C_A}\right)^{0.28 + \left(0.002 \times \sum_{j=1}^{5} SF_j\right)}\right) \quad \text{(E.36)}$$

where:

$$\chi_t = \begin{cases} 1 & , \quad t = 2 \\ \prod_{k=2}^{t-1}(1 - \hat{p}_k'), & \quad t > 2 \end{cases} \quad \text{(E.37)}$$

This captures the time-to-market savings from adding a new phase to a project to improve quality.

E.6 Defaults

Although the ROI model can seem overwhelming initially, it is actually straightforward to use. The model does not require information that would not normally be available to a project manager.

One initial set of simplifications for using the ROI model are the defaults. Below we present a series of defaults that can be used.

The first default is for the expression:

$$\frac{C_3 + C_4}{C_A} \tag{E.38}$$

The review of available data presented in Chapter 7 revealed that a large proportion of total development effort is devoted to rework. As a conservative estimate, we assume that 50 percent of the development effort is rework.

The next default is the proportion of post-release effort that is devoted to rework (or fixing bugs):

$$\frac{C_5}{C_B} \tag{E.39}$$

Again, the data review in Chapter 7 indicates that we can safely assume 50 percent of total post-release costs are being devoted to rework.

Another default concerns the effectiveness of inspections. A comprehensive literature review (this is presented in Appendix C) has found that the average effectiveness of design and code inspections is 0.57 (i.e., inspections tend to find, on average, 57 percent of the defects in the artifacts that are inspected). Thus, the value for:

$$\hat{p}_{\text{design inspection}} = \overline{\left(\left| \frac{\lambda_{f,i}}{\alpha_{f,i}} \right| \right)} = 0.57 \tag{E.40}$$

and

$$\hat{p}_{\text{code inspection}} = \overline{\left(\left| \frac{\lambda_{f,i}}{\alpha_{f,i}} \right| \right)} = 0.57 \tag{E.41}$$

We use as the default for β the value 0.1 (i.e., about one in ten fixes introduce new defects). Fagan[2] notes that one in six fixes in an inspection introduces another defect. Jones[3] notes that 5 percent of code inspection fixes may yield new defects, 3 percent of design inspection fixes may yield new defects, and 5 percent of test-based changes may yield new defects. One study found that 27 percent of the correction effort during software maintenance was devoted to bad fixes.[4] We err on the conservative side by choosing a value of one in ten fixes.

Again, based on a comprehensive review of published industrial data (this is presented in Appendix C), we estimate that the *average* effort to find and correct a defect during inspections is given by:

$$\hat{\varepsilon}_{\text{code inspection}} = \overline{\left(\left|\frac{E_{f,i}}{\lambda_{f,i}}\right|\right)} = 1.5 \left(\text{person-hours}\right) \qquad (E.42)$$

$$\hat{\varepsilon}_{\text{design inspection}} = \overline{\left(\left|\frac{E_{f,i}}{\lambda_{f,i}}\right|\right)} = 1.5 \left(\text{person-hours}\right) \qquad (E.43)$$

$$\hat{\varepsilon}_{\text{testing}} = \overline{\left(\left|\frac{E_{f,i}}{\lambda_{f,i}}\right|\right)} = 6 \left(\text{person-hours}\right) \qquad (E.44)$$

The RCR value indicates how much reuse costs as a proportion of new development cost. This value is estimated to be around 0.2. This means that reuse costs only 20 percent of new development costs, on average. This value is obtained from Poulin.[1]

E.7 Illustration

Before presenting a simple illustration of ROI calculations, we make a number of observations about the ROI models.

The customer ROI model in Equation E.22 will always be positive. This means that the implementation of any practice that reduces defects will always result in customer cost reductions.

The financial ROI models behave differently, depending on whether one is looking at pre-release or post-release savings. If we assume a defect detection life cycle looking like Figure E.3, and using the default values, the maximum value for effort per defect for any new practice to give a positive return is:

$$\hat{\varepsilon}_1 = \left(1 - \beta\right) \times \hat{\varepsilon}_2 \times \hat{p}_2 \qquad (E.45)$$

Using our defaults, this gives:

$$\hat{\varepsilon}_1 = 5.4 \times \hat{p}_2 \qquad (E.46)$$

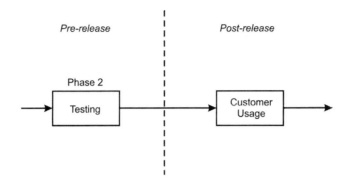

FIGURE E.3 **Defect detection life cycle showing a simple project that has only testing.**

The interesting point about this equation is that it does not depend on the effectiveness of the technology that will improve quality (i.e., Phase 1). For example, if we say that $\hat{p}_2$ for testing is 0.5, then the maximum effort per defect for code inspections is 2.7 hours. If the cost per defect increases above that, then the new technology will not provide a positive pre-release return, irrespective of its effectiveness.

Post-release ROI is always positive if the practices introduced have non-zero effectiveness. Therefore, any quality improvement practices that work, even a little, will reduce post-release costs.

Note also that if the pre-release effort savings are negative then by definition the schedule will be extended rather than decreased.

To help provide some context for this ROI model, we will look at an example of introducing code inspections. We assume that the defect detection life cycle before introducing code inspections looks like Figure E.3. And after the introduction of code inspections, the defect detection life cycle is as depicted in Figure E.4.

We will use the default values for each of our models. The customer ROI is given by:

$$\text{Percentage Saving} = \hat{p}_1' \times 75 = 0.57 \times 0.9 \times 75 = 38.5\% \qquad (\text{E.47})$$

Therefore, through the introduction of code inspections, the customer's cost savings from bugs is around 38 percent.

The pre-release cost savings are given by:

$$\text{PreRelease ROI}_2 = 0.57 \times \frac{(6 \times \hat{p}_2 \times 0.9) - 1.5}{6 \times \hat{p}_2} \times 0.5 \approx 11\% \qquad (\text{E.48})$$

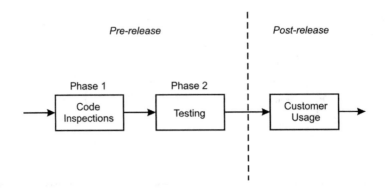

FIGURE E.4 **A defect detection life cycle consisting of code inspections and testing.**

If we assume that testing finds 50 percent of the defects, then approximately 11 percent of the post-release costs are saved by the introduction of code inspections. We can also consider post-release costs:

$$\text{PostRelease ROI}_2 = \frac{\hat{p}_1' \times C_5}{C_A} = 0.57 \times 0.9 \times 0.5 \approx 26\% \qquad \text{(E.49)}$$

Therefore, code inspections will save, on average, approximately 26 percent of the post-release costs as well.

We can then translate the pre-release cost savings into a schedule reduction as follows. If we assume that the project has nominal values on all of the Scale Factors in the SCEDRED model, we can estimate that:

$$\text{Schedule ROI} = 1 - \left(1 - 0.11\right)^{0.28 + \left(0.002 \times 0.32794\right)} \approx 3\% \qquad \text{(E.50)}$$

This shows around 3 percent reduction in delivery time after the introduction of code inspections. Unless the duration of the project is very long, this indicates that the quality improvements come at minimal impact on the schedule.

E.8 Assumptions and Limitations

The above ROI models make a number of assumptions. While we endeavored to ensure that the models are as accurate as possible, some assumptions were inevitable to produce something that was actually usable. These can be relaxed in future revisions of the model.

It should be noted that all the assumptions that we have made are conservative. This means that they would result in a smaller estimate of ROI rather than inflating it. Therefore, if a business case is attractive under the current models, it would certainly be attractive when the assumptions are relaxed.

Poulin[2] also considers another benefit of reuse: *service cost avoidance.* This is the potential saving from not having to maintain reused code. It is common that there is a different organization, group, or project that is maintaining a reuse library. To the extent that a project that reuses some of this code does not get involved in maintenance, then these maintenance costs are saved. Our models do not take this into account. Therefore, the benefits of reuse are underestimated.

An important assumption that we have made is that a defect escaping from a particular defect detection phase will potentially be discovered by a subsequent phase further down the series. For example, a defect that escapes from code inspections can be found through testing. However, different defect detection phases are not equally good at finding the same types of defects. Therefore, a defect that is quite easy to find during inspections may be extremely difficult to find during testing. The consequence is that we have underestimated the true cost of escapes because a defect that escapes inspections and is not found by testing will be detected by the customer (which is very expensive). To the extent that this assumption affects the results of the ROI analysis, the calculated ROI values will be conservative.

For all defect detection activities we have assumed that the cost per defect is fixed. This means that as the number of defects entering a defect detection activity decreases, the total effort spent on that defect detection activity goes down proportionately. For example, if the cost per defect is $20, and we reduce the number of defects entering that activity from 50 to 30, then the cost saving is $400.

One implication of this assumption is that as the number of defects approaches zero, so does the total effort spent on that activity. Strictly speaking, this is not accurate because the defect detection activity will go on anyway, even if there are no defects detected. For example, one must still test even if no defects are discovered during testing. In practice, this assumption is not problematic because the number of defects entering a defect detection activity rarely, if ever, approaches zero.

We make the added assumption that there is no defect amplification. For most purposes, this is acceptable unless one wishes to explicitly take into account defect detection techniques at the design and requirements stages of a project (such as design and requirements inspections).

References

1. Poulin, J. *Measuring Software Reuse: Principles, Practices and Economic Models,* Addison-Wesley, 1997.
2. Fagan, M. Advances in software inspections. *IEEE Transactions on Software Engineering,* 12(7):744–751, 1986.
3. Jones, C. *Estimating Software Costs,* McGraw-Hill, 1998.
4. Basili, V. et al. Understanding and predicting the process of software maintenance releases, in *Proceedings of the Eighteenth International Conference on Software Engineering,* pp. 464–474, 1996.

Appendix F

Evaluating Schedule Reduction

Schedule reduction in our model is based on the published COCOMO II model. We have basically taken COCOMO II and modified the equations to account for effort reductions.

The tables and questionnaires included in this appendix allow one to accurately evaluate the schedule reduction benefits from implementing quality practices. The SCEDRED equation includes a term that is the sum of the Scale Factors. The information here is used to calculate the exact values for these Scale Factors.

The characteristics that can be used to evaluate the PREC, FLEX, TEAM, and RESL Scale Factors are summarized in Tables F.2, F.3, F.4, and F.5, respectively. One would use a subjective weighted average of the responses to each of the features to score the factors according to Table F.1. The Table F.1 scores are then summed to compute the Scale Factor value that is used to calculate schedule reduction.

The fifth scale factor, which is also included in the Scale Factor sum, is process maturity (PMAT). The calculation of PMAT is a bit more involved and involves evaluating the process maturity of the organization. This is done through a questionnaire modeled after the ones used by the Software Engineering Institute.

Traditionally, the SW-CMM ratings scales have used Yes/No response categories.[1] The ratings scales in our questionnaires use a frequency scale.[2]

TABLE F.1 Explaining How to Compute the Scale Factors for the Schedule Reduction Estimates

Scale Factor	Very Low	Low	Nominal	High	Very High	Extra High
PREC	Thoroughly unprecedented 6.2	Largely unprecedented 4.96	Somewhat unprecedented 3.72	Generally familiar 2.48	Largely familiar 1.24	Thoroughly familiar 0
FLEX	Rigorous 5.07	Occasional relaxation 4.05	Some relaxation 3.04	General conformity 2.03	Some conformity 1.01	General goals 0
RESL	Little (20%) 7.07	Some (40%) 5.65	Often (60%) 4.24	Generally (75%) 2.83	Mostly (90%) 1.41	Full (100%) 0
TEAM	Very difficult interactions 5.48	Some difficult interactions 4.38	Basically cooperative interactions 3.29	Largely cooperative 2.19	Highly cooperative 1.1	Seamless interactions 0
EPML	Lower Level 1 7.8	Upper Level 1 6.24	Level 2 4.68	Level 3 3.12	Level 4 1.56	Level 5 0

TABLE F.2   Characteristics for Evaluating the PREC Scale Factor

Feature	Very Low	Nominal/High	Extra High
Organizational understanding of product objectives	General	Considerable	Thorough
Experience in working with related software systems	Moderate	Considerable	Extensive
Concurrent development of associated new hardware and operational procedures	Extensive	Moderate	Some
Need for innovative data processing architectures and algorithms	Considerable	Some	Minimal

TABLE F.3   Characteristics for Evaluating the FLEX Scale Factor

Feature	Very Low	Nominal/High	Extra High
Need for software conformance with preestablished requirements	Full	Considerable	Basic
Need for software conformance with external specifications	Full	Considerable	Basic
Combination of the inflexibilities above with premium in early completion	High	Medium	Low

Previous work has found that the binary scale was being used inconsistently because some project in an organizational unit would be implementing a practice, but not all projects. Therefore, should this be a "Yes" or a "No" response? The frequency scale that we use allows the respondent to make clear how often the practice is being used. The frequency scale is summarized in Table F.6.

This scale was empirically evaluated to demonstrate its validity and reliability.[2] This article reported on two studies to evaluate the scale. The first study used an initial version of this scale. Four expert judges grouped a series of goal-level questions into the KPAs without being told to which KPA the questions belong. If the judges are able to do that with accuracy, then this demonstrates convergent and discriminating validity. The judges had a 75 percent accuracy. The second study with a different set of four judges and the final version of the scale reached an accuracy of 84 percent.

TABLE F.4 Characteristics for Evaluating the TEAM Scale Factor

Feature	Very Low	Low	Nominal	High	Very High	Extra High
Consistency of stakeholder objectives and culture	Little	Some	Basic	Considerable	Strong	Full
Ability, willingness of stakeholders to accommodate other stakeholders' objectives	Little	Some	Basic	Considerable	Strong	Full
Experience of stakeholders in operating as a team	None	Little	Little	Basic	Considerable	Extensive
Stakeholder teambuilding to achieve shared vision and commitments	None	Little	Little	Basic	Considerable	Extensive

TABLE F.5   Characteristics for Evaluating the RESL Scale Factor

Feature	Very Low	Low	Nominal	High	Very High	Extra High
Risk management plan identifies critical risk items, establishes milestones for resolving them	None	Little	Some	Generally	Mostly	Fully
Schedule, budget, and internal milestones through PDR* or LCA** compatible with risk management plan	None	Little	Some	Generally	Mostly	Fully
Percent of development schedule devoted to establishing architecture, given general product objectives	5	10	17	25	33	40
Percent of required top software architecture available to project	20	40	60	80	100	120
Tool support available for resolving risk items, developing and verifying architectural specs	None	Little	Some	Good	Strong	Full
Level of uncertainty in key architecture drivers: mission, user interface, COTS, hardware, technology, performance	Extreme	Significant	Considerable	Some	Little	Very Little
Number and criticality of risk items	> 10 Critical	5-10 Critical	2-4 Critical	1 Critical	>5 Non Critical	<5 Non Critical

* PDR = Product Design Review
** LCA = LifeCycle Architecture

TABLE F.6 Definition of the Question Anchors (Response Categories) for the PMAT Scale Factor

Response Category	Anchor Definition
Almost always	The practice or goal is well established and consistently performed as a standard operating procedure (over 90 percent of the time)
Frequently	The practice is performed relatively often, but sometimes is omitted under difficult circumstances (about 60 to 90 percent of the time)
About half	The practice is performed about half the time (about 40 to 60 percent of the time)
Occasionally	The practice is performed less often (about 10 to 40 percent of the time)
Rarely if ever	The practice is performed rarely if ever
Does not apply	You have the required knowledge about the organization and the question but you feel that the question does not apply or that this KPA was not assessed at all
Do not know	You are uncertain about how to answer the question or you do not have the required information

TABLE F.7 Converting the Responses into Values Used for Calculating PMAT

Response Category	KPA% Value
Almost always	100
Frequently	75
About half	50
Occasionally	25
Rarely if ever	1
Does not apply	Ignored
Do not know	Ignored

Reliability was demonstrated in the article with the Cronbach alpha coefficient for the goal level questionnaire at 0.70. This is a respectable value for reliability. In addition, this scale is used in the COCOMO II cost estimation model.[3]

TABLE F.8 Table to Help with the Conversion of the EPML Rating into a PMAT Rating

PMAT Rating	Maturity Level	EPML
Very Low	ML1 (lower half)	0
Low	ML1 (upper half)	1
Nominal	ML2	2
High	ML3	3
Very High	ML4	4
Extra High	ML5	5

Therefore, from the practical, reliability, and validity viewpoints, this frequency scale has many advantages over previous scales. The COCOMO[3] approach computes what is called the Equivalent Process Maturity Level (EPML). The first step in computing the EPML is to convert the response to each rating question to a percentage according to the schedule in Table F.7.

The EPML is then computed as:

$$\text{EPML} = 5 \times \left(\sum_{i=1}^{n} \frac{\text{KPA\%}}{100} \right) \times \frac{1}{n} \qquad (\text{F.1})$$

where n is the total number of items for which there was a response. If there was a response on either of the last two response categories, then the question is ignored and not included in the n.

The EPML is then converted to a rating based on the scheme in Table F.8.

The following tables contain the complete questionnaires that can be used to collect the maturity responses and then convert them into an EPML score based on Equation F.1. The scoring scheme for the response categories is presented in Table F.7.

The remainder of this appendix contains the questionnaire that can be used to collect PMAT data. The questions are grouped by KPA.

References

1. Zubrow, D. et al. Maturity Questionnaire. Technical Report, Software Engineering Institute, CMU/SEI-94-SR-7, 1994.
2. Krishnan, M. and Kellner, M. Measuring process consistency: implications for reducing software defects. *IEEE Transactions on Software Engineering*, 25(6):800 815, 1999.
3. Boehm, B. et al. *Software Cost Estimation with COCOMO II*, Prentice Hall, 2000.

Questionnaire

	Do Not Know	Does Not Apply	Rarely If Ever	Occasionally	Almost Half	Frequently	Almost Always
Requirements Management							
Are system requirements allocated to software used to establish a baseline for software engineering and management use?	❏	❏	❏	❏	❏	❏	❏
As the system requirements allocated to software change, are the necessary adjustments to software plans, work products, and activities made?	❏	❏	❏	❏	❏	❏	❏
Software Project Planning							
Are estimates (e.g., size, cost, and schedule) documented for use in planning and tracking the software project?	❏	❏	❏	❏	❏	❏	❏
Do the software plans document the activities to be performed and the commitments made for the software project?	❏	❏	❏	❏	❏	❏	❏
Do all affected groups and individuals agree to their commitments related to the software project?	❏	❏	❏	❏	❏	❏	❏
Software Project Tracking and Oversight							
Are the project's actual results (e.g., schedule, size, and cost) compared with estimates in the software plans?	❏	❏	❏	❏	❏	❏	❏
Is corrective action taken when actual results deviate significantly from the project's software plans?	❏	❏	❏	❏	❏	❏	❏
Are changes in the software commitments agreed to be all affected groups and individuals?	❏	❏	❏	❏	❏	❏	❏

	Do Not Know	Does Not Apply	Rarely If Ever	Occasionally	Almost Half	Frequently	Almost Always
Software Subcontract Management							
Is a documented procedure used for selecting subcontractors based on their ability to perform the work?	❏	❏	❏	❏	❏	❏	❏
Are changes to subcontracts made with the agreement of both the prime contractor and the subcontractor?	❏	❏	❏	❏	❏	❏	❏
Are periodic technical interchanges held with subcontractors?	❏	❏	❏	❏	❏	❏	❏
Software Quality Assurance							
Are SQA activities planned?	❏	❏	❏	❏	❏	❏	❏
Does SQA provide objective verification that software products and activities adhere to applicable standards, procedures, and requirements?	❏	❏	❏	❏	❏	❏	❏
Are the results of SQA reviews and audits provided to affected groups and individuals (e.g., those who performed the work and those who are responsible for the work)?	❏	❏	❏	❏	❏	❏	❏
Are issues of noncompliance that are not resolved within the software project addressed by senior management (e.g., deviations from applicable standards)?	❏	❏	❏	❏	❏	❏	❏
Software Configuration Management							
Are software configuration management activities planned for the project?	❏	❏	❏	❏	❏	❏	❏
Has the project identified, controlled, and made available the software work products through the use of configuration management?	❏	❏	❏	❏	❏	❏	❏

	Do Not Know	Does Not Apply	Rarely If Ever	Occasionally	Almost Half	Frequently	Almost Always
Does the project follow a documented procedure to control changes to configuration items/units?	❑	❑	❑	❑	❑	❑	❑
Are standard reports on software baselines (e.g., software configuration control board minutes and change request summary and status reports) distributed to affected groups and individuals?	❑	❑	❑	❑	❑	❑	❑
Organization Process Focus							
Are the activities for developing and improving the organization's and project's software process coordinated across the organization (e.g., via a software engineering process group)?	❑	❑	❑	❑	❑	❑	❑
Is your organization's software process assessed periodically?	❑	❑	❑	❑	❑	❑	❑
Does your organization follow a documented plan for developing and improving its software process?	❑	❑	❑	❑	❑	❑	❑
Software Process Definition							
Has your organization developed, and does it maintain, a standard software process?	❑	❑	❑	❑	❑	❑	❑
Does the organization collect, review, and make available information related to the use of the organization's standard software process (e.g., estimates and actual data on software size, effort, and cost; productivity data; and quality measurements)?	❑	❑	❑	❑	❑	❑	❑
Training Program							
Are training activities planned?	❑	❑	❑	❑	❑	❑	❑
Is training provided for developing the skills and knowledge needed to perform software managerial and technical roles?	❑	❑	❑	❑	❑	❑	❑

	Do Not Know	Does Not Apply	Rarely If Ever	Occasionally	Almost Half	Frequently	Almost Always
Do members of the software engineering group and other software-related groups receive the training necessary to perform their roles?	❏	❏	❏	❏	❏	❏	❏
Integrated Software Management							
Was the project's defined software process developed by tailoring the organization's standard software process?	❏	❏	❏	❏	❏	❏	❏
Is the project planned and managed in accordance with the project's defined software process?	❏	❏	❏	❏	❏	❏	❏
Software Product Engineering							
Are the software work products produced according to the project's defined software process?	❏	❏	❏	❏	❏	❏	❏
Is consistency maintained across software work products (e.g., is the documentation tracing allocated requirements through software requirements, design, code, and test cases maintained)?	❏	❏	❏	❏	❏	❏	❏
Intergroup Coordination							
On the project, do the software engineering group and other engineering groups collaborate with the customer to establish the system requirements?	❏	❏	❏	❏	❏	❏	❏
Do the engineering groups agree to the commitments as represented in the overall project plan?	❏	❏	❏	❏	❏	❏	❏
Do the engineering groups identify, track, and resolve intergroup issues (e.g., incompatible schedules, technical risks, or system-level problems)?	❏	❏	❏	❏	❏	❏	❏

	Do Not Know	Does Not Apply	Rarely If Ever	Occasionally	Almost Half	Frequently	Almost Always
Peer Review							
Are peer reviews planned?	❏	❏	❏	❏	❏	❏	❏
Are actions associated with defects that are identified during peer review tracked until they are resolved?	❏	❏	❏	❏	❏	❏	❏
Quantitative Process Management							
Does the project follow a documented plan for conducting quantitative process management?	❏	❏	❏	❏	❏	❏	❏
Is the performance of the project's defined software process controlled quantitatively (e.g., through the use of quantitative analytic methods)?	❏	❏	❏	❏	❏	❏	❏
Is the process capability of the organization's standard software process known in quantitative terms?	❏	❏	❏	❏	❏	❏	❏
Software Quality Management							
Are the activities for managing software quality planned for the project?	❏	❏	❏	❏	❏	❏	❏
Does the project use measurable and prioritized goals for managing the quality of its software products (e.g., functionality, reliability, maintainability and usability)?	❏	❏	❏	❏	❏	❏	❏
Are measurements of quality compared to goals for software product quality to determine if the quality goals are satisfied?	❏	❏	❏	❏	❏	❏	❏
Defect Prevention							
Are defect prevention activities planned?	❏	❏	❏	❏	❏	❏	❏
Does the project conduct causal analysis meetings to identify common causes of defects?	❏	❏	❏	❏	❏	❏	❏

	Do Not Know	Does Not Apply	Rarely If Ever	Occasionally	Almost Half	Frequently	Almost Always
Once identified, are common causes of defects prioritized and systematically eliminated?	❏	❏	❏	❏	❏	❏	❏
Technology Change Management							
Does the organization follow a plan for managing technology changes?	❏	❏	❏	❏	❏	❏	❏
Are new technologies evaluated to determine their effect on quality and productivity?	❏	❏	❏	❏	❏	❏	❏
Does the organization follow a documented procedure for incorporating new technologies into the organization's standard software process?	❏	❏	❏	❏	❏	❏	❏
Process Change Management							
Does the organization follow a documented procedure for developing and maintaining plans for software process improvement?	❏	❏	❏	❏	❏	❏	❏
Do people throughout your organization participate in software process improvement activities (e.g., on teams to develop software process improvements)?	❏	❏	❏	❏	❏	❏	❏
Are improvements continually made to the organization's standard software process and the project's defined software processes?	❏	❏	❏	❏	❏	❏	❏

Appendix G

Expecting and Interpreting Evidence

Whenever a new technology or methodology is introduced and starts to gain widespread interest, one starts to hear strong demands for evidence that demonstrates the efficacy of that technology before it is adopted. That dynamic occurred in the 1980s and early 1990s when the Capability Maturity Model for Software (SW-CMM) first came out, and there were many voices against its adoption because of the lack of evidence supporting its efficacy. Now one is hearing similar arguments about agile practices and the evidence supporting their efficacy.

An article published in the early 1980s lamented the dominance of personal experiences, intuition, and "common sense" (as opposed to empirical evidence from observational studies and experiments) that, in some instances, became etched as axioms of software engineering.[1] Almost 15 years later, an editorial by Davis[2] in *IEEE Software* encouraged software engineers to ignore empirical evidence, noting that "If it makes sense, do it!" His call was for intuition and common sense to guide the adoption of software engineering technologies. Historically, reliance on so-called intuition has played a big role in justifying software engineering technologies, with advocates and opponents each expressing their personal views, exemplified with personal experiences. An apt characterization is that "Much conventional wisdom in software engineering resembles folklore more than science".[3] To most observers, this is not a good state in which to be.

Reliance on intuition as the sole tool for evaluating software engineering technologies, and for understanding why some technologies work and others do not, is fundamentally flawed. Imagine your doctor giving you a concoction he or she came up with while in medical school with the reassuring words, "Trust me, I have a gut feeling this will work: it worked wonders on my rats." Glass makes the point eloquently: "You know that your intuition is trustworthy and I know that mine is, but what about all those other unwashed pseudo-experts out there? Do you want to trust the intuition of a computing journalist? A vendor marketer? An academic researcher who has never worked on a real project? A brain-dead practitioner who can't program his way out of a 1000-line project? A noted guru whose biases are different from yours? The guy sitting next to you on the airplane?"[4]

As noted by Zelkowitz and Wallace,[5] in a mature discipline, we need to do more than simply say: "I tried it, and I liked it."

In fact, there are two extremes. One is not to rely on evidence at all — the "just do it" view. At the other end are the extreme scientists who insist that every technology should be evaluated and that it be demonstrated conclusively that it works before being unleashed onto the world. Reality is, however, a mix of both.

It is quite unrealistic to expect that compelling evidence will be available at the same time as when a technology is first introduced. Evidence typically evolves with the rate of adoption of a technology. For example, to study a practice and how it works in real software projects, there must be someone actually using it. To put some perspective on how the evolution of evidence follows the evolution of a technology, we will consider the SW-CMM as an example.

G.1 The SW-CMM Example

Some of the comments that have appeared about the SW-CMM in the early years after its introduction would make one think that the practical use of process assessments, especially using the SW-CMM, was proceeding in an evidential vacuum. For example, in the context of SW-CMM based assessments, Hersh[6] stated: "Despite our own firm belief in process improvement and our intuitive expectation that substantial returns will result from moving up the SEI [CMM] scale — we still can't prove it." Fenton[7] noted that evaluating the validity of the SEI's process maturity scheme was a key contemporary research issue. Jones, commenting on the SW-CMM effort at the SEI, stated that "Solid empirical information is lacking on the quality and productivity levels associated with the SEI five levels of maturity."[8] In relation to process assessments, Pfleeger makes the point that "many development organizations grab new, promising technologies well before there is clear evidence of proven benefit. For instance, the U.S. Software Engineering Institute's Capability Maturity Model was embraced by many companies well before the SEI and others began empirical investigations of the nature and magnitude of its process improvement effects." [9] More recently, Gray and Smith render severe criticism of process assessments, mainly due to a presumptive lack of empirical evidence.[10] For example, they state that "The whole CMM-style approach is based on untested assertions and opinions, [...] there is a lack of evidence to support the notions of repeatability and reproducibility of software process assessments. [...] Currently, software process assessment schemes are being applied and resultant process improvement plans being drawn up and acted upon without answers to the questions of repeatability and reproducibility being in place. [...] the validity of the SEI's maturity model remains unproven. [...] If anyone states that existing process assessment schemes or the attempted world standard [ISO/IEC 15504] are based on a full understanding and sound theoretical underpinnings, let it go in one ear and out the other."

The above criticisms were undoubtedly rather severe and relentless. It is fair to say that at the outset, when the CMM effort was first introduced to the software engineering community, there was indeed little empirical evidence supporting its use. Initially, there were case studies in military organizations (the first users of the CMM). Then the number of case studies and experience reports started to increase rapidly as more commercial organizations adopted the SW-CMM. Eventually, very good surveys and observational studies were performed that strengthened the evidence. Therefore, most of the strong empirical evidence supporting the CMM did indeed come after wide initial adoption. It took time. An extensive review of that body of work has been published.[11] In fact, especially when compared to other widely used software engineering technologies such as object-oriented techniques, the process assessment field is now remarkably rich with empirical evidence.

G.2 Evidence in Software Engineering

Is the case of the CMM unique? The answer is a categorical no. That empirical results lag the actual adoption of technology is not a problem unique to software engineering. In the allied discipline of management information systems, this particular problem has been well recognized.

Specifically, Benbasat and Zmud, two noted academics, state that rapid technological change "results in our chasing after practice rather than leading practice, and [this] typically leads to reporting results from (rigorous) studies involving new technologies years after the technology's acceptance (and, occasionally, rejection) by practice. [...] Needless to say, pronouncements in the future about today's technological and associated business challenges are just not going to be considered relevant by most practitioners."[12]

Should managers then wait for the strong evidence before acting, or should they go ahead without the evidence? It depends on the willingness to take risks.

When one considers the classical technology adoption stages,[13] it becomes clear that strong empirical evidence serves the needs of early majority adopters who follow rather than lead, and who are willing to try new things only when others demonstrate them to be effective.[9] Organizations that have a low tolerance for risk will wait for the evidence. It will be difficult for them to accept a technology without it.

Innovators and early adopters need no such assurances (their evidence threshold is much lower). Herbsleb notes: "If, for example, we are trying out a new technology that we believe has enormous potential, it may be a serious error for managers to wait until conclusive results are available. Management is the art of placing good bets, and as soon as a manager is convinced that the likelihood of significant benefits outweighs the risks and justifies the cost, managers should act."[14]

Therefore, the type of evidence needed to convince companies to adopt technologies depends on the risk profile of the company. The nature of evidence evolves as the technology is adopted. For example, large-scale surveys and observational studies are very unlikely to occur during the early days of a technology, so it is unrealistic to expect that kind of evidence early on.

References

1. Moher, T. and Schneider, G. Methodology and experimental research in software engineering. *International Journal of Man-Machine Studies*, 16:65–87, 1982.
2. Davis, A. Eras of software technology transfer. *IEEE Software*, pp. 4–7, March 1996.
3. Stringini, L. Limiting the dangers of intuitive decision making. *IEEE Software*, pp. 101–103, January 1996.
4. Glass, R. Good numbers and bad. *Journal of Systems and Software*, 44:85–86, 1998.
5. Zelkowitz, M. and Wallace, D. Experimental methods for validating technology. *IEEE Computer*, pp. 23–31, May 1998.
6. Hersh, A. Where's the return on process improvement?. *IEEE Software*, p. 12, July 1993.

7. Fenton, N. Objectives and context of measurement/experimentation, in *Experimental Software Engineering Issues: Critical Assessment and Future Directions*, Rombach, H.D., Basili, V., and Selby, R., Eds., Springer-Verlag, 1993.

8. Jones, C. Gaps in SEI programs, *Software Development*, 3(3):41–48, March 1995.

9. Pfleeger, S. Understanding and improving technology transfer in software engineering. *Journal of Systems and Software*, 47:111–124, 1999.

10. Gray, E. and Smith, W. On the limitations of software process assessment and the recognition of a required re-orientation for global process improvement. *Software Quality Journal*, 7:21–34, 1998.

11. El Emam, K. et al. Validating Object-oriented Design Metrics on a Commercial Java Application, National Research Council of Canada, ERB-1080, 2000.

12. Benbasat, I. and Zmud, R. Empirical research in information systems: the practice of relevance. *MIS Quarterly*, 23(1):16, March 1999.

13. Raghavan, S. and Chand, D. Diffusing software-engineering methods. *IEEE Software*, pp. 81–90, July 1989.

14. Herbsleb, J. Hard problems and hard science: On the practical limits of experimentation. *IEEE TCSE Software Process Newsletter*, 11: 18–21, 1998.

Index